'*The Fight For Beauty* is a remarkable book: passionate, persuasive and brave. It cleverly braids the personal record of a campaigning life with the modern history of Britain's belief – and disbelief – in the importance of landscape beauty. It lays bare some of the political and economic forces that shape the contemporary countryside, makes alarmingly clear the vulnerability of the aesthetic when fed into the crunching cogs of the fiscal, and stirringly shows us the need to fight *hard* to keep certain places and values intact, or to turn things around. It offers fascinating glimpses behind the scenes of some of the big modern political episodes concerning landscape – and it even makes planning exciting.'

Robert Macfarlane

'In this deep-rooted and urgently important book, Fiona Reynolds shows that she is the heir to the great tradition: Wordsworth, Ruskin, Morris and Muir all tread these pages, not as voices from the ancient past but as standard-bearers for all that might be best in the future. She proclaims beauty for what it is: an ideal, a battleground, a practical goal, the necessary frame for a civilised existence.

'It is a fascinating story told by someone who has lived and worked at the heart of the struggle for more than 30 years: clear, analytical, principled and impassioned but never dodging the economic and political realities. It constitutes a naked appeal to those in power and, more than that, to all of us who can choose the people who will be in power. Will we accept the responsibility of changing our lives to protect the interests of those who will follow us? Beauty is not a luxury but a compelling force for good. This deeply inspiring book needs to transform the government of Britain.'

Adam Nicolson, author of *Sea Room*

Items should be returned on or before the date shown below. Items not already requested by other borrowers may be renewed in person, in writing or by telephone. To renew, please quote the number on the barcode label. To renew online a PIN is required. This can be requested at your local library.
Renew online @ **www.dublincitypubliclibraries.ie**
Fines charged for overdue items will include postage incurred in recovery.
Damage to or loss of items will be charged to the borrower.

Leabharlanna Poiblí Chathair Bhaile Átha Cliath
Dublin City Public Libraries

Leabharlann Sráid Chaoimhín

Kevin Street Library

Comhairle Cathrach
Bhaile Átha Cliath
Dublin City Council

Tel: 01 222 8488

Due Date	Due Date	Due Date

THE FIGHT FOR BEAUTY

OUR PATH TO A BETTER FUTURE

FIONA REYNOLDS

ONEWORLD

A Oneworld Book

First published in North America, Great Britain and
Australia by Oneworld Publications, 2016

ISBN 978-1-78074-875-7
eISBN 978-1-78074-876-4

Typeset by Hewer Text UK Ltd, Edinburgh
Printed and bound by Clays Ltd, St Ives plc

Oneworld Publications
10 Bloomsbury Street
London WC1B 3SR
England

To my father, Jeff Reynolds

'not blind opposition to progress, but opposition to blind progress'
(John Muir, 1838–1914)

Contents

Preface   xi

1   From admiration to defence   1

2   The calls and claims of natural beauty   30

3   National Parks – a nobler vision for a better world   66

4   How nature and the wider countryside lost out   95

5   How farming made and destroyed beauty   122

6   The curious case of trees   160

7   The coast – a success story   193

8   Cultural heritage – how caring for the past
     creates a better future   229

9   Urbanisation and why good planning matters   261

10   The case for beauty   305

Acknowledgements   319

Bibliography   321

Index   329

Preface

Beauty. It is a word full of resonance. We use it with ease in everyday conversation but it is, nevertheless, the kind of word that can make us stop and think. Beauty can stop us in our tracks in wonder, create enduring memories and raise our expectations of ourselves and each other. When we say 'how beautiful', whether of a building, painting, view or butterfly, we are caught in a moment of admiration. Beauty is capable of lifting our spirits and touching emotions that lie deeper and are more meaningful to us than almost anything else in life.

Yet you would have to search hard to find the word beauty in any official document. Indeed, in formal dialogue we seem to be deeply uneasy talking about something that feels so personal and emotional. With so few exceptions that they can be counted on the fingers of one hand, no politician today gives speeches about beauty. And it's become a no-go zone in legislation too. But it wasn't always like that. Beauty was a word and a concept that people in previous centuries used freely and confidently, and Acts of Parliament were passed whose aims were simply and clearly to protect the beauty of Britain's countryside, wildlife and history. Today we have fallen into bureaucratic habits and we use instead words like biodiversity, ecosystem services, natural capital and sustainable development.

Perhaps as a result, that clear-sighted commitment to protect beauty has been lost. And beauty has been lost too. In the second half of the twentieth century we became obsessed with material-ism, preoccupied by a culture that values consumption more than intangible benefits, and we presided over a period of devastating losses to nature and the beauty of our countryside and heritage, while too much of what we built ranged from the undistinguished to the downright ugly.

Yet twice before people have fought for beauty and it has meant and achieved something. The first time was in the high Victorian era when the calamitous consequences of industrialisation clashed with human and social needs, with devastating consequences. Luminaries including John Ruskin, Octavia Hill and William Morris led a public debate about the questionable morals and damaging results of mechanisation and the commercial exploita-tion of the country's resources. Among other things their advocacy led to the birth of the conservation movement, including the National Trust, and helped create one of the main instruments for protecting beauty, the land use planning system.

The second time was in the aftermath of the Second World War when the government's post-war reconstruction plan committed, alongside jobs, housing, the NHS, the welfare state and the univer-sal right to education, to 'preserve and enhance the beauty of our countryside'. A vision of shared prosperity, including cultural as well as material benefits, was articulated and implemented, born of a commitment to values wider than economic growth and to soci-ety's need for more than money.

Yet in the decades that followed the clarity of that vision was lost, and the fight for beauty had to be revived time and time again as new threats emerged.

So beauty matters. But what, in this context, does it mean? John Ruskin's moment of epiphany about beauty came when as a young man he watched a storm gather in the Chamonix Valley:

> Spire of ice – dome of snow – wedge of rock . . . a celestial
> city with walls of amethyst and gates of gold – filled with
> light and clothed with the peace of God. And then I
> learned . . . the real meaning of the word Beautiful . . . It
> was then that I understood all which is the type of God's
> attributes – which in any way or in any degree – can turn
> the human soul from gazing upon itself . . . and fix the
> spirit – in all humility – on the types of that which is to be
> its food for eternity; – this and this only is in the pure and
> right sense of the word BEAUTIFUL.

His was not just an aesthetic but a deeply spiritual experience. In describing beauty he recognised the obligations of humans to do more than satisfy our own demands and to fix our spirit instead on what will sustain us for eternity.

My own, immature but no less heartfelt, epiphany came at the age of seven when I climbed my first mountain. My father took my older sister and me, soon after dawn, to climb Cnicht, a miraculous little Matterhorn-shaped mountain nestled in the hills of Snowdonia behind Porthmadog. It was the mid-1960s and we proudly laced our school shoes and stowed our Pac-A-Macs, specially purchased for holiday walking. Cnicht is just over 2,250 feet high and rises steeply, its summit hidden behind a series of ridges and mini-summits as you ascend. We took most of the morning to scale it, the excitement of breaching each horizon dashed as another loomed before us. But the moment when we reached the top has never left me. The peaks and ridges of Snowdon and the Glyderau to the north; the bulk of Cader Idris to the south; the Moelwyns to the east littered with the poignant remains of mining communities; and the azure blue sweep of Cardigan Bay to the west, with Harlech's sandy beach and our tiny holiday cottage containing our mother and two small sisters (our youngest sister, the fifth in our family, was not yet born) in the foreground.

I had never before seen such beauty, never before felt the shiver of nature's exquisite perfection, never before experienced the sense of striving then reaching a summit, from which we could survey, it felt, the whole glorious world.

That moment, and many other experiences in my happy, countryside- and exploration-filled childhood, shaped my life and stimulated my love of beauty. My passion was fuelled when as a student an ordinary Ordnance Survey map, with its contour lines and settlements, textual clues and ribbon-like roads, rivers and footpaths suddenly came alive to me, revealing all the layers of our history, should one care to look closely enough, in a fascinating palimpsest. And again when for the first time I read W. G. Hoskins' *The Making of the English Landscape*, with his beautiful descriptions of an evolved and evolving countryside, ending in his rallying call to defend it from the imminent threat of irreversible damage.

So when in 1980 I got my first job after leaving university, as Secretary to the Council for National Parks (now the Campaign for National Parks), I already had rooted in me something indefinable but purposeful. I soon realised that what I had become part of was more than a job. I had joined a movement of people whose pursuit of beauty had shaped their whole lives, and I was only too ready to add my eager voice to theirs. Through my later roles, as leaders of both the Council for the Protection of Rural England (now the Campaign to Protect Rural England) and the National Trust (for which I had volunteered for fifteen years before my twelve years on the staff), my passion for beauty and my determination to defend it grew alongside my understanding of and absorption by the forces that shape it. As a devotee of Hoskins I always believed that beauty was generous in scope, embracing all the elements of landscape, nature and cultural heritage, but I also became drawn into a progressively deeper understanding of beauty. I came to see that seeking beauty requires us to harmonise the complex demands we make of our land and natural and built resources, and to leave a legacy for future generations of which we can be proud, and which gives them hope.

These are not objectives that everyone shares. And in my life as a campaigner, very often the argument was not about beauty but about the economy; and why that should take precedence. So defending beauty was, too often, a fight.

But it always felt a worthwhile fight, and it felt more worthwhile the more I understood the motives and purpose of my predecessors. I learned to admire their vision and prescience, and their courage in standing up for what they believed in. Theirs is a story that needs to be told. So here it is: the story of the movement I joined, interwoven in more recent times with my own. As a result it is mostly about England, where the majority of my campaigning life has been spent, but I include Wales, Northern Ireland and Scotland where I was directly involved.

It is, ultimately, the story of a determined and recurring fight for beauty and it ends with a call to arms to revive that fight today. For despite a long and honourable history of attempts to bring beauty into the heart of our thinking, we live in a world where the economy and consumerism have become dominant forces shaping our lives today. We are using the resources of this planet as if we had three to depend on. The threat of climate change looms large yet our vision for the future appears rooted in materialism rather than the quality of our lives. We seem to be stuck in a place where the only thing that matters is economic progress, but this fails to understand the human spirit's need for succour of other kinds. Yet as this book will show, adopting a perspective shaped by beauty has achieved much and could achieve much more, giving us greater hope for the future. As John Muir so wisely said, it is not a question of 'blind opposition to progress, but opposition to blind progress'.

If we care about our future, we need to fight for beauty. It matters to us all, and as this book will show it can help us find a better path. Indeed, not only is beauty more than skin deep it is, potentially, the means of our salvation.

1

From admiration
to defence

'*That* is what you are doing with your scenery!' With his paintbrush held aloft, John Ruskin, the writer, art historian and philosopher, shocked his audience by defacing a painting by his hero and national celebrity J. M. W. Turner. It was a landscape of Leicester Abbey, and across its glass frame he scrawled a monstrous iron bridge, a heavily polluted river and billowing smoke.

The only surviving account of this event, a lecture Ruskin gave at Oxford University, comes from a student who was present, the young A. E. Housman, who would go on to write one of the best-loved elegies to England, *A Shropshire Lad*. But for the moment, he and his fellow students were awed by the Slade Professor of Fine Art's blatant confrontation of modern civilisation. 'The atmosphere is supplied – thus!' Ruskin continued, dashing a flame of scarlet across the picture, which became first bricks and then a chimney from which rushed a puff and cloud of smoke all over Turner's sky. Housman describes how Ruskin threw down his brush amidst a tempest of applause, his students enthralled by the idea that beauty could matter as much, if not more, than the unconstrained pursuit of wealth.

Those were radical ideas in the 1870s, but support was building for Ruskin's views. For as well as bringing great wealth and innovation, industrialisation was casting a pall over a nation whose countryside was internationally admired; whose poets, artists and writers were renowned for celebrating it; and whose identity was shaped by its beauty. The fight for beauty had begun, and Ruskin was at the heart of it.

The beauty of Britain's nature and landscape has long captivated the people of this country and has taken many forms. Chaucer wrote lyrically of the countryside's awakening in the spring as part of the inspiration for 'folk to goon pilgrimages'; and mediaeval craftsmen painted and sculpted exquisite flowers, leaves and creatures into the friezes, pillars and gargoyles of cathedrals and country churches. As well as vivid descriptions of nature and landscape in his sonnets and plays, Shakespeare's evocative settings – whether the leafy Warwickshire Forest of Arden or the bleakness of Macbeth's Scottish hills – are central to the appreciation of his texts. Thomas Traherne, a century later (he was born in 1636), captures the religious underpinning of much appreciation of landscape and nature in *Centuries of Meditation*: 'This visible World is wonderfully to be delighted in, and highly to be esteemed, because it is the theatre of God's righteous kingdom.'

Beauty was a word freely used and invoked, whether by young men in search of Arcadia as they travelled the continent on the Grand Tour, educating and preparing themselves for their future lives, or by the many people inspired by the increasingly popular school of landscape painting, led by Thomas Gainsborough in England and Richard Wilson and Thomas Jones in Wales. Thomas Gray's romantic 1719 'Elegy Written in a Country Churchyard', celebrating the beauty of nature and everyday country life, reached unprecedented heights of popularity, becoming one of the most quoted poems of the English language.

The early eighteenth century was a time of burgeoning interest in aesthetics, and Edmund Burke, in his 1757 *Philosophical Inquiry into the Origin of our Ideas of the Sublime and Beautiful*, drew a distinction between what was considered beautiful, derived from love or pleasure; and what was sublime, triggered by pain or terror. Burke presented the sublime and the beautiful as antithetical, with the sublime inspiring delight at terror perceived but avoided, emotions echoed in Daniel Defoe's descriptions of Westmoreland [sic] in his *Tour through the Whole Island of Great Britain* as 'a country eminent only for being the wildest, most barren and frightful of any that I have passed over in England, or even in Wales itself'. Beauty, on the other hand, was triggered by the warmer emotions of love and sensuality, and it was clear that the human-created world could be made to replicate, in a milder form, and closer to home, the affirming power of nature.

The gentleman's park, for instance, was a conscious attempt to enhance the natural landscape, sweeping away earlier manor houses and the structured form of fifteenth- and sixteenth-century

An engraving of the dramatic scenery that inspired
thoughts of the sublime: Thomas Smith of Derby's view of
Ennerdale (© UK Government Art Collection).

gardens and replacing them with classical houses and 'landscapes' decorated with temples and monuments: expertly designed but natural-looking prospects which reconstructed the elements of ancient Arcadia in the countryside of Britain.

The person most in demand to create such idylls was 'Capability' Brown, the 'omnipotent magician' as William Cowper dubbed him after his death. Born in Northumberland, Brown trained under William Kent at Stowe, in Buckinghamshire, and went on to design or contribute to at least eighty landscape gardens in England. His wide, sweeping lawns with their perfectly placed serpentine lakes, and their neo-classical buildings carefully positioned to create an idealised view, represented the pinnacle of many eighteenth-century landowners' aspirations. But he would have rebelled against the idea that his creations were entirely artificial. He was inspired by Alexander Pope's instruction that landscape design should draw on the underlying 'genius of the place', a concept which shapes much thinking about landscape to this day:

> Consult the Genius of the Place in all;
> That tells the Waters or to rise, or fall;
> Or helps th' ambitious Hill the heav'ns to scale,
> Or scoops in circling theatres the Vale;
> Calls in the Country, catches op'ning glades,
> Joins willing woods, and varies shades from shades;
> Now breaks or now directs, th' intending Lines;
> Paints as you plant, and, as you work, designs.
>
> > (Alexander Pope, 'Epistle IV', addressed
> > to Lord Burlington, *Moral Essays*, 1731)

By the end of the eighteenth century tastes were changing and new ideas about beauty were emerging, favouring the countryside's own qualities rather than those which were imposed upon it.

William Gilpin, priest, artist and schoolmaster, proposed the 'picturesque' as something of a third way between the sublime and the beautiful, reflecting the naturalistic character of the British countryside, created without apparently conscious intervention: 'Picturesque beauty is a phrase but little understood. We precisely mean by it that kind of beauty which would look well in a picture. Neither grounds laid out by art nor improved by agriculture are of this kind.'

In the 1760s Gilpin published accounts of his visits to the Lake District and the Wye Valley, prompting thousands of eager tourists who were drawn by his descriptions to explore the picturesque beauty of England's countryside. Of the ancient trees of the New Forest he wrote: 'Such Dryads! Extending their taper arms to each other, sometimes in elegant mazes along the plain; sometimes in single figures; and sometimes combined.' Many followed his lead, clutching their sketchbooks and Claude glasses to frame the perfect view. His cause was taken up by Uvedale Price, a Herefordshire squire, who praised the 'real' countryside as a work of art, and also Humphry Repton, with whom he travelled down the Wye, because he (Repton) 'really admired the banks in their natural state, and did not desire to turf them, or remove the large stones'. And as the French Revolution and Napoleonic Wars restricted continental travel, enthusiasm for the landscapes of Britain was re-energised.

By the end of the eighteenth century the whole population could be said to be falling in love with nature and the British landscape. In addition to the tourists following Gilpin's scenic routes, Gilbert White's *Natural History of Selborne* and Thomas Bewick's *History of British Birds* inspired a new generation of nature lovers. White's finely observed, unsentimental prose described, named and publicised many species for the first time; and Bewick's beautiful engravings formed a popular and widely used reference book, encouraging the fashion for bird identification. As the eighteenth century gave way to the nineteenth, the Romantic poets inspired a new generation of landscape and nature lovers, their outpourings devoured by a nation hungry to appreciate their pastoral, beautiful imagery of England.

And this was no superficial appreciation: William Wordsworth's 'Lines Written a Few Miles above Tintern Abbey' (1798) enjoin us not only to appreciate nature but to accept its moral depths:

> to recognise
> In nature and the language of the sense,
> The anchor of my purest thoughts, the nurse,
> The guide, the guardian of my heart, and soul
> Of all my moral being.

Wordsworth also brought something new. He had been born in Cockermouth in the Lake District in 1770 and grew up with a deep love of nature, travelling widely in France, Switzerland and Germany before settling again in his childhood home. By the time he published, in 1810, his best-selling *Guide through the District of the Lakes* he was tapping into a population hungry for the appreciation of its own countryside. He gave people routes and viewpoints, places to stay and sights to see. And his statement that the Lake District was 'a sort of national property in which every man has a right and interest who has an eye to perceive and a heart to enjoy' hinted at a universal stake in its landscape. Because while his predecessors as writers and poets had helped the nation to love nature, Wordsworth's readers got something more. This revered place, his beloved Lake District, was coming under threat, and the stage was set for the first great clash about beauty. Admiration was about to tip into defence, and Wordsworth's was the voice that brought this about.

William Wordsworth, whose passion for the Lake District
tipped admiration of its beauty into defence.

During the early nineteenth century a new breed of business
opportunists spotted the commercial potential of the age-old
industries of the Lake District: slate quarrying, and mining for
copper and other valuable minerals. They also wanted stylish
places to live in the Lake District's beautiful valleys. Wordsworth,
whose passion for long, solitary walks meant that he knew the
Lakes intimately, was among the first to raise the alarm, speaking
out in his *Guide* against the construction of ugly villas in its beautiful valleys. In 1844 he fired off eloquent letters to *The Morning Post*
objecting to a railway line that might link Kendal to Windermere
and spoil for ever the solitude of a wilderness 'rich with liberty'. In
the same year he wrote the sonnet with which his passion for the
Lake District has been ever since associated:

> Is then no nook of English ground secure
> From rash assault? Schemes of retirement sown
> In youth, and 'mid the busy world kept pure

As when their earliest flowers of hope were blown,
Must perish; – how can they this blight endure?
And must he too the ruthless change bemoan
Who scorns a false utilitarian lure
'Mid his paternal fields at random thrown?
Baffle the threat, bright Scene, from Orrest-head
Given to the pausing traveller's rapturous glance:
Plead for thy peace, thou beautiful romance
Of nature; and, if human hearts be dead,
Speak, passing winds; ye torrents, with your strong
And constant voice, protest against the wrong.

(Wordsworth, 'On the Projected
Kendal to Windermere Railway', 1844)

Wordsworth had already railed against the 'spiky larch', a new tree brought in to launch commercial timber growth in the Lakes, and for the rest of his life he fulminated against the despoliation of the landscape he loved.

As the fight in the Lakes began, the 'rash assault' was gathering pace across Britain's industrialising landscape. Mechanisation and the growth of manufacturing during the late eighteenth and early nineteenth centuries brought great wealth to those able to reap the profits of trade and manufacturing. But their social and aesthetic consequences were often dire, especially in the rapidly growing cities and towns. Mills and factories colonised riversides and green fields, and filthy smoke and pollution choked their surroundings. Houses thrown up for mill and factory workers were often poor, mean and overcrowded.

To some the vision was apocalyptic. In 1798 the Reverend Robert Malthus published his *Essay on the Principle of Population* arguing that population growth would outstrip food supplies and the world would end in chaos and misery. His reasoning was based on simple mathematics: because population multiplies geometrically and food production arithmetically the population would inevitably collapse when food supplies failed, 'The power of population is indefinitely greater than the power in the earth to produce subsistence for man.' He was one of the first to recognise that there were limits to the Earth's capacity to cope with human demands.

His essay, though, provoked a storm of protest. Marx and Engels argued that the crisis was due not to 'natural' causes but to capitalism denying resources to the poor; while the capitalists argued that Malthus had failed to recognise that increases in productivity would feed the poor. His critics were proved right and Malthus wrong. Extreme poverty was due at least as much to unequal access to food as to its availability (the same is true today), and food production expanded dramatically during the nineteenth century due to technological innovations.

What no one could fail to observe, though, were the 'processes of misery and vice' experienced by those whose basic needs were not met. Within the teeming cities filthy, polluted air wreaked havoc with people's health, and children employed in the factories and mills suffered appalling injuries and were deprived of sunlight, play and freedom. Medical facilities were virtually non-existent, or too expensive, and babies were routinely doped with opiates so their mothers could work. Average life expectancy fell as many died young, their lives broken by working in the mines, mills or factories, and child mortality rose through a combination of poverty, sickness and accidents.

Apocalyptic, too, was the physical footprint of urbanisation. George Cruikshank's 1829 cartoon *London Going Out of Town, or The March of Bricks and Mortar* captures the disastrous consequences as newly built but already-decaying tenements stand gloomy and forlorn; a kiln fires a barrage of hot bricks over a cornfield, whose haystacks, terrified, call out 'Confound these hot bricks! They'll fire all my hay ricks'. A tree is cast to the ground

LONDON going out of Town. — or — The March of Bricks & Mortar.

George Cruikshank's 1829 cartoon captured the horror of
unplanned urbanisation. (Courtesy of the Museum of London)

crying 'Oh! I'm mortally [sic] wounded' and a robotic army advances
from the city into the countryside, while trees sway wildly and cattle
and sheep flee from fields which have already become building sites.

Britain was a land of inconsistencies and contrasts. Enormous
wealth sat alongside desperate poverty; objects and architecture of
great beauty contrasted with the pitiful squalor of poor people's homes
and the implements of drudgery; and the glorious, verdant forests and
landscapes with the filth of rapidly growing, overcrowded cities.

Out of this cacophony came a powerful voice for beauty. John
Ruskin was born in 1819 and observed at first hand this world of rapid
change and social division. Though variously a scientist, philosopher
and educator, he was always obsessed by beauty. As a precocious child
he had measured the blue of the sky with a cyanometer, and his early
written works, especially *Modern Painters*, were underpinned by references to his own love of beauty as well as celebrating artists such as
Turner who best represented the brilliance of nature's stormy skies and

swirling seas. His early sensibility to art and architecture (he wrote his first book, *Poetry and Architecture*, as a teenager) matured into a passionate love for the countryside and an intense hatred of the obsession with money, machinery and mechanisation that threatened to drive all that was beautiful out of the world. And his awakening to the deeper meaning of beauty at Chamonix shaped his whole life, framed by a profound commitment to social justice as well as aesthetics. Not for him was beauty defined by the elite; it was close to home and belonged, as of right, to everyone.

Drawing on deep though constantly challenged religious and ethical beliefs, Ruskin became a social reformer and campaigned for beauty, justice and moral virtue. He saw no division between the three. 'Beauty,' he wrote in Volume II of *Modern Painters* (1846) 'is either the record of conscience, written in things external, or it is the symbolizing of Divine attributes in matter, or it is the felicity of living things, or the perfect fulfilment of their duties and functions. In all cases it is something Divine.'

But only a decade later his mood had switched to despair:

John Ruskin's was the powerful voice who raised expectations and demands for beauty in the nineteenth century. (Courtesy of the Wellcome Library)

Once I could speak joyfully about beautiful things, thinking to be understood; – now I cannot any more; for it seems to me that no-one regards them. Wherever I look or travel in England or abroad, I see that men, wherever they can reach, destroy all beauty. They seem to have no other desire or hope but to have large houses and to be able to move fast. Every perfect and lovely spot which they can touch, they defile.

(*Modern Painters*, Volume V, 1856)

Ruskin took up the mantle of Wordsworth's defence of the Lake District after the poet's death in 1850, scorning in particular the railways that were defiling the places he loved. He condemned plans (never fulfilled) to build railways to connect the Honister slate quarries in the Newlands Valley with the railway line at Braithwaite, running tracks through Borrowdale along the pristine western shoreline of Derwentwater; and to link Keswick and Windermere by rail:

The stupid herds of modern tourists let themselves be emptied, like coals from a sack, at Windermere and Keswick. Having got there, what the new railway has to do is shovel those who have come to Keswick to Windermere, and to shovel those who have come to Windermere to Keswick. And what then?

His riposte to the Midland line through Monsal Dale in the Peak District which was built in 1863 was similar: 'now, every fool in Buxton can be in Bakewell in half an hour and every fool in Bakewell in Buxton.'

Ruskin was sickened by the destruction of beauty in the countryside, but he also deplored the unplanned, inhumane growth of cities. In *The Seven Lamps of Architecture* he described how it was 'not possible to have any right morality, happiness, or art, in any country where the cities are . . . clotted and coagulated'; arguing that instead 'you must have lovely cities . . . limited in size, and not casting out the scum and scurf of them into an encircling eruption of shame, but girded each with its sacred pomoerium, and with garlands of gardens full of blossoming trees and softly-guided streams.'

To put his ideas into practice, Ruskin set up the Guild of St George, for which he wrote a monthly bulletin, *Fors Clavigera*. Its aim was to acquire land and beautiful objects so that its members could live according to its (surprisingly authoritarian) principles.

> We will try to take some small piece of English ground: [he wrote in 1871] beautiful, peaceful and fruitful. We will have no steam-engines upon it, and no railroads; we will have no untended or unthought-of creatures on it; none wretched, but the sick; none idle, but the dead. We will have no liberty upon it; but instant obedience to known law, and appointed persons; no equality upon it, but recognition of every betterness that we can find, and reprobation of every worseness.

Ruskin envisaged a world where social justice, human effort and a deep appreciation of nature and the intrinsic beauty of art and architecture would unite to create a society in harmony with itself. Members of the Guild would live wholesome and rewarding lives dependent on the forces of nature – water, human and horse-power, not machines – in communities committed to education, fairness and collective decision-making.

Ruskin's utopian vision struggled to gain a footing, however. Although he invested a tenth of his own fortune in the Guild he failed to attract much support. By 1884 the Guild numbered only fifty-six members and its assets were small: a few cottages in Barmouth left by Fanny Talbot (who later also donated to the National Trust its first property, Dinas Oleu); a few small farms including two, plus forest land, in the Wyre Forest near Bewdley; a mill on the Isle of Man; and the St George's Museum in Sheffield, furnished with objects acquired by Ruskin. Disappointment that the Guild did not thrive in his lifetime (though it continues today, doing much good work) was a source of sadness to Ruskin and contributed to his failing health and declining mental state.

All the same, Ruskin's public persona was extraordinarily influential. He was a prolific writer and correspondent and an impassioned and charismatic public speaker. His lectures in the great cities of Britain were attended by thousands, and his eloquence inspired many followers. There are frequent references to Ruskin in *Hansard*, his lectures inspiring not just students but those occupying the highest offices of public life as he called for beauty to be taken seriously.

And he left a powerful legacy. Not least was the way his ideas found practical expression in a new architecture. He personally sponsored Oxford's new Museum of Natural History, drawing on the principles of perfection he had articulated in *The Seven Lamps of Architecture* and *The Stones of Venice*, written in veneration of mediaeval Venice as it crumbled in the first half of the nineteenth century. Many cities commissioned magnificent buildings – though he hated some of them – as homages to his championship of the Gothic: Manchester Town Hall, Bradford City Hall, St Pancras Station and the Albert Memorial in Kensington Gardens.

Perhaps more important, though, were the people he inspired: people who would carry forward his ideas as his own health declined, ensuring that his passion for beauty remained alive as Britain shuddered into a new century. And linked to these people were organisations whose foundation and purposes drew heavily on his ideas.

Among his most prominent followers were William Morris, inspirer of the Arts and Crafts movement which has left its own legacy in beauty; and the three founders of the National Trust: Octavia Hill, Robert Hunter and Canon Hardwicke Rawnsley.

Morris was at the heart of the pre-Raphaelite movement of painters and designers. As an Oxford undergraduate he was inspired by mediaeval history and buildings as well as Ruskin's writing. He trained as an architect and in 1861, with his close friends the artists Edward Burne-Jones and Dante Gabriel Rossetti, and the architect Philip Webb, he founded the decorative arts firm that would become Morris and Co. The company shaped the fashion for interior decoration throughout the Victorian period and beyond, creating tapestries, wallpaper, fabrics, furniture and stained-glass windows. 'Beauty,' Morris wrote, 'which is what is meant by art . . . is no mere accident to human life, which people can take or leave as they choose, but a positive necessity of life.' And he memorably enjoined his clients to 'have nothing in your house that you do not know to be useful or believe to be beautiful.'

In 1877 he established the Society for the Protection of Ancient Buildings (SPAB) to promote sensitive principles of repair and preservation, seeking 'truth not pastiche'. SPAB was directly inspired by Ruskin's *The Seven Lamps of Architecture*, which attacked restoration and urged new skills of trusteeship and sensitive conservation. It was known as 'Anti-Scrape', rejecting earlier, brutish tendencies to restore by destroying the patina of age and evolution. By the 1880s, as Ruskin's health was declining, Morris became a revolutionary activist, socialist and radical writer. His epic *News from Nowhere* described his utopian vision, no less ambitious than Ruskin's, set in a future London. It depicted an epoch after a socialist revolution; a land of beauty and art. Like Ruskin, Morris was profoundly anti-urban; rejecting the evils of nineteenth-century cities as symbolic of greed, misery and destructive competitiveness. At the first meeting of the London Committee of the Kyrle Society he addressed the members by saying 'he could not be otherwise than discontented, while the aspect of London was so squalid'.

The Kyrle Society for the Diffusion of Beauty was named after the English philanthropist Robert Kyrle, whose work to improve and embellish the town of Ross-on-Wye was widely admired, and was set up in 1876 by Miranda Hill, Octavia's sister. Its purpose was, straightforwardly, 'to bring the refining and cheering influences of natural and artistic beauty to the people'. Drawing heavily on Ruskin's ideas its members provided art in public places, decorated hospitals and schools, organised choirs and laid out gardens. Its four committees – decorative, musical, literature distribution and open spaces – were all energetic, but its open spaces branch left the greatest legacy, securing the clearing and opening of sixty-two London burial grounds (which had hitherto been kept locked and closed because they were so filthy and dangerous) as gardens for the poor. Arguably its finest hour came when it raised nearly £10,000 from a public appeal to establish and open Vauxhall Park in 1890, though it reluctantly handed the park over to the Lambeth Vestry as the Kyrle Society was not constituted to own and manage land. The Society stimulated the formation of many branches to champion beauty in towns and cities across the country, often joining with local antiquarian and historical societies to press for the protection of important local buildings, green spaces or vernacular architecture during the endless process of urban building and remodelling. Many of today's civic societies began life as local branches of the Kyrle Society.

At a national level, though, its ideas were embraced and ultimately subsumed by the National Trust, an organisation whose birth and purposes are deeply Ruskinian. Its three founders were each, in their own way, indebted to him, and their personal commitment to beauty established deep roots within the Trust.

The first was Octavia Hill, who met Ruskin when she was a teenager. Born in Wisbech in 1838, she seemed destined for a philanthropic life. Her maternal grandfather, Thomas Southwood Smith, was the first doctor to demonstrate the link between infectious diseases like typhoid and poor living conditions. Her father, James Hill, was a committed follower of Robert Owen's philanthropic ideas but he became bankrupt and largely disappeared from Octavia's life when she was a child. Caroline, her mother, was her role model and mentor, and she encouraged the fourteen-year-old Octavia to supervise a classroom of girls making toys within the Ladies' Guild she had established in the Working Men's College in Russell Place.

When John Ruskin, as a friend of the Christian Socialist preacher F. D. Maurice, visited the Guild in 1853 Hill was captivated by him. She was already a disciple of Maurice's, passionately supporting his belief in people's entitlement to decent living conditions and educational opportunities. She was more than ready to follow Ruskin, and when he invited her to visit him at his house in Denmark Hill and become one of his copyists she accepted, slaving to produce accurate copies of the Italian Masters. For years she tried to combine this work, for which she was not temperamentally suited, with her own philanthropic efforts. She and Ruskin became close but he knew she was destined for other things and early in their relationship he wryly remarked, 'If you devote yourself to human expression, I know how it will be, you will watch it more and more, and there will be an end to art for you. You will say "*Hang* drawing!! I must go and help people." ' Hill denied it but he was right. Less happily, in the 1870s, they fell out after he accused her of questioning his ability to conduct any practical enterprise successfully. Again she denied the charge but it was hardly untrue. It created a rift between them that was never fully to heal.

At the heart of Hill's beliefs was the importance of bringing beauty to people, and as a teenager she used to lead groups of ragged schoolchildren out of London on a Sunday, sometimes as far as Romford or Epping Forest and back, to let them experience clean air, growing grass, trees and flowers. This remained a guiding

The young Octavia Hill brought beauty and dignity into people's lives by buying up housing in poor condition and providing decent homes for families to live in (courtesy of the National Trust) – pictured above is her first project, Paradise Place, as it is today.

motive throughout her life: 'The need of quiet, the need of air, the sight of sky and of things growing seem human needs, common to all.'

But she also saw with piercing clarity that what people most lacked was clean, wholesome conditions at home. With Ruskin's financial backing, at the age of thirty-two she bought three squalid cottages in the inappropriately named Paradise Place in the heart of Marylebone and set them up as tenancies. She was an unusual and interventionist landlord, marked for her humanity and practicality. She improved the houses before her tenants moved in and insisted they maintain them as decent and clean places to live. Against the conventions of the day she collected the rent herself and, by knowing her tenants personally, was often able to help resolve their problems and find them work. She was intolerant of those who did not live by her high moral standards, but she was a world away from the Dickensian landlords of the time, believing in dignity and self-reliance. Her passion was to relieve ugliness as well as poverty:

> let us hope that when we have secured our drainage, our cubic space of air, our water on every floor, we may have time to live in our homes, to think how to make them pretty, each in our own way . . . because all human work and life were surely meant to be like all Divine creations, lovely as well as good.

She made sure her housing schemes were near to places where people could walk and find beauty. The Red Cross Cottages she built in Southwark, today still occupied, scrunched below The Shard, all have their own patch of garden as well as a communal open space that brings brightness and pleasure to a densely packed inner London borough. She would insist on a window-box or a tiny courtyard for the children to play in if that was all that was possible.

Though fundamentally philanthropic, Hill ran her housing schemes (by 1874 she had over three thousand tenancies in fifteen sites in London) as a business, returning to Ruskin and her other investors a reliable five per cent a year. As her business expanded it became more sophisticated, but she never deviated from the principle of employing women rent-collectors whose personal touch was crucial to her tenants' ability to thrive. She was extraordinarily assiduous: working long hours, maintaining relationships with hundreds of volunteers and supporters, fundraising endlessly, and writing every year to account for her activities in her *Letters to Fellow Workers*.

Octavia Hill was soon drawn into the emerging preservation movement, because she was appalled by the way London's green spaces – she called them 'out-door sitting-rooms' – were being built over. Her housing schemes depended on having nearby 'places to sit in, places to play in, places to stroll in and places to spend a day in', yet with the pressures for new housing these were being gobbled up by voracious developers.

When the fields around Swiss Cottage were threatened with development she urged her influential friends to help her 'save a bit of hilly ground near a city, where fresh winds may blow, and where wild flowers are still found and where happy people can still walk within reach of their home'. In the summer of 1875 she had persuaded the owner to sell the land to her if she could raise enough money. But after she had raised an astonishing £8,000 in three weeks he reneged on his agreement, leaving her in despair.

It was through this and other campaigns that she met the lawyer Robert Hunter, and through the Kyrle Society pursued the fight to save London's open spaces. Hunter and Hill were a good campaigning pair. The diminutive Hill, less than five feet tall, was a compelling speaker and fundraiser. And increasingly alongside her was the sharp legal mind and experience of Robert Hunter, who had led the campaign to prevent common rights being extinguished as solicitor for the Commons Preservation Society.

Hunter was younger than Hill, born in 1844, and he was a delicate and studious child after contracting a near-fatal illness at two. A prodigy, he lapped up his formal education and became a scholar at University College, London, paying as much attention to social causes as to his studies, the reason for his attraction to the law.

In 1866, while an articled clerk to a firm of London solicitors, he spotted a competition sponsored by the businessman Henry Peek, seeking original essays on the subject of commons preservation. Peek (later an MP) was a common right-holder in Wimbledon where the common was facing the threat of enclosure by the Lord of the Manor, Lord Spencer. Hunter was young and untested and did not win the prize but his brilliant essay was one of six to be privately published by Peek, and before long he was articled to one of the Commons Preservation Society's own lawyers, Philip Lawrence.

Sir Robert Hunter. (Courtesy of the National Trust)

The Commons Preservation Society had only recently been established (its 1865 foundation making it the oldest conservation group in England) but it was already forging a feisty reputation, fighting the enclosures that threatened to extinguish common rights and thereby allow London's open spaces to be built on. The society became famous for its battles to save Wimbledon Common, Hampstead Heath and Epping Forest as spaces for public recreation. Hunter's speciality, in which he delighted, was seeking out people who remembered common rights being exercised, and bringing them before the courts to testify that the rights that owners and builders wanted forgotten were still valid. He also condoned the Society's use of direct action, tearing down fences installed by landowners at Tooting, Knole and Berkhamsted, arguing in his essay that 'any commoner whose rights are molested is clearly entitled to throw down the whole fencing or other obstruction erected.'

Hunter's career took off and in 1882 he was appointed Solicitor to the Post Office, where he demonstrated the same intelligent, questioning and painstaking approach, winning respect for his integrity and commitment to public service. He was by now working with Octavia Hill, and their bitter disappointment over Swiss Cottage Fields was followed in the early 1880s by another, when they tried to save the site of John Evelyn's former home and garden, Sayes Court in Deptford. Though his house had long ago been demolished and rebuilt, later being used as a workhouse, the garden bore traces of Evelyn's work and was of immense historical importance. Evelyn's descendant wanted to give the house and garden to the nation, but as Hunter (after an exhaustive effort to identify a legal means of safeguarding it) had to convey to Hill, there was no secure means of doing so. The chance to save Sayes Court was lost, and what remained of it was bulldozed after the Second World War.

Stung by these failures, Hunter and Hill concluded that there needed to be a body able to acquire and hold in perpetuity properties like Sayes Court and the green spaces that were so valuable to urban residents. This needed to be a legal entity (Hunter suggested a company) in order to protect the public interests in land and open spaces. Hill didn't like the word 'company', feeling that it spoke too much of business. Instead she suggested a trust, perhaps 'Commons and Gardens Trust'? Hunter memorably pencilled across her letter '?National Trust. R.H.'

That was in 1885, a full ten years before the National Trust came into being. The impetus to get it off the ground was supplied by the firebrand campaigner Canon Hardwicke Rawnsley.

Rawnsley was the youngest member of the trio (born in 1851) and was also a devotee of Ruskin, having studied under him at Oxford. But he was no academic, and after going down from Oxford with a poor third-class degree he followed his father and grandfather into the church. He began work as an assistant in a hostel for down-and-outs in Soho. Ruskin referred him to Octavia Hill and she took him on as an assistant to one of her most devoted managers, Emma Cons. But Rawnsley drove himself too hard and suffered a nervous collapse, so Hill arranged for his convalescence with friends on the shores of Windermere.

Recovered, Rawnsley returned to work, this time in a mission for the poor of Bristol founded by Clifton College. Like Hill, he took poverty-stricken children for walks in the countryside and campaigned for open spaces for their recreation. He also saved the fourteenth-century church tower of St Werburgh from demolition. But his hot temper and outspoken defence of his badly behaved charges got him into trouble and he was dismissed. Jobless, and again helped by Hill, he was offered the living of St Margaret at Wray in the Lake District. And from there he began to campaign for the beauty of the Lake District, drawing on Wordsworth's inspiration.

Canon Hardwicke Rawnsley in a 1915 pastel portrait by
Frederick Yates. (Courtesy of the National Trust)

Rawnsley led the charge against the continuing 'rash assaults'. It
was not just intrusive railways and quarrying to which he objected:
tourists, already numerous, flocked to the railway and threatened
to disrupt the peace and harmony of the Lakes. The line to
Windermere so decried by Wordsworth in 1844 had been built in
1847 and an estimated ten thousand day trippers visited
Windermere on Whit Sunday 1883; many, ironically, attracted by
Wordsworth's popular *Guide to the Lakes*.

But neither tourists nor railways posed the most offensive assault
on the Lake District. That came from a public body. The row was
triggered by Manchester Corporation's acquisition in 1877 of the
Thirlmere catchment, followed by its application to Parliament for
powers to construct a reservoir and take fifty million gallons a day by
aqueduct to Manchester. Thirlmere was the central lake, the inspiration of poets and painters; it was the heart of this revered landscape.

The plans to dam the lake and flood the valley aroused huge opposition. It was orchestrated by Robert Miller Somervell, of the 'K' shoes

Thirlmere before the reservoir was built. (© Martin and Jean Norgate)

family in Kendal, supported by the now famous defenders of beauty: William Morris, Thomas Carlyle, John Ruskin, Octavia Hill, Robert Hunter and Hardwicke Rawnsley. But as even they recognised, the moral case to supply clean water to Manchester was overwhelming and their combined efforts, which included stalling the Bill in the House of Commons for several months in 1878, failed to prevent the valley from being flooded. And its construction set in train further assaults on beauty: a new road (now the A591) was blasted through the heart of the Lakes and in 1908 the Corporation planted two thousand conifers, the first of millions, believing – extraordinarily – that native broadleaved trees would pollute the water supply.

The Lake District needed a watchdog and Rawnsley provided one. In 1887 he joined the protests against blocked footpaths to Latrigg above Keswick and argued the case for keeping ancient footpaths open. He fought off quarrying threats at Loughrigg, a dam across the river Duddon and ugly new roads around Thirlmere. His campaigns made him a local hero, and he was soon nicknamed the Defender of the Lakes. Before long he was the leading light of the Lake District Defence Society, which had grown out of the Thirlmere Defence Society to fight for the whole of the Lake District's beauty.

The spring of 1883 saw Rawnsley's instalment as Vicar of Crosthwaite, the parish church of Keswick. Here, in the heart of the Lake District, he was able to fulfil his ambitions for the revival of traditional crafts as well as the protection of landscape beauty. He and his wife Edith founded the Keswick School of Industrial Arts and the Ruskin Linen Industry (Ruskin had established himself at Brantwood, on Coniston Water, in 1872), providing a northern centre for the Arts and Crafts movement. And just as Beatrix Potter did later, Hardwicke Rawnsley threw himself into Lake District life. He was present at every show and sheep shearing, sports day and sheepdog trials. Passionately committed to teaching children about nature, he founded schools and a May Queen ceremony.

In 1889 Rawnsley topped the poll as an independent Liberal in the Keswick election for the new Cumberland County Council, mandating his defence of the Lake District. His friendship with Octavia Hill and Robert Hunter grew, and by 1893 he was attending regular meetings with them in London. That the National Trust was finally founded in February 1895 was due as much to Rawnsley's energy, fuelled by his passion for the Lake District, as to Hill and Hunter's greater experience.

The Trust's founders, though, were always clear about their debt to Ruskin and were keen to remember him, especially in the hallowed ground of the Lake District. 'One [place],' wrote Hill, 'which the years will we believe render always more valuable, [is] the simple stone erected to John Ruskin on Friar's Crag at Derwent Water, where first he learned the beauty of that nature that he was to love so much and describe so eloquently.'

The Act which gave the Trust its legal standing also drew heavily on Ruskin's vision, and confirmed the centrality of beauty to the Trust's objectives:

> The National Trust shall be established for the purposes of promoting the permanent preservation for the benefit of the nation of lands and tenements (including buildings) of beauty or historic interest and as regards lands for the preservation (so far as practicable) of their natural aspect, features and animal and plant life.
>
> (National Trust Act, 1907)

Apart from the emphasis on beauty, the Act contains three significant phrases: 'promoting', giving the Trust a proactive energy; 'permanent preservation', requiring the foresight both to determine what merits preservation and the means to sustain it for ever; and 'for the benefit of the nation', confirming the social purpose of safeguarding beauty for everyone. By these words Ruskin's passionate beliefs were given statutory force, and the universal right to beauty was recognised.

The Trust's early priorities were not the great country houses and estates with which it is often associated today. Its leaders continued to safeguard vital patches of countryside as the cities sprawled, and rescued precious mediaeval vernacular buildings representing, in the Arts and Crafts movement's words, 'the twin virtues of beauty and utility; the value of craftsmanship, honesty and virtue' as many were razed to the ground in the name of progress.

The Trust's very first property was a gift from Fanny Talbot, a donor to Ruskin's Guild of St George. She gave a little bit of land, Dinas Oleu above Barmouth, that would be forever open to the public. Its first building was Alfriston Clergy House: a mediaeval cruck house, almost falling down; it was purchased for ten pounds and the Trust commissioned the SPAB to restore it, confirming its commitment to the Anti-Scrape approach.

Although the National Trust was tiny, from the beginning its future looked secure. The founders were skilled at fundraising and winning support, and they populated its committees with members of the aristocracy, MPs and representatives of the great universities, ensuring advocacy for beauty in high places. Octavia Hill persuaded her friend Princess Louise, Queen Victoria's daughter, to honour the ceremony marking the acquisition of the Trust's first property in the Lake District, Brandelhow, in 1902. The National Trust became the place where thinking and prominent people came together to consider the state of conservation in the nation:

The acquisition and opening of Brandelhow in the Lake District, attended by Princess Louise, marked one of the National Trust's early successes. Here it is pictured today. (Courtesy of the National Trust/Joe Cornish)

what was under threat, what could be saved, what issues needed to be raised in Parliament, and what needed to be said to the press and the public. As a result, their legacy, like Ruskin's, is far greater than the National Trust itself. It is about the principle and the importance of beauty, the right to defend what matters and the universal human need for beauty and places where it may be experienced.

These were the ideas and the spirit that gave birth to the fight for beauty; a fight that would continue undimmed into the twentieth century.

2

The calls and claims of natural beauty

'The [objects of the] Bill before the House ... are, first, to preserve and enhance the beauty of the countryside; and second, to enable our people to see it, get to it, and enjoy it.' With these words, the most conscious Act for beauty ever brought about by a British government was introduced into Parliament by Lewis Silkin, Minister of Town and Country Planning, on 31 March 1949.

If the fight for beauty in the nineteenth century was launched in response to the uncontrolled and unforeseen side-effects of industrialisation, the spark that reignited it in the twentieth century was the way housing and other development – much though it was needed – seemed completely to disregard the character and quality of a countryside that was held in exceptional esteem. The years up to and following the First World War, caught up in its horror, saw an extraordinary upsurge in affection for the English countryside. This was captured most poignantly by the war poets, whose elegies brought to life its romantic beauty, and what it meant to those offering their lives and liberty. But theirs were not the only voices speaking up for beauty: concerns about the pace and scale of change led to a remarkable consensus that urban sprawl was bad for the country, bad for the economy and bad for people; and that the country and its people deserved better. So protecting the beauty of the countryside and enabling people to enjoy it were among the package of transformational measures put in place by the 1945 post-war government as part of its promise to deliver a better world. But as the twentieth century advanced that clear-sighted consensus broke down, and new pressures on beauty materialised, leaving the inspiration Ruskin had provided far behind.

Ruskin's star had been fading for some time before he died quietly at his home, Brantwood, in the Lake District in 1900, and those who ushered in the twentieth century were preoccupied by new challenges. Redressing the social ills of the previous century was, rightly and understandably, at the heart of them. While the Empire was still confident, even brash (Lord Curzon's Durbar in Delhi in 1903 to celebrate the coronation of Edward VII was the most extravagant on record), at home the economy was far from secure, and in politics the power bases were shifting, the traditional ruling classes ousted by new parties passionate about social justice. The 1906 election saw victory for the Liberals and the first group of elected Labour politicians entering Parliament, all with a reforming agenda. The Chancellor from 1908 was David Lloyd George, who introduced the first welfare measures: free school meals and clinics, pensions and better conditions for workers including, for the first time, health insurance and unemployment benefit.

But the connections between social justice and beauty so strongly advocated by Ruskin were not completely lost. Early attempts to organise a response to the dire living conditions in Victorian cities coalesced in the first Planning Act, which was passed in 1909. Its purposes could have been written by Ruskin and Hill, since it aimed:

to provide a domestic condition for the people in which their physical health, their morals, their character and their whole social condition can be improved by what we hope to secure in this Bill. The Bill aims in broad outline at, and hopes to secure, the home healthy, the house beautiful, the town pleasant, the city dignified and the suburb salubrious.

These aims were easier described than addressed, because the reality was so harshly different. And the Bill was not just focused on providing better housing and sanitation; the government also wanted to reduce the rate at which land was being consumed for building. This was a serious problem. John Burns, MP for Battersea and President of the Local Government Board, warned at the Planning Bill's Second Reading in May 1908:

> In fifteen years 500,000 acres of land have been abstracted from the agricultural domain for houses, factories, workshops and railways . . . if we go on in the next fifteen years abstracting another half a million from the agricultural domain, and we go on rearing in green fields slums . . . in many respects more squalid than those found in Liverpool, London and Glasgow, posterity will blame us for not taking this matter in hand in a scientific spirit. Every two and half years there is a County of London converted into urban life from rural conditions and agricultural land. It represents an enormous amount of building land which we have no right to allow to go unregulated.

It was a warning for which there was no answer, however, because there was no mechanism to manage the process of development:

apart from a very few safeguards for public health, developers could simply buy land and build on it. The first Planning Acts of 1909 and 1919 attempted to get to grips with this and were preoccupied with urban renewal, proposing housing schemes for urban areas to deliver both slum clearance and new public housing – the forerunner of the council house – built to higher standards including sanitation. Outside towns and cities, however, there were no schemes: developers continued to build where and what they wanted, favouring quickly built housing from cheap materials, and so the outskirts of London and other major cities were taken over by a new phenomenon – sprawl.

Into the midst of this process came the First World War, triggered by an assassination in the far-off Balkans, which was to have such devastating consequences for the blooming youth of Britain and their families. Initially there was a rush to enlist, to serve one's country, and because it was expected to be a short, sharp conflict; but the long years between 1914 and 1918 became almost wholly preoccupied with battles on land and sea, in Palestine, Arabia, Turkey and France, with casualties far worse than anyone foresaw at the war's start. By the end, British deaths stood at over 700,000, a twelfth of those who had fought. Families throughout the land lost fathers, sons and brothers, husbands and sweethearts.

But those who went into battle were fighting for an England they loved. Into the maelstrom went troops carrying copies of Housman's *A Shropshire Lad*, its nostalgic descriptions of rural life and young men going to early deaths creating an all-too vivid parallel with the awful realities of the war. The poets Robert Graves, Wilfrid Owen and Rupert Brooke wrote both harrowing accounts of the brutal conditions in the trenches and also evocative lines recalling the lives and landscapes of the England they had left behind. Edward Thomas mused as he agonised about whether to enlist: 'It seems foolish to have loved England up to now without knowing it could perhaps be ravaged and I could and perhaps would do nothing to prevent it.'

And for those who did return from the war it was to disappointment and frustration. The loss of the family's breadwinner caused hardship; the country's 'new' workforce (largely women) had to be demobilised to create jobs for returning servicemen, who had themselves to be re-absorbed into a workplace still more focused on munitions than peace-time manufacturing. Moreover in 1918 an intense flu pandemic killed an estimated fifty million people worldwide and nearly a quarter of a million people in the UK. For many, returning home from the wastelands of northern France was a dismal story of hopes still further dashed.

Desperate to establish order and confidence, the government elected in 1918 (a Liberal/Conservative coalition led by Lloyd George) promised 'A Land fit for Heroes' to those returning from the battlefields. Within this pledge were plans for housing: 'Homes fit for Heroes', in part a military-inspired response to the poor physical condition of many army recruits, in part a response to the urgent need to provide decent housing for those who had suffered during the war, and in part a fulfilment of earlier commitments to slum clearance. The returning soldiers deserved to be treated as heroes, but they were also seeking the England they loved and had fought for. In the absence of many tangible benefits, novelists and poets met their need for nurture and reassurance. Thomas Hardy wrote prolifically about rural society and the landscapes of Dorset; Mary Webb's famous account of vernacular Shropshire, *Precious Bane*, was honoured by a preface by no less a figure than the Prime Minister, Stanley Baldwin; while Henry Williamson's elegiac story *Tarka the Otter* was universally popular.

But the government's ambitious plans for state-led renewal proved impossible to deliver. Although there was an immediate post-war economic lift, the economy soon spiralled into depression. The core elements of international trade – coal, iron and steel – interrupted during the war, never revived, leading to a collapse in domestic production and manufacturing. Other countries began to produce textiles and build ships more cheaply than Britain could, and an unhappy domestic workforce resorted to strikes – most famously in 1926 – adding to the pressures on workers and businesses. The international financial crisis swept Britain into depression, leaving no money for heroes. The slums were not cleared and the government could not build the houses it promised. And in the countryside farming faltered in the doldrums, land unkempt and uncared-for. Rural poverty was widespread, rural businesses struggled, and housing and services were poor. Investment was urgently needed but there was no structure to shape where and how it should be made.

Into the vacuum came the opportunists. If the government had no money to invest in housing, others saw no such restraint. Urban slum clearance was expensive and required formal planning schemes, while land in the countryside stood ready to be seized. Land speculators spotted the opportunity and began to build cheap housing, new roads and the paraphernalia associated with them. With no controls to manage it, the tentacles of sprawl seemed unstoppable. J. B. Priestley in *Our Nation's Heritage* (1939) described the process and its results:

> First we construct a specially broad and straight road . . . as soon as the road is finished . . . firms of builders buy the land on each side of the road, and begin hastily throwing up hundreds of bungalows and the like . . . so that very soon the road that was made to escape the town has

become a sort of town itself. This is called Ribbon
Development and it is going on all over England.

He, like others, believed that what was happening was even worse
than the industrialisation of the previous century: 'our twentieth
century spoiling, especially our 1920, 1930, spoiling, has been
much worse [than the nineteenth century spoiling],' he wrote,
'instead of concentrating the nasty attack on a few districts, it has
set to work to ruin the look of the whole island.'

The new developments were vastly more land-hungry than
the housing they replaced, and industry and its associated housing was also leaving the cities for greenfield sites. New houses
were certainly needed: a million were built in the 1920s and
ambitions were much higher for the 1930s. But the lack of any
control over their location or design horrified many observers.
Clough Williams-Ellis (the architect who created the Italianate
village in Snowdonia, Portmeirion), wrote 'since the War, indeed
[England] has been changing with an acceleration that is catastrophic, thoroughly frightening the thoughtful among us and
making them sadly wonder whether anything recognisable of
our lovely England will be left for our children's children.' He
was not the only person who found it deeply ironic that the
country had been saved from the Germans only to be ruined by
its own citizens.

In his autobiography, *Architect Errant*, Williams-Ellis dubbed
the new breed of defenders of beauty (all were knighted for their
work) 'The Seven Knights Errant' of the movement. Sir Patrick
Geddes, Sir Raymond Unwin, Sir Charles Reilly, Sir Guy Dawber,
Sir Lawrence Weaver, Sir Patrick Abercrombie and Sir Herbert
Griffin were all concerned with architecture or planning or both.
They were intellectuals, philanthropists and thinkers, and although
inspired by Ruskin they were not anti-urbanites, believing

passionately in cities but arguing for a greater commitment to city design and civic life. Their ambition was to extend the new discipline of land-use planning and urban design to protect England's countryside.

The most vocal advocate of rural planning was Patrick Abercrombie. The son of a Manchester stockbroker, he was apprenticed to architects in Manchester and Liverpool for six years before joining the staff of the University of Liverpool, where in 1915 he became Professor of Civic Design. In 1916 he won an international competition to redesign Dublin, which led to a city plan in 1922, and he followed its success with similar plans for Plymouth, Hull, Sheffield, Bath, Edinburgh and Bournemouth. But he was also passionate about the countryside, and in 1926 he published a pamphlet, *The Preservation of Rural England*, a polemic which decried the 'ribbon of residential growth unrolling along the roadside', but which also proposed the constructive suggestion that planning could provide the answer.

His pamphlet opened with a question: 'The English countryside is undergoing a change . . . Is this inevitable change to destroy the existing aspect of the countryside or is it possible during transition to preserve its character or even in places to create a new kind of beauty? It is at any rate a matter than cannot be left to chance.' It closed with a warning: 'There is . . . no time to be lost if the English countryside is not to be reduced . . . to the same state of dreary productiveness to which the English town sank during the industrial revolution.'

Abercrombie's central idea was that the government should apply the 'same principles of constructive planning and conservation to the country as are already familiarly in use for town and suburb'. He did not want to stop new development, but to guide it to appropriate places, believing that most, including roads, 'if skilfully engineered . . . will in time drop into the landscape'. But he concluded that the art of persuasive planning in rural areas required 'a sympathy for historic tradition and an appreciation of landscape beauty', making it quite unlike town planning thus far.

Later that same year the Council for the Preservation of Rural England (CPRE) was founded to carry forward his aims, with Abercrombie as its first Honorary Secretary. Its purposes were:

> to co-ordinate the efforts of many national Associations, Institutions and Societies, each of which is interested in preserving rural scenery from some special danger or in protecting the artistic and historic features of country towns and villages. It is not intended to object to the reasonable use and development of rural areas: it is the abuse and bad development of such areas that require restrictions.

Its objects were to organise action to secure protection for rural scenery and country towns and villages; to act directly, or as a centre of advice for others; and to arouse, form and educate public opinion in pursuit of its objects. One of its first publications, with the refreshingly straightforward title *War on Ugly Building*, stated that CPRE aimed 'to preserve beauty and see that what is added to the face of the land is not unbeautiful'.

CPRE's inaugural meeting was held on 7 December 1926 at the Royal Institution of British Architects where it established its Council, composed of the organisations who would work together to preserve rural England. These included official bodies such as the Ministry of Housing and Local Government, the Forestry Commission, Generating Board and local authorities; and charities like the National Trust, Commons Preservation Society, ramblers' bodies, the Women's Institute and the Boy

Scouts. There were also professional bodies including the Royal Institute of British Architects (RIBA) and the town planning organisations, as well as the Automobile Association (AA) and the National Farmers' Union.

CPRE was influential from the start, earning the endorsement of Neville Chamberlain, later to become Prime Minister but then Minister of Health with responsibility for housing. In addressing its inaugural meeting he effectively invited CPRE to make the case in terms that he could advance within the government:

> I most heartily give my support and approval to the objects of this new Council . . . the very fact that I do my work in the town and I take my recreation in the country is perhaps a reason why I should be, as I am, deeply concerned at the persistent and rapid defacement of the countryside, which is proceeding today at a pace far in excess of anything we have ever known before in our history . . . I consider that the formation of a body such as this is a real step forward from the practical point of view . . . and that it will bring nearer the time when we can begin to think about legislation which will enable greater restrictions to be placed upon individual liberty than perhaps public opinion would tolerate today.

With such warm official backing CPRE got off to a flying start. It was soon being consulted on specific proposals as well as being asked to help develop general principles for rural planning. Its activists were drawn from the ranks of Clough Williams-Ellis' Knights Errant: its first General Secretary was Herbert Griffin, who served for fifty years, and its first President was Guy Dawber. CPRE quickly set up county branches and sister organisations in Wales and Scotland (an Ulster Society for the Preservation of the Countryside was established a decade later, in 1937). Some of its

A 1934 CPRE design guide showing how not to build new housing in the Peak District. (Courtesy of CPRE) affiliates pre-dated it, including the Friends of the Lake District, which had grown out of the Lake District Defence Association, and the Sheffield Association for the Protection of Local Scenery, which was established in 1925 to campaign against ugly roads, buildings and suburban development around Sheffield. Before long there were CPRE branches in nearly every county, run by enthusiastic and knowledgeable volunteers.

This local effort was essential for the promotion and protection of beauty. CPRE was arguing strongly for national principles: that town planning should apply to rural areas; ribbon development and urban sprawl should be curtailed; cities should be divided from the countryside; and the design of new development should be improved. But the only way of making practical progress was by harnessing the eyes and ears of local people, who could make objections and propose alternatives to ugly development, whether in different locations or to a better design. A hallmark of CPRE's early days was an array of design guides produced by friendly local architects, encouraging vernacular traditions and the use of local materials, and discouraging the ugly.

But as the pressures persisted it was clear that the CPRE's third object, educating public opinion, would be as important as its immediate practical work.

Sprawl, especially in the South East, was the chief concern. Abercrombie had predicted that 'it can only be a matter of time before the main roads in the home counties are completely taken up, and soon this green and pleasant land of ours will only be glimpsed through an almost continuous hedge of bungalows and houses.' And it was London's expansion that inspired Clough Williams-Ellis to write his polemic *England and the Octopus*, published in 1928. His target was the poor quality of development, not the people who badly needed housing, but the book is full of unpleasant and deprecating descriptions of 'mean and perky' little houses and 'blasphemous bungalows' appearing like a 'higgledy-piggledy' rash across England's beautiful countryside. His *Devil's Dictionary* was a recitation of ugliness: outdoor advertisements, aerodromes, broadcasting aerials, the electric power grid and petrol pumps, alongside ideas about how to make things beautiful, with harmonious architecture and (intriguingly) feng shui featuring prominently. He claimed, though, endorsed by the accompanying *Epistola Epilogica* penned by Patrick Abercrombie, that the chief cause of ugliness was ignorance, not evil intent. Thus the challenge was simply, if ambitiously, to educate everyone to embrace the cause of beauty.

The problem was not just the lack of planning but the poor quality of much of what was built. G. M. Trevelyan, the newly appointed Regius Professor of History at Cambridge University and

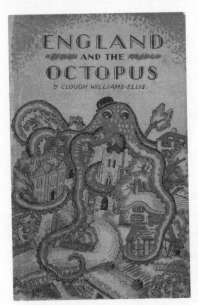

Clough Williams-Ellis' *England and the Octopus* drew provocative attention to the problems of urban sprawl and poorly designed new housing.

Chairman of the Estates Committee of the National Trust, railed against the utilitarianism of the modern world in his rhetorical pamphlet *Must England's Beauty Perish?* (1929). He wrote, echoing Ruskin:

> action taken for purely economic reasons no longer as of old creates new beauty, but destroys old beauty and substitutes modern ugliness . . . Concrete is cheaper than stone. A wire fence can be more quickly set up than a hedge or a stone wall. A curving road is regarded as a public nuisance because it impedes the pace of the motor. A bungalow or a red brick villa are more easily run up than a house of the old local material. Electric power marches across the country on poles that scrape the sky. It pays better to plant conifers than beech or oak – and so forth through innumerable instances.

That was a plea for support for the National Trust, but in his 1931 lecture 'The Calls and Claims of Natural Beauty' he, like Priestley, blamed the car for the new evils:

> Two things are characteristic of this age, and more particularly of this island. The conscious appreciation of natural beauty, and the rapidity with which natural beauty is being destroyed. No doubt it is partly because the destruction is so rapid that the appreciation is so loud . . . the advent of the motor car, though it enables the dweller in our unhappy cities to enjoy relief in the country more easily, is plastering the countryside with horrors of bungalows, advertisements and ugly houses in the wrong places at a pace of which the Victorians might have perhaps been proud, but which they were fortunately unable to rival for lack of the internal combustion engine.

There was, therefore, no time to wait for the population to be educated. The fight for beauty was urgent. And, slowly, it began to gain purchase. Throughout the 1930s and 1940s CPRE marshalled the arguments against uncontrolled housebuilding and ribbon development, for establishing green belts to contain city expansion and to control outdoor advertisements. And the government responded: the 1932 Planning Act extended planning powers to rural as well as urban land, though it was to prove pathetically weak; and the Restriction of Ribbon Development Act 1935 provided the first line of defence against Abercrombie's 'ribbon of residential growth'.

The government continued to believe in planning schemes to decide where new development should take place. But the idea remained better in theory than in practice. Schemes took years to prepare and required Parliamentary approval, so few got past the draft stage and many developers ignored them. Almost worse, once a scheme was agreed there was no control over what was built, making it impossible to secure good design. The result, whether makeshift houses in scattered plots on the clifftops at Peacehaven, or street after street of identikit bungalows, ranged from the undistinguished to the downright ugly. Many agreed that people deserved better than the desultory quality of the thousands of identical 'labour-saving homes' that triggered Betjeman to write:

> Come, friendly bombs and fall on Slough
> It isn't fit for humans now,
> There isn't grass to graze a cow
>> Swarm over, Death!
> Mess up the place they call a town –
> A house for ninety-seven down
> And once a week for half a crown
>> For twenty years . . .
>>>> (John Betjeman, 'Slough', 1937)

And, for the first and only time in planning's existence, the rush to ensure there was enough land for housing ran out of control too. Though in the twenty years from 1919 to 1939 four million houses were built, the majority in and around London, by 1937, in the half of the country covered by draft planning schemes, enough land was zoned for housing to accommodate 350 million people for a population of only forty-five million. Rural and urban planning had yet to prove their worth.

By the late 1930s the country was once again distracted by preparations for war. This time those in charge were determined that things would be different. Not only would the war be managed differently but its consequences would be anticipated. Never again would heroes return to the chaos that had greeted the survivors of the last war. Never again would poor organisation prevent the delivery of essential services. And it was clear what people would be fighting *for*: the graphic designer Frank Newbould was commissioned to produce a series of evocative recruitment posters for the War Office – *Your Britain, Fight for it Now* – laden with images of the romantic beauty of England's unspoiled countryside.

This time the government was determined to plan for the peace even as the war began. The leader of the war-time coalition government, Winston Churchill, applied to post-war planning the same characteristics that shaped the orchestration of Britain's war effort: positive intervention, clear strategy and effective organisation. In 1941 he established the Committee on Wartime Reconstruction and he told its members, including Clement Attlee, leader of the Labour Party, that their work was as important as delivering Britain's war victory. Uniting them all was the determination to build a better, fairer Britain for all its citizens, and among their objectives was protecting the beauty of the countryside for people to enjoy.

There were many strands to the Committee's work, some predating the war. Already commissioned was the Committee on Social Insurance and Allied Services, chaired by William Beveridge, a Ruskin devotee, his proposals addressing the five 'Giant Evils' of 'Squalor, Ignorance, Want, Idleness and Disease' that afflicted the country. His report was published in 1942 and laid the foundations for a comprehensive welfare state and National Health Service. But many other elements related to land and the distribution of jobs, houses and services. The central role of the Ministry of Works in supporting the Committee reflected the realisation that the wise use of land should be at the heart of an effective reconstruction programme.

To that end, three pieces of work informed the Reconstruction Committee's thinking. First was the Barlow Commission (set up in 1937, chaired by Sir Anderson Montague-Barlow) which addressed the unacceptable contrast between the thriving South East of the country and the depressed areas of the North, given the government's desire to spread the benefits of jobs and housing. It was not a harmonious committee (Patrick Abercrombie was one of several members who called for more radical and urgent solutions) but on three points it was united: there needed to be a mechanism for national planning; dispersal outside the South East was essential; and measures were needed to anticipate and stop regional depression.

Second, the Uthwatt Committee was commissioned in 1939 and its report was published in 1941. It advised on Compensation and Betterment, proposing ways of sharing the proceeds of development value, the dramatic increase in the value of land when planning permission was granted. Its recommendations were implemented in 1947 but it proved too difficult to extract profits from developers and owners and the system was abandoned in 1959.

And third, Lord Justice Scott led a committee whose report *Land Utilisation in Rural Areas* was published in 1942. While they all fed in to the post-war legislative package, the Scott Committee was most influential in shaping the government's thinking and decisions about beauty. Its wide terms of reference encompassed the social, economic and aesthetic problems facing the country-side. The report eulogised about land: 'land is one of the prime essentials of human subsistence. From the soil and from under the soil come practically all the materials on which mankind depends'; and it eulogised about the particular beauty of the English coun-tryside: 'the landscape . . . is a striking example of the interdepend-ence between the satisfaction of man's material wants and the crea-tion of beauty.'

Scott's primary concern was the agricultural depression and the resuscitation of farming, rural life and living conditions in the countryside which had not improved since the First World War. So he looked at the provision of piped water and electricity, housing, roads, schools and industry (which his Committee wanted to steer to the towns) as well as the case for improved rural planning, public access, national parks and nature reserves, all of which he endorsed. Optimistically if not naively he believed that it should be possible to protect what was beautiful while addressing people's material needs, and that a prosperous farming industry posed no threat to beauty. Echoing Morris, his report concluded: 'we consider that the land of Britain should be both useful and beautiful and that the two aims are in no sense incompatible.' But the Scott Committee's failure to anticipate the breakdown of the relationship between farming and conservation was to have more severe consequences than anyone appreciated at the time.

A passionate albeit short-lived figure in post-war reconstruction was Sir John (later Lord) Reith, who had left the BBC in 1938 and was recruited to join the wartime effort in government. In 1940 he was appointed the first Minister of Works, the department at the centre of post-war reconstruction. Though only in the post for two years before Churchill dropped him from the Cabinet, he left an important legacy in his commitment to a 'national plan for the optimum use of land' as a central plank of post-war reconstruction. His later role in getting New Towns off the ground was also influential.

The principles Reith espoused came to fruition in the 1944 White Paper *The Control of Land Use*. This was an unusually clear document in stating both what was right and what was wrong about the use of land. And it sat firmly on the side of the campaigners for beauty, being deeply critical of urban sprawl for multiple reasons:

> The wrong use of land [it said] [resulted] in much loss, both to individuals and to the nation, of well-being, of time and of money. Good agricultural land was unnecessarily wasted, and the appearance of the country spoiled, by sporadic and unsightly building; public authorities were put to undue expense by the need of supplying water and other services strung out along the principal highways; road accidents (especially among children) were multiplied; valuable hours were lost each working day, and the traffic of great cities congested, because of the distance at which workers lived from their work; the standard of health was affected, and the decency of living impaired, by overcrowding.

By contrast:

> Provision for the right use of land, in accordance with a considered policy, is an essential requirement of the

government's programme of post-war reconstruction. New houses, whether of permanent or emergency construction; the new layout of areas devastated by enemy action or blighted by reason of age or bad living conditions; the new schools which will be required in the Education Bill now before Parliament; the balanced distribution of industry which the government's recently published proposals for maintaining active employment envisage; the requirements of sound nutrition and of a healthy and well-balanced agriculture; the preservation of land for national parks and forests; and the assurance to the people of enjoyment of the sea and countryside in times of leisure; a new and safer highway system better adapted to modern industrial and other needs; the proper provision of airfields – all these related parts of a single reconstruction programme involve the use of land, and it is essential that their various claims of land should be so harmonised as to ensure for the people of this country the greatest possible measure of individual well-being and national prosperity.

This was a remarkably firm endorsement of the concerns that had underpinned the early twentieth-century fight for beauty. Moreover its ideas foreshadowed the ambitions for and elements of harmonisation that would shape the whole post-war plan. And as the planner Gordon Cherry commented in 1974: 'Never before (and never since) had a statement of national planning objectives been quite so clearly stated; it was indeed a remarkable affirmation.' Protecting the beauty of the countryside, through the 'right use of land,' was one of its goals.

So when Clement Attlee, as much to his surprise as Churchill's disappointment, became Prime Minister in July 1945 in the

Labour landslide, he inherited the work of the Reconstruction Committee and implementing its ideas became the primary objective of his government. And beauty was embedded in the government's aims.

What motivated Attlee? He was the quiet man of British politics, an unlikely leader though an excellent administrator and committee man. His background, unlike many in the early Labour movement, was middle class: his father was a lawyer who rose to become President of the Law Society. Attlee attended Haileybury College near Hertford before University College, Oxford, and was led to both Ruskin and socialism by his brother Laurence. He took Clem to the East End in 1905, soon after leaving Oxford, to visit the Stepney Boys' Club, which was supported by Haileybury College to help poor boys in an area of desperate poverty. Attlee became first intrigued then committed, and by 1907 (after a failed attempt at training for the Bar) he was both its manager and a committed socialist. Apart from his war service he dedicated himself to social and political work in the East End, becoming Secretary of the Stepney Branch of the Independent Labour Party in 1908 and Labour MP for Limehouse in 1922.

Like many early Labour MPs, Attlee devoured the works of Ruskin and Morris, especially Ruskin's *Unto this Last*. In his common-sense autobiography *As it Happened* he writes most elegiacally when describing the countryside of his childhood and school days; influences that surely informed his leadership of the first majority Labour government.

The reconstruction programme was ambitious, requiring laws designed not only to meet citizens' basic human needs but also their spiritual, physical and cultural well-being. And thanks to the work of the Reconstruction Committee and its focus on the 'right use of land' they were based on an approach seeking harmonisation, to address and improve *all* the elements of people's lives, meeting both their material and non-material needs.

So in the five years following the war – as well as legislating for a universal right to education (1946), National Insurance (1946) and pensions (1947), the National Health Service (1948) and measures to revive agriculture (1947) – the government introduced comprehensive Town and Country Planning (1947) and the National Parks and Access to the Countryside Act (1949).

The last two Acts in particular represented pioneering ambitions for beauty, introducing the first clear and comprehensive framework for land use planning, and new (though long fought-for) measures to protect the countryside, designate national parks, safeguard nature and wildlife, and provide legal access to the countryside. If it seems impressive to us that these elements were central to the post-war offering, it was transparently clear why to its proponents. Introducing the National Parks Bill, the Minister, Lewis Silkin, told Parliament that:

> the enjoyment of our leisure in the open air and the ability
> to leave our towns and walk on the moors and in the dales

The 1945 Attlee Cabinet. (Courtesy of Keystone/Stringer, Getty Images)

without fear of interruption are . . . just as much a part of positive health and wellbeing as are the buildings of hospitals or insurance against sickness . . . This is not just a Bill. It is a people's charter – a people's charter for the open air, for the hikers and the ramblers, for everyone who loves to get out into the open air and enjoy the countryside.

In creating National Parks Silkin was responding to a thirty-year clamour for the legislation from people who, having endured two world wars, now wanted and deserved to enjoy the countryside they had fought for. Since images of the countryside had spurred troops on with their romantic portrayal of a rural England untouched by modern life or damaged by ugly development, it was only right that in peacetime the countryside should in some sense belong to them.

These were heroic goals at a time when heroic leadership was needed. And harmonisation – a process of balancing social, economic and cultural goals – was at the heart of them. But how successful would this ambition be? It was certainly heartfelt, marking an unprecedented commitment to renewal and reconstruction. Perhaps never before or since has motivation for such a collective, integrated approach been stronger: Britain had survived the threat of invasion and attack; many lives had been lost or irreparably damaged; and its people had endured the stresses of rationing, evacuation, conscription and loss.

But beyond the immediate period of post-war austerity the mood of collective endeavour for collective benefit was soon challenged, and the contradictions within and between the package of policies began to show.

By the 1950s Britain's working people were having their first real taste of growth not only trickling down but reaching them. Indeed, by 1957 Prime Minister Harold Macmillan was telling the nation that they had 'never had it so good'. He was right. Between 1951 and 1973 the British economy grew by an unprecedented 2.8% a year, unemployment was at record low levels (two per cent or below), and inflation was also low (less than four per cent) by historical comparisons. The new measure of GDP (Gross Domestic Product), urged on the government by John Maynard Keynes, confirmed that the economy was steadily improving. And not least because of the post-war reforms each generation was also healthier, longer lived and better educated than their parents. Between 1951 and 1973 infant mortality halved, life expectancy rose by five years for both men and women, and average hours worked fell while wages rose.

Golden years economically, this was also a time of rising consumerism and the growth of technology and labour-saving devices in the home. In those same two decades car ownership rose from forty-six households per thousand head of population to 247 (it is now over five hundred); and most households acquired washing machines, refrigerators and televisions. Leisure time expanded and people enjoyed trips out into the countryside, causing new headaches as car-borne millions swarmed into popular beauty spots. And the countryside itself was changing as, despite the Scott Committee's optimism, there was nothing to constrain the technological transformation that was overtaking farming and forestry, damaging its beauty.

Small wonder, then, that the government's aspirations to protect beauty faced many challenges. As later chapters will show, the conservation of all aspects of beauty was central to the 1940s vision but the tools provided were not strong enough to counter the demands that were driven by the new wealth and mobility and the rapid rate of technological advances.

In fact the safeguards for beauty introduced in the 1940s proved hopelessly inadequate in the face of the pressures on land and natural resources that flowed as the economy grew from the 1950s onwards. National Parks were a shadow of what their advocates had envisaged. Historic buildings were lost to urban and rural redevelopment, and agriculture (even in National Parks) became increasingly industrialised as farmers were paid to remove hedges, ponds and semi-natural vegetation to grow cereal crops and to plough the heather-clad hills for intensive sheep production. Though planning helped manage the pressures, the demands for houses, jobs, roads and factories were intense; much design was poor and architectural standards were low. New forests of alien species were planted and ancient woodlands were felled or under-planted with commercial timber crops. Seas were over-fished. Pollution killed rivers and tarnished beaches. Rare birds and plants were pushed to the brink of extinction. Oil, coal and building materials were extracted at an ever faster rate and energy consumption escalated. By the 1970s there was a crisis, for both natural beauty and the wider environment.

The alarm was sounded with increasing urgency both at home and internationally. In 1972 the United Nations convened the Stockholm Conference on the Human Environment. And Malthusian ideas of a catastrophic readjustment in response to a soaring population re-surfaced. *The Limits to Growth* burst onto the scene in 1972, its frightening forecasts exacerbated by the oil crisis and fuel's rapidly increasing cost. Its genesis was a Massachusetts Institute of Technology *Project on the Predicament of Mankind* under the auspices of the Club of Rome, looking at the effects and impacts of worldwide growth.

The project modelled growth rates, dependencies and feedback loops to investigate the five major trends of industrialisation, population growth, malnutrition, depletion of non-renewable resources and a deteriorating environment. Like Malthus' theory, its conclusions rested on mathematics, because the researchers observed exponential rates of growth in each trend. Their calculations showed that if 1960s trends continued the limits to growth on Earth would be reached within a hundred years in the form of an uncontrollable crisis. Though they argued that a state of global equilibrium was feasible, based on 'satisfying the basic material needs of each person and enabling each person to reach their human potential', no time should be lost in seeking it.

As before, though, *The Limits to Growth* failed to anticipate the ingenuity and adaptability of humans. The issue on which the authors were most accurate was population growth, where they forecast a world population of seven billion by the year 2000. In fact the six-billionth child was born in 1999 and the seven-billionth in October 2011. But growth levels of industrial output of seven per cent per annum in the 1960s were not sustained; agricultural productivity increased faster than they predicted; new sources of non-renewable resources (including fossil fuels as well as rare minerals) were found; and measures were taken, at least in more mature economies, to address pollution.

The authors were right, though, to predict that the unequal distribution of wealth, food and natural resources would persist. And that addressing certain forms of pollution would stretch human creativity and political will to the limit. Presciently, *Limits to Growth* commented, 'it is not known how much CO_2 or thermal pollution can be released without causing irreversible changes in the earth's climate'.

They also recognised that humans need to grow in some way, even if not materially, concluding with the observation that:

> any human activity that does not require a large flow of irreplaceable resources or produce severe environmental degradation might continue to grow indefinitely. In

particular, those pursuits that many people would list as the most desirable and satisfying activities of man – education, art, music, religion, basic scientific research, athletics, and social interactions – could flourish.

Though the legacy of *The Limits to Growth* was not a new definition of progress, it did lead to a strengthening of the environmental movement. In the UK Friends of the Earth was founded in 1971, with a returnable-bottles campaign, and Greenpeace launched the *Rainbow Warrior* in 1978 to oppose commercial whaling. The World Wildlife Fund (now the Worldwide Fund for Nature), though founded earlier, in 1961, grew rapidly in the 1970s and 1980s.

But the very sources of human ingenuity that rescued the human population from disaster also triggered the renewal of tensions and a revival of the fight for beauty. In particular rising agricultural productivity, encouraged by the 1947 Agriculture Act, caused the conservation bodies catastrophically to fall out with those who had created the beauty of the landscape in the first place: the farmers. Unforeseen by the Scott Committee, the tensions between farming and conservation dominated the last three decades of the twentieth century. And these were by now deep tensions, illustrated by Marion Shoard's conclusion in *The Theft of the Countryside* (1980): 'the English landscape is under sentence of death . . . Indeed, the sentence is already being carried out. The executioner is not the industrialist or the property speculator . . . Instead, it is the figure traditionally viewed as the custodian of the rural scene – the farmer.'

And so, towards the end of the twentieth century, the fight for beauty was re-energised. And once again it was about the two preoccupations that had consumed the fight since Wordsworth first captured its dynamic: whether human demands have always to be met; and the quality (or otherwise) of what we do. The fight for beauty was not about stopping progress, but about whether beauty was overlooked or marginalised in decisions about change. So our fights were about the location and numbers of houses, industry and power stations; the damage caused by pollution on land and sea; road expansion; quarries; and the commercialisation of agriculture and forestry. At the same time we were fighting *for* public access and better protection for archaeology, historic buildings, nature and landscapes, and for higher quality development and good design. But the obstacles often felt insuperable.

I know because this was when I joined the movement. In 1980, straight out of university, I became Secretary to the Council for National Parks, a small charity lobbying for the protection of National Parks. Later I took on leading roles in both CPRE and the National Trust. For thirty-five years I have worked for or closely with some of the leading conservation charities in this country, and that is the experience on which I draw as I describe the fight for beauty and make the case for why beauty matters today.

But the fight for beauty in the twentieth century was not all about conflict, or indeed all about stopping things. It was also a time of learning and experimentation, about developing the techniques of conservation and the skills needed to protect natural resources and our environment. As campaigners we became expert in all manner of legal, policy and practical matters, and the conservation movement, both statutory and voluntary, became increasingly professional. And we started to win back some of beauty's ground.

The terms on which we did so were rooted in the post-war aspirations for harmonisation and integration, ambitions which still resonated in parts of Whitehall and Westminster. The aspiration for balance, and of seeking to achieve multiple benefits, including beauty, still carried some weight. Many fights were won with help, particularly from the European Union, which through the 1980s and 1990s set increasingly rigorous standards for clean air, clean water, the protection of birds and habitats, and measures for dealing with acid rain and chlorofluorocarbons (CFCs), which damaged the ozone layer. And as later chapters will show, as a result of our lobbying, the worst damage caused by the Common Agricultural Policy was stopped when the European Commission began to pay some farmers to look after the beauty of the countryside and nature alongside food production. The European Commission also introduced new processes to assess environmental impact, helping reduce the damage caused by new infrastructure.

Land use planning, arguably the most important practical tool in the post-war government's armoury, was always contentious and there were periodic attempts to weaken it, but thanks to our strong defence of them, green belts – the protective rings around major cities created to stop sprawl and create a clear urban edge – remained intact and most are still upheld today. Successive Secretaries of State for the Environment accepted the case for better policies, including for the protection of beauty: in 1990 Chris (now Lord) Patten commissioned the first-ever White Paper on the Environment, introducing the concept of 'greening' policy across government, imposing new duties on departments not previously known for their sympathy to these aims. John Gummer (now Lord Deben), stopped out-of-town superstores almost in their tracks in 1993, switching supermarkets' commercial investment into high streets. And in 1996 he introduced a 'brownfield first' target, requiring that at least fifty per cent of new housing should be built on previously developed land; it was increased by John (now Lord) Prescott to sixty per cent in 1998 and later rose still higher. Increasing numbers of local authorities adopted design guides to improve the quality of architectural design and the materials of new housing. All these processes – the inching forward, the knocking back – are described in later chapters.

But although we won some important safeguards, beneath all these arguments one trend is clear. There has been a marked shift away from the use of the word beauty in policy and legislation, towards a new language which may please the bureaucrats but leaves the human spirit cold. These new words have a technical meaning – for example biodiversity, sustainable development, ecosystem services and natural capital – but we have lost the simple, unaffected power of beauty that was capable of inspiring millions, including (in their day) politicians. Once, a belief that beauty mattered resonated across the entire population, infusing the pre-, inter- and immediate post-war period, and led to commitments to the 'right use of land' and measures for beauty in post-war legislation and policy. Today to talk of beauty in policy circles risks embarrassment: it is felt both to be too vague a word, lacking precision and focus; and, paradoxically given its appeal by contrast with official jargon, elitist. Yet in losing the word 'beauty' we have lost something special from our ability to shape our present and our future.

And now, at the start of the twenty-first century, we face another profound challenge. Climate change. Just as Malthus and the Club of Rome concluded, the consequences of our consumption – now of fossil fuels – threatens humanity's existence. But this time it seems unlikely that reliance on our resourcefulness and new technology (though vital) will be enough. Our ability to respond and adapt to these pressures requires cultural as well as technical changes, and our obsession with material progress may compromise our ability to make them. By contrast, an approach framed by reference to beauty, including the search for non-material and cultural satisfaction, could help us.

We have been aware of evidence of the Earth's warming, wrapped in trapped carbon dioxide, since the 1970s. The United Nations held its first environment conference in Stockholm in 1972, after which the United Nations Environment Programme (UNEP) was established. After scientists identified the hole in the ozone layer the UN secured the 1987 Montreal Protocol, restricting chemicals that damaged it, and the process began to curtail the gases that cause warming, the so-called greenhouse gas emissions, especially carbon dioxide. Finally, in 1988, UNEP set up the Intergovernmental Panel on Climate Change (IPCC) to provide an independent scientific view on climate change. Its First Assessment in 1990 concluded that temperatures had risen by 0.3–0.6°C over the previous century, and that human-created emissions were adding to the atmosphere's natural complement of greenhouse gases and were likely to result in further warming.

The Earth Summit in Rio de Janeiro in 1992 was the first United Nations conference to tackle climate change, and governments agreed there the United Nations Framework Convention on Climate Change with the objective of 'stabilisation of greenhouse gas concentrations in the atmosphere at a level that would prevent dangerous anthropogenic interference with the climate system'. As a first step, developed countries agreed to return their emissions to 1990 levels and through the 1997 Kyoto Protocol the nations that ratified the treaty (the USA did not) agreed to reduce emissions by five per cent by 2008–12.

With each further report of the IPCC (its Fifth Assessment was published in 2013) there has been further confirmation of temperature rise. The latest figures confirm a rise of between 0.65–1.06°C between 1880 and 2012, and newly record both an unprecedented warming of the sea and record levels of Antarctic ice shrinkage. The IPCC confirms that scientists are now ninety-five per cent certain that humans are the 'dominant cause' of global warming since the 1950s. There is also now a firm consensus, endorsed by the 2015 Paris Conference, that we must limit further warming to below 2°C if we are to retain the possibility of humanity surviving and adapting to the changes this will bring, and we must limit greenhouse gas emissions to a level that can be absorbed by carbon sinks. As a result the tables have turned. Far from *The Limits to Growth*'s forecasts that we would run out of fossil fuels, today's challenge is how to keep around four-fifths of the known reserves in the ground.

The UK has played a positive role in international and European negotiations and by 2010 we had reduced our own emissions of carbon dioxide by almost a quarter from 1990 levels. Some of our success came from the 'dash for gas' which substituted for burning coal during the 1990s and 2000s. And thanks to the Climate Change Act, passed in 2008, we have legally binding and credible future ambitions for carbon dioxide reductions even if it is not always clear how we will achieve them. The Act sets progressively lower carbon budgets: the first, for 2008–12 was 3,018 Megatonnes of carbon dioxide equivalent (Mte), and that for 2023–27 will be 1,950 Mte, a fifty per cent reduction against base levels. The UK also has a longer term target of an eighty per cent reduction on 1990 levels by 2050, though the government's withdrawal of subsidies for many elements of renewable energy in 2015 will make this even harder to achieve.

Technology will undoubtedly help us move towards these targets, especially through the development of renewable sources of energy, but there is no easy fix. We cannot simply carry on as we have been doing. We will need to maintain carbon stores in our land and woodlands, save energy and live less carbon-hungry life-styles if we are to control greenhouse gas emissions and stay below the 2°C limit. So as the 2015 Paris Conference confirmed, we cannot avoid the need for changes in how we manage land, use resources – especially but not only energy – and live our daily lives. These are cultural questions, not technical ones.

Yet those who champion solutions to climate change, not least because of the need to convince businesses to invest in new technology and prompt politicians to act, tend to emphasise the technical and financial cases for addressing climate change, focusing on its science and talking to people about technological solutions.

These discussions risk missing something important. As Oliver Letwin pointed out in 2005, in one of very few political speeches about beauty:

> discussion of the environment has remained resolutely mechanical. There is the science of far-off events – admittedly of colossal significance, but none the less technical for that . . . the language of politics needs to reflect the felt experience of the environment as sensations and impressions that are capable of moving us to delight and awe . . . we need to conduct politics as if beauty matters.

He was right. Inspiring people through a love of beauty will help motivate us to live healthier, more rewarding lives. To be as satisfied by taking a walk as by shopping, and to enjoy a more reflective pace of life rather than always striving for more material wealth. To use our passion for beauty to make the places where we live more attractive and better for the planet; and to help us leave a better legacy for future generations.

As later chapters will show, there is potential for huge synergy between taking beauty seriously and the patterns of land management, resource consumption and human behaviour that will move us in the right direction to save the planet. But we cannot pretend it will be easy; it never has been. Sometimes there will be clashes between beauty and sustainability. Some people find wind farms ugly (I do, in the wrong place) and coastal barrages can damage long-protected nature reserves. But rather than use these tensions as a reason not to take action, we need to confront them and find the solutions that certainly exist.

There is, though, another, deeper challenge that we must address and that is the rise of a state of being that believes only the economy is really important. Some call this 'economism': a word that is not widely used but seems remarkably apt. Even without the threat of climate change it poses a warning to us, as the American economist Albert Jay Nock wrote in his 1943 autobiography *Memoirs of a Superfluous Man*:

> I have sometimes thought that here may be the rock on which Western civilisation will finally shatter itself. Economism can build a society which is rich, prosperous, powerful, even one which has a reasonably wide diffusion of material well-being. It cannot build one which is lovely, one which has savor and depth, and which exercises the irresistible power of attraction that loveliness wields.

We have not yet reached this 'rock' but we could do so. Because for the last fifty years we have been drifting towards an ever more materialistic and instrumental view of the world and our lives. We measure success solely through GDP, yet as Diane Coyle in *GDP: A Brief but Affectionate History* points out, it 'does not measure the nation's assets or balance sheet, only its flow of income, expenditure, and production from year to year'. It flatters us into thinking things are going well when in fact, unnoticed and unrecorded, we are destroying our underlying wealth of renewable and non-renewable resources. And as Senator Bobby Kennedy said of its USA equivalent, Gross National Product (GNP) in 1968: '[it] measures neither our wit nor our courage, neither our wisdom nor our learning, neither our compassion nor our devotion to our country, it measures everything in short, except that which makes life worthwhile.'

Public dialogue may be conducted as if only the economy matters but we all know there is more to life than this. John Ruskin fought for social justice and beauty as counters to the single-minded pursuit of wealth. And as Octavia Hill reminded us, human lives need more than material things: 'We all want beauty for the refreshment of our souls.' And in our day-to-day behaviour many of us show that we value beauty, and seek experiences and surroundings that give us pleasure.

We need to learn from and develop these instincts. In a world where there are not enough resources for us to have everything we could conceivably want, we will need to be happy with less. And we face deeper human challenges too. After decades of improved health and quality of life some of the progress made in the twentieth century is beginning to unravel. Scientists are now predicting poorer health and shortening life spans, and the current generation is likely to be the first to be less materially well off than its parents. There are particular concerns about our children, with conditions such as rickets, obesity and mental health problems becoming more prevalent.

We know these problems are real, and we also know that they could be addressed if we focus on the long term and a more rounded approach to what progress means. It is not about stopping progress but about recognising that there is more to progress than things we can measure. It is time to learn from the way we responded in the nineteenth and twentieth centuries to new challenges and pressures. For on both occasions the arguments for beauty, resting on the need for enrichment of our lives, the wise use of resources, especially land, and social justice, helped us find solutions.

It is the time, and the place, to revive the arguments for beauty.

3

National Parks – a nobler vision for a better world

Exmoor's heather moorland was looking its best in the gleaming, golden September sunshine. The intense purple of the heather, interspersed with the still-flowering yellow gorse, created a glorious, flowing, tactile blanket, buzzing with insects and home to many birds and small mammals, which clothed the undulating plateau as far as my eye could see. This, it was clear, was why Exmoor was such a valued landscape, yet as we breached the horizon, walking into the next valley, we were greeted by a profoundly different picture. Here was the sharp green of limed grassland, dense with sheep but poor in plant and animal life, showing vividly where the 'improvers' had been at work. Exmoor's stunning moorland was disappearing, and only days into my first job as Secretary to the Council for National Parks I had come to see what the row was about. My guide was Guy Somerset, chairman of the Exmoor Society, whose campaign to protect it was about to reach its crunch point.

Exmoor became a National Park in 1954, the rationale for its choice its glorious plateau of heather moorland, then covering about a third of the Park. It is one of three big upland semi-natural landscapes in South West England (the others are Bodmin and Dartmoor) and suited perfectly one of the primary aims of National

Park designation: to protect the country's remaining stretches of open country with their dramatic views, vibrant colours and exhilarating offer of freedom and escape.

National Parks are at the heart of the debate about beauty and represent, in many ways, the high point of what its advocates were able to achieve. And although they got off to a faltering start, their achievements are now impressive. The Act that designated them has two clear purposes: protection of their beauty and provision of access to them, vital public needs which were accepted and then implemented by a series of governments.

The story of how this happened is longer, more complicated and more contested than it should have been. It is the story of two impressive and persistent lobbies, driven by the hunger for beauty that pervaded Britain in the late nineteenth and early twentieth centuries; and the challenges they faced. But from the outset their vision was pure and their case straightforward, based on two popular, pressing needs: the protection of beautiful landscapes and giving the people of Britain access to the hills.

The campaign for National Parks in Britain in the early twentieth century was inspired by what was happening across the Atlantic. In 1864, as the American Civil War raged, President Abraham Lincoln signed an Act of Congress ceding the Yosemite Valley and the Mariposa Grove of ancient sequoias to the State of California to be used as a public park provided that it would be 'inalienable for all time'. The first National Park in the world, Yellowstone, was designated by President Ulysses Grant in 1872 'as a public park or pleasuring-ground for the benefit and enjoyment of the people' in which 'timber, mineral deposits, natural curiosities, or wonders' would be kept 'in their natural condition'. More parks followed, and in 1916 President Woodrow Wilson established the National Parks Service to 'promote and regulate the use of the Federal areas known as national parks, monuments and reservations' whose purpose was 'to conserve the scenery and the natural and historic objects and the wild life therein and to provide for the enjoyment of the same in such manner and by such means as will leave them unimpaired for the enjoyment of future generations.'

An influential force was the Scottish émigré, John Muir, who in the 1870s challenged America's aggressive exploitation of its western wildernesses, asking 'Why should man value himself as more than a small part of the one great unit of creation?' He urged on the nascent National Parks movement, founded the Sierra Club and shamed successive presidents into a more serious commitment to preservation. Muir, like Ruskin, was a passionately spiritual man, believing that 'everybody needs beauty as well as bread, places to play in and pray in, where nature may heal and give strength to body and soul.'

The vast open spaces and monumental landscapes of the United States' National Parks were a world away from the man-made, settled landscapes of Britain, but these words and the vision they represented inspired those who were struggling to protect beautiful places here. Wordsworth's influential *Guide to the Lakes*, with its claims that it was a 'sort of national property' spurred the movement on. And although the parks eventually created here were very different, the movement in Britain was driven by exactly the same motives as in the USA: conservation and enjoyment.

While, as we have seen, the case for protecting the cultural and aesthetic qualities of the landscape owed its origins to Wordsworth and Ruskin, that for access came from the grassroots, and was truly an urgent need. Since the early nineteenth century the working population had sought to escape their poor living and working conditions in the cities by finding joy and freedom on foot or bicycle outside them. This was particularly the case in the northern cities where the fells rose enticingly from almost the city boundaries. But the limits to people's enjoyment were brutally clear, since the hills were effectively closed to them.

Since the middle of the nineteenth century there had been repeated, failed, attempts to legalise free access to mountains and open country, and rising frustration that landowners were able to exclude people from places – often former common lands which had been enclosed in the eighteenth and nineteenth centuries – which were felt to 'belong to no man'. And as we have seen, the battle to protect common land and prevent it from being enclosed paved the way for the wider conservation movement.

The Commons Preservation Society's success was that it combined legal and campaigning skill with generating popular support for its work. It achieved much in and around London, saving large parts of Wimbledon Common, Hampstead Heath and Epping Forest, and with them the ancient rights of timber and turf collection, grazing and charcoal-making. But arguably its greatest achievement was to demonstrate that commons were important to the public as a whole as well as to those with common rights, establishing a link between commons and public access that has endured.

Safeguarding access to common land, however, did not satisfy the demands for the right to walk in the hills. In 1884 James Bryce, an Aberdeenshire lawyer and MP, introduced the first of many attempts to legalise access to the Scottish mountains, where the Clearances, the forced eviction of tenants and enclosure of common lands, were in full flow. A landowner-dominated Parliament repeatedly rebuffed him. Similar treatment was doled out to Tom Ellis, Liberal MP for Meirionnydd, who introduced the Mountain Access and Footpath Bill for Wales in 1888. In 1908 the cause was taken up by Charles Trevelyan, lawyer, Liberal MP and elder brother of G. M. Trevelyan, who introduced four successive Access to Mountains Bills. They all failed. There were many further attempts before eventually, in 1939, an Access to Mountains Act reached the statute book. But it allowed only for modest, controlled access to be negotiated in defined areas and – to the ramblers' fury – introduced a set of new offences and fines for people found to be trespassing. This only reinforced their determination to press for what they really wanted: free and unconstrained access to open country. For the ramblers were by then a growing force, representing large numbers of working-class people who were desperate, in their limited free time, to get out into the countryside that was tantalisingly visible from their homes and factories yet too often out of bounds.

The first local access bodies were set up in York in 1824 and Manchester in 1826 to preserve and fight obstructions to ancient footpaths. But they soon had wider ambitions. G. S. Phillips, Secretary of the Huddersfield Mechanics Institute in the 1840s, spoke for many when he said 'whoever may own the land, no man may own the beauty of the landscape.'

These emotions were widely shared among those who constituted the access movement, including members of countless local rambling, history and botanic societies, enthusiastic about the countryside but angry with those who denied working people what they saw as their legitimate right to walk on land in their own country in search of simple refreshment. After the First World War the denial of access to the hills was perplexingly inconsistent with the idea of a land 'fit for heroes' and so the ramblers and the cyclists began to campaign for change.

The glorious unenclosed moors of the Peak District were at the centre of their demands. In 1930 there were sixty-two thousand acres of open moorland of which less than one per cent was legally open for access. Yet half the population of England lived within fifty miles of it. In frustration ramblers began to trespass, and became used to being turned back by gamekeepers.

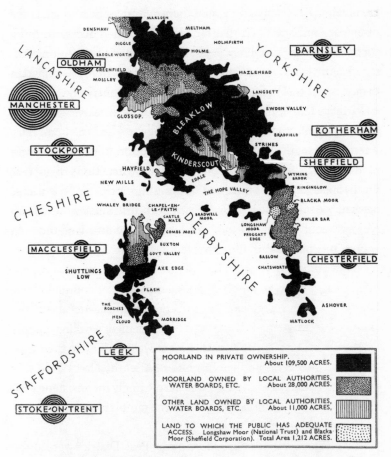

The Peak District was all but closed to public access in 1930, in spite of the huge demand from people living in neighbouring cities.

After one such event, the Lancashire District of the British Workers' Sports Federation reflected that if their numbers had been larger the gamekeepers would not have been able to stop them. So they made plans for a large-scale, peaceful protest in the form of a mass trespass on Kinder Scout, land owned by the Duke of Devonshire, on 24 April 1932. The idea was controversial: the more moderate Ramblers' Federation was keen to retain credibility with the landowners and urged its members not to take part, a decision that was to fracture the movement for years.

In fact eight hundred people joined in and as predicted the Duke's gamekeepers stopped them as they reached the open hills. There was a scuffle and six people were arrested, of whom five were members of the Young Communists' League. These five were imprisoned for six months and became folk heroes of the access movement. One, Benny Rothman, was still leading walks up Kinder Scout in his eighties. In an emotional and well-received speech on the seventy-fifth anniversary of the Mass Trespass in

The Mass Trespass on Kinder Scout in April 1932
paved the way for access to the hills.

2007, in front of Benny and a large crowd of ramblers, including me, the 11th Duke of Devonshire winningly apologised on his grandfather's behalf.

The Mass Trespass alone did not move the debate forward, however, and it took repeated demonstrations combined with increasingly effective lobbying in Parliament before the government began to listen. Famously, one rally held in the Winnats Pass in Castleton in 1932 attracted ten thousand people. In 1935 the Ramblers' Association was formed, uniting local footpath groups and federations in a formal campaigning alliance.

The Second World War at last brought progress, helped by the fact that one activist, Tom Stephenson (a journalist and later secretary to the Ramblers' Association for more than twenty years) became Press Officer to the Minister of Town and Country Planning in 1943. He brought the voice of the rambler into Whitehall, persuading Lewis Silkin, the Minister, to receive a deputation from the Ramblers' Association in 1945. Finally Silkin promised to introduce legislation to create access to wild country and to define and protect the public path network. He also agreed to make provision for long-distance footpaths, advocated by Stephenson in his 1935 article 'The Long Green Trail' which envisaged a path stretching the length of the Pennines. Stephenson even persuaded several MPs and Ministers – Hugh Dalton, Arthur Blenkinsop, Fred Willey and Barbara Castle among them – to join him on a three-day walking tour from Teesdale to Hadrian's Wall in May 1948 to demonstrate how popular the legislation would be. The experience was written up by Barbara Castle in *The Spectator* after they returned. Her article wittily describes the varying motives and walking abilities of her colleagues and their journalist companions: 'Take forty-five miles of Pennine Way, together with four or five Parliamentary wayfarers of varying degrees of public prominence, and you have all the ingredients of a first-class news story.'

Tom Stephenson of the Ramblers' Association led a party of politicians on a three-day walk along the putative Pennine Way in May 1948. With him were Hugh Dalton, Barbara Castle, George Chetwynd, Fred Willey, Julian Snow and Geoffrey de Freitas. (Courtesy of Ramblers Association)

So Lewis Silkin delivered his promises, and in 1949 Parliament passed the National Parks and Access to the Countryside Act, including specific measures to secure legal access to the countryside. But from the beginning it contained disappointments. As promised it set up a pioneering system, now the envy of many countries, to define and protect the rights-of-way network as it was in the late 1940s. But it did not provide free access to open land either within or outside National Parks. Once again the objections of the landowners and farmers prevailed. Instead the arrangements for negotiated access put in place by the 1939 Act were improved. But few access agreements were ever made outside the Peak District, and it was another fifty years before the Countryside and Rights of Way Act 2000 provided the free access, at least to mapped open country, for which Bryce had argued in the 1860s, finally offering the experience of beauty and freedom the factory workers had sought.

The access story ran alongside efforts to protect Britain's best landscapes as National Parks, which also took many years and much heartache before they reached the statute book. After the excitement generated by the USA pioneers, it took Ramsay MacDonald, leader of the second minority Labour government, to promise 'the preservation of natural beauty' in the Labour Party's 1928 manifesto, *Labour and the Nation*, before the official wheels began to turn. In 1929 he commissioned Lord Addison, then Parliamentary Secretary to the Minister of Agriculture and earlier the first-ever Minister of Health, to look into the feasibility of National Parks and facilities for countryside recreation. The voluntary bodies – the newly established CPRE, its sister in Wales (CPRW) and the National Trust in particular – responded enthusiastically, submitting detailed evidence on why National Parks should be designated and where. In response, Addison proposed National Parks as one component of a nationwide scheme of parks, open spaces and playing fields. He recommended two kinds of designation: National Reserves and Nature Sanctuaries in more remote and unspoiled countryside, primarily for preservation; and Regional Reserves, attractive countryside closer to the main centres of population where public access would also be encouraged.

While the government was generally positive it had much else on its plate and used the excuse of the recently passed 1932 Town and Country Planning Act to defer making a decision on National Parks. Then, much to the frustration of the voluntary bodies, the recession curtailed further action. But the appetite for National Parks was growing and in 1936 CPRE and CPRW formed the Standing Committee on National Parks, chaired by the eminent lawyer Sir Norman Birkett KC (he would later be one of the judges in the Nuremberg Trials) to lobby for their creation.

The government clearly hoped it could rely on the 1932 Act to stop unsympathetic development in the prospective National Parks, but the Standing Committee produced case after case to show that it was not doing so. It cited poorly designed holiday camps and uncontrolled housing development nibbling away at beautiful countryside. But at least as often it was the government's own activities, nationally or locally, that caused most damage to the proposed park areas: the Ministry of Defence's training grounds in Dartmoor and Northumberland, municipal reservoir construction in the Peak and Lake Districts, and the installation of power lines, new roads and controversial forestry plantations.

In the end, frustrated by the delays, one of the Standing Committee's members, John Dower, an architect and town planner who had married into the Trevelyan family, wrote a booklet, *The Case for National Parks*, in 1938. It was prefaced by an emotional appeal by G. M. Trevelyan in words that echoed Ruskin's: 'But it is no less essential for any national health scheme to preserve for the nation walking grounds and regions where young and old can enjoy the sight of unspoiled nature. And it is not a question of physical exercise only, it is also a question of spiritual exercise and enjoyment. It is a question of spiritual values.'

The Standing Committee took the booklet and a draft Bill round the country to garner support, engaging the press and the public in a series of well-attended public meetings. A film was made promoting National Parks which was shown in the West End and at the New York World Fair. Public enthusiasm for National Parks grew, but once again action was halted, this time by the outbreak of war.

So in the early 1940s the case for National Parks had to be made again. This time, though, it was to Lord Reith, the Minister of Works, whose sympathy for the wise use of land and resources made him more receptive. Moreover Reith brought John Dower, invalided out of the army because he had contracted TB, into the

Ministry as a war-time civil servant. In 1942 Reith asked him to write an official report on National Parks which was published in 1945. Drawing on his earlier work, Dower proposed a legal definition for National Parks, the areas to be designated (mostly in the remote, upland, unspoiled areas of England and Wales that he surveyed personally, despite his failing health), and how they should be run. He proposed a strong National Parks Commission to define, designate and oversee the protection of the parks, as well as management structures for each park. Unlike Addison he proposed that all the parks should be for the twin purposes of preservation and public access.

So ideas for National Parks were poised and ready to be picked up by the incoming Labour government in the post-war reconstruction programme. As Norman Birkett eloquently put it in his 1945 Rede lecture at Cambridge University, at which he chose to focus on National Parks:

> After the experiences of the past six years, it is altogether praiseworthy that there should be a great stirring in men's minds, a vast quickening of man's social conscience. And even if it were thought that this is put too high, it is at least inevitable that after so much suffering so nobly borne, it should be felt that some compensation might be found for so large a calamity, that something nobler should emerge for those who had endured so much, that there should be in the somewhat wistful phrase – a better world.

It was to this better world that National Parks were designed to contribute, alongside the National Health Service, education and social-welfare reforms. And to clinch the arguments the Minister Lewis Silkin commissioned Sir Arthur Hobhouse, Chairman of the County Councils' Association, to prepare the National Parks legislation. So at last their final shape emerged. Hobhouse proposed twelve National Park areas, mostly in the northern and western uplands of England and Wales, and upheld most of Dower's recommendations including the establishment of a central National Parks Commission supported by local management within each National Park. His proposals formed the backbone of the 1949 Bill, though the details were weakened during its passage through Parliament.

But pass it did, and finally, with the National Parks and Access to the Countryside Act 1949, the long-argued case for National Parks in Britain reached fruition. The importance of protecting landscape beauty and providing public access for the physical and spiritual refreshment of the nation had been recognised, and in the next decade ten National Parks, covering ten per cent of the land area of England and Wales, were designated by the new National Parks Commission. Its members, some of them die-hards of the movement for beauty like Francis Ritchie and Tom Stephenson of the Ramblers' Association and Pauline Dower (née Trevelyan, John Dower's widow), relished their task, travelling the country, surveying areas and deciding on boundaries. First they designated the Peak District, then the Lake District, Snowdonia, Dartmoor, Pembrokeshire Coast, North York Moors, Yorkshire Dales, Exmoor, Northumberland and the Brecon Beacons. The missing two from Hobhouse's list were the New Forest and South Downs, which were finally designated half a century later in 2005 and 2010 respectively.

The Act also established Areas of Outstanding Natural Beauty, the only statutory designation actually to use the word beauty in their title. Their origin lay in Addison's ideas about different categories of designation, but while they were considered equal to National Parks in landscape terms they were given no provisions for access and no special bodies to manage them. Yet these were well-known areas such as the Cotswolds, Chilterns, and the North and South Downs which were already popular and would only become more so. Without proper governance or management they were, from the outset, weaker than the National Parks and their designation process began slowly, too, starting with Gower (1956) and the Quantocks. But the idea quickly became popular, and by the mid-1960s twenty-one AONBs had been designated. It took fifty years after the 1949 Act for the importance of AONBs to be fully recognised, but since 2000 many have been given boards or committees and specialist staff to manage their conservation work.

Meanwhile the National Parks, officially our best protected landscapes and central to the fight for beauty, faced a series of debilitating compromises. Partly this was due to administrative weakness: when it was set up in 1950 the National Parks Commission had fewer powers, staff and resources than Dower had argued for. And partly it was political. Though the Peak District National Park was established with a Joint Planning Board supported by its own staff as envisaged by the Act, the Minister buckled in the face of local authority objections to setting up boards elsewhere. He first ceded a 'special planning board' rather than a full board for the Lake District (with no staff), and then in Snowdonia and all the subsequent parks established only commit-tees of each county council (so sometimes resulting in multiple committees) for each park. This meant there was no coherent approach to land use planning across multi-county parks from the beginning, and it was impossible to implement proactive manage-ment of the park areas. All the parks were meagrely funded and only the Peak District was able to build up a professional staff and expertise in the new field of park protection.

Subsumed within local authority management, the National Parks were unable to muster the arguments, resources or authority to defend themselves against the major developments everyone assumed would not be allowed. And these were the main threats to the early parks. Though some already damaged areas were excluded when the parks were designated (for example the slate tips around Blaenau Ffestiniog in Snowdonia – now, rightly, considered worthy of inclusion – and the biggest limestone quarries of the Peak District), being inside a National Park did not stop new uglinesses being permitted. Caravan sites soon colonised large parts of the Snowdonia and Pembrokeshire coasts, and the National Grid began to criss-cross the country, with particularly controversial sections in Snowdonia and the Pennines. Permissions were granted to extract minerals: potash in the North York Moors; to extend china clay extraction on Dartmoor; and limestone from the Yorkshire Dales and Peak District. An early warning station was allowed on Fylingdales Moor in the North York Moors in 1962, and the Trawsfynydd nuclear power station in Snowdonia in 1963. The North Hessary Tor television mast on Dartmoor was given permission on the casting vote of the Chairman of the National Park Committee. Laudable though the post-war ambitions were for

The newly designated National Parks were, disappointingly, not no-go areas for major development: the Trawsfynydd nuclear power station was built in the Snowdonia National Park in 1963. (Courtesy of Wikimedia Images)

the protection of their beauty, National Parks were failing to live up to their promise.

What did not fail, though, was the public's appetite for access to beautiful places. Not only were the Parks hugely popular for walkers and cyclists, as predicted, but the newly prosperous and mobile middle-classes were also keen to visit, especially by car. Honeypot sites like Hutton-le-Hole in the North York Moors and Dovedale in the Peak District were soon overwhelmed. It was not long before the need to protect beauty and promote public access became, rather than complementary aspects of a single policy, objectives in conflict with each other as the weight of numbers, congestion at beauty spots and erosion on popular walks escalated.

The need, it was soon clear, was for help with the management of people in the landscape. And somehow the pressure on National Parks had to be eased. That needed action outside the National Parks as well as within. A White Paper, *Leisure in the Countryside*, in 1966 proposed that the National Parks Commission should become the Countryside Commission, with a remit embracing the protection and enjoyment of the whole countryside of England and Wales. This came about in the Countryside Act in 1968 and many local authorities responded with alacrity to the availability of modest funds and advice, establishing dozens of Country Parks with recreational facilities for the public near towns and cities.

But the National Parks were still beautiful areas needing protection and the means in place were simply not strong enough. The job of the Standing Committee on National Parks (SCNP), far from being complete when the 1949 Act was passed, became that of a watchdog, monitoring development proposals in the National Parks and calling the park administrators and Ministers to account over decisions – and there were many – that were not in line with park purposes. There were soon active local groups in each National Park: monitoring, reporting concerns and invoking the power of their influential members. Among many, Sylvia Sayer was a redoubtable campaigner for Dartmoor, and Esmé Kirby for Snowdonia. SCNP meanwhile continued to lobby nationally against pylons, TV masts, reservoirs and new or improved roads; as well as threats posed by mass tourism such as power boats, caravan sites, car parks and pop festivals. It did not always object in principle, but looked for constructive alternatives: one of Lord Birkett's last achievements before he died in 1962 was to negotiate for new pumping stations at Ullswater and Windermere to be put underground.

The newly established Countryside Commission was just as concerned about National Parks as its predecessor, and one of its first acts was to ask Jack Longland, a new member of the Commission and a leading climber, to review their administration. He recommended that each National Park should be administered, as originally intended, by an independent board with its own staff and resources.

But administration was a symptom of the problem, not the cause. The beauty of the parks was suffering through bad decisions, often made in Whitehall. Again the Countryside Commission proposed a review, this time of how 'national considerations . . . should affect park policies'. Its ideas were hijacked by the Secretary of State for the Environment, Peter Walker, who descended by helicopter to the shores of Windermere to address the National Parks Conference in 1971, announcing that his Under-Secretary Lord Sandford, a naval officer and former clergyman, would carry out the review. He was asked to consider 'how far the National Parks had fulfilled the purpose for which they were established, to consider the implications of the changes that have occurred and may be expected in social and economic conditions and to make recommendations as regards future policies'.

Lord Sandford's committee toured the parks and heard widespread concern about their poor effectiveness. It received many complaints about quarrying, holiday camps and caravan sites, military training, reservoirs, road construction and ugly housing development as well as controversial power stations and national infrastructure projects. Sandford concluded that 'many large scale intrusions of an incongruous nature had been allowed, usually by decisions taken at a national level.' His panel also noted continuing conflicts between recreation and conservation, and his report is best remembered for the 'Sandford Principle' which stated that 'where irreconcilable conflicts exist between conservation and public enjoyment, then conservation interests should take priority.' Since then the parks have shown how large numbers of people can be managed without destroying their beauty, including through innovative transport systems like the Snowdonia Sherpa bus service, which minimises the number of car parks needed in this sensitive mountain area; and cleverly engineered path improvements, such as the Lake District's *Fix the Fells* programme, which have cured the ugly scars which once disfigured popular mountain routes.

Today the National Parks are success stories and they have found solutions to many of the problems of their early days, including the installation of robust, aesthetically pleasing footpaths such as the one being put in place here on Cat Bells in the Lake District by the National Trust. (Courtesy of the National Trust/Paul Harris)

The Sandford Report was unequivocal in endorsing the need to protect National Parks – 'the presumption against development which would be out of accord with parks must be strong; . . . in the most beautiful parts . . . it should amount to a prohibition to be breached only in the case of a most compelling necessity' – and it also sought a big increase in resources, noting that National Parks expenditure (in 1971–72 a paltry £1.2 million a year) was running at less than a third of what Hobhouse had expected would be needed back in 1947.

Finally things started to improve. Jack Longland's more ambitious recommendations were not accepted but the 1972 Local Government Act (implemented in 1974) gave each Park a single National Park Authority: boards in the Peak and Lake Districts, and a single committee, though still under the control of the county councils, in the other parks. It also introduced a National Park Officer to head a professional, expert staff and the obligation to prepare a National Park Plan for the whole area of the Park, for the first time enabling a proactive approach. And Lord Sandford's endorsement of National Park principles gave the parks a leg-up in status and recognition.

These changes, removing the worst shortcomings in the implementation of the 1940s ideal, were a step forward for National Parks. But they did not diminish the arguments about protecting their beauty. Indeed when I arrived at CNP in 1980, the parks still faced serious challenges, hugely frustrating for places that were intended to be the best protected in Britain.

One of the most vivid was Exmoor's moorland crisis, and its fight about beauty was about to be taken into the heart of Westminster. Only weeks after my visit I was climbing the staircase to the House of Lords Gallery to watch the Second Reading of the Wildlife and Countryside Bill. It was November 1980 and feelings were running high.

I was excited. It was the first time I'd been inside the House of Lords and I was awed by its Victorian Gothic splendour, hushed atmosphere and echoing corridors. I'd never seen a live debate and I was keenly awaiting my first sight of democracy in action. But those I was with, CNP's chairman Alan Mattingly (then Director of the Ramblers' Association) and other members of its council, were less impressed. They'd seen a more ambitious Countryside Bill fall in 1979 with the Labour government and were disappointed by the contents of this one. They wanted to hear what the House of Lords made of it and gauge the prospects for its improvement. For those who cared about beauty, much rested on this legislation and how it would progress.

Part of the Bill's origins lay in the Exmoor row. Exmoor's history is littered with attempts to tame its moorland, and its designation as a National Park did little to deflect the energy of the agricultural improvers. But the pace of agricultural technology had moved on, and now the very future of the moorland was at stake.

Within ten years of its designation there was a particularly provocative proposal, to plough a glorious 220-acre stretch of heather moor at Countisbury near Lynmouth, in the heart of the park. The owner's aim was to turn the moorland into grass, vastly increasing its productivity. Exempt from any form of control, farmers were not required to tell anyone what they planned to do, and certainly not the National Park committees. Unhelpfully there were three of these for Exmoor: one for the Somerset part of the park, one for Devon and a Joint Advisory Committee to take an overview, all firmly under the control of the two county councils. The committees soon discovered that they were powerless to do anything to stop the land being 'improved', and a suggestion that the land might be bought for the park by Devon County Council met with no sympathy.

This was the first proposal to set alarm bells ringing, but far from the last. By the 1960s the Exmoor Society (Exmoor's voluntary watchdog) was sufficiently concerned to commission research into the rate of moorland loss. The study, by part-time farmer and academic Geoffrey Sinclair, calculated that in the past ten years Exmoor had already lost over nine thousand acres of moorland, nearly seven per cent of the feature that was its *raison d'être*. And not only was there no mechanism for the Park Committees to protect the moorland, the Ministry of Agriculture was actually giving grants to farmers to destroy it. The profits generated from improved grassland, which could carry many more sheep (for which farmers were also paid, per head) than moorland, were irresistible. Over the next ten years a further 2,500 acres were converted and the moorland was fragmenting fast. Lord Porchester was appointed by the government to investigate the problem.

He did so against the background of growing public outrage about how one of the country's foremost landscapes could be so damaged by government subsidies. Because thanks to adroit press work on the part of the acerbic and brilliant duo of Chris Hall, a former government press officer and now Director of CPRE, and Malcolm MacEwen, a journalist and independent member of the Exmoor National Park Committee as well as a leading light of the Exmoor Society, the story of Exmoor's moorland loss became a national *cause célèbre*. It shed light on the weakness of the National Parks and the tensions between two contradictory government policies. The consequences of the Scott Committee's belief that prosperous farming would protect the landscape had been exposed. The row set the scene for decades of debate about whether and how beauty should moderate the contrived economics of farming.

So far as the Wildlife and Countryside Bill was concerned, the answer was that it would not. My colleagues' scepticism on that first day in the House of Lords was fully justified. Following Lord Porchester's study (he reported in 1977) the then government had drafted a Countryside Bill enabling Ministers to make Moorland

Conservation Orders to protect upland landscapes, but in 1980 all that the Wildlife and Countryside Bill proposed was that farmers should notify the relevant Park Board or Committee if they wanted to reclaim moorland. Under pressure from the National Farmers' Union, the government conceded that farmers should be compensated if they were persuaded not to go ahead, and that the compensation should be equal to the profits they had foregone. This would have bankrupted the National Parks if implemented.

Lobbying as the Bill went through, we tried to resuscitate the idea of legal powers of protection, even as a last resort, such as existed for the built environment. But our efforts were in vain. Even an amendment to this effect moved by the Conservative Peer Lord Ridley on behalf of the Association of County Councils (of which he was chairman, and which also wanted Exmoor protected), was defeated, by the narrow margin of ninety-seven votes to ninety-one. I was there when the votes were counted, sitting below the Bar; it felt a crushing moment of defeat. All the government conceded, in the end, picking up another of Lord Porchester's recommendations, was that the moorland in all the National Parks should be mapped, to inform the National Park Committees' responses to farmers' notifications. The only defence of the beauty of these vital landscapes was a map.

The gradual, grudging process by which farming and farm policies were eventually moderated to reduce these conflicts is the subject of chapter five, but it was not our only fight. Throughout the 1980s, while I was at CNP, we faced a series of battles with official bodies, private companies and unsympathetic public policies which took very little notice of National Parks designation and proposed damaging developments that should have had no place in National Parks. For example, despite government commitments in 1976 that trunk roads should avoid National Parks and even though an alternative was available, the government decided to drive the controversial Okehampton bypass through the northern edge of the Dartmoor National Park. And, regardless of commitments to protect the Parks from incongruent developments, those wanting to quarry for road aggregate (the stone that provides the bed of trunk roads and motorways) seemed able to flout National Park protection. So we faced proposals for expanding limestone quarries at Coolscar in the heart of Wharfedale in the Yorkshire Dales, and Topley Pike near Buxton in the Peak District. We made some progress: the result of two public inquiries into the Coolscar case, to which I gave evidence, was a tortuously extracted condition that such high-quality limestone should only be used for specialist end-uses for which there was no alternative, such as in the chemicals industry. More than thirty years later both quarries have closed and will eventually deliver wildlife and landscape benefits, but at the time no such happy outcome was in prospect.

Today's equivalent controversy is the issue of fracking, the extraction of shale gas by forcing high-pressure injections of water, sand and chemicals into rocks to release the gas inside them. Arguments have raged about fracking since it was first proposed that the technique be imported from the USA, both because it represents a further exploitation of fossil fuels, and because of the potential risks of the process, still untested in densely populated countries where there are fears about water contamination and ground disturbance. Initially it seemed that National Parks would be better protected: in January 2015, after heated protests against applications to test the potential for fracking in the South of England and Lancashire, the government conceded that fracking would be banned in National Parks, Areas of Outstanding Natural Beauty, Sites of Special Scientific Interest (SSSIs) and areas near to groundwater sources. Yet only months later, following the 2015 General Election, it reneged on its promise to protect SSSIs, and has modified its protection for National Parks by allowing fracking adjacent to – or below the surface of – their boundaries.

Throughout the 1980s we endlessly campaigned to strengthen National Parks so that they could fulfil the aspirations successive governments and people had for them. And finally the moment of breakthrough approached. In 1989 the Countryside Commission set up a Review Panel under the chairmanship of Professor Ron Edwards of Cardiff University. I was asked to join, by then having left CNP to become Assistant Director at CPRE; my first child, Alice, arrived at almost the same time as the report, a year later.

The Edwards Review's conclusions were as gloomy, in their own way, as Sandford's had been: 'We had to conclude that National Park Authorities have faced serious impediments in pursuing their aims, and that the Parks themselves have not lived up to the expectations of their founders . . . we saw evidence of deteriorating environmental quality, permanent damage to the landscape and poor local relationships.' We saw, however, the potential for a more confident and successful future for the National Parks within a wider European and global context. We argued that, in spite of their imperfections, National Parks remained an important ideal to strive for and that the experience of the British National Parks in protecting man-made and managed landscapes had been under-recognised and was of international significance. We felt that the benefits National Parks offered the nation had been seriously underestimated, and we proposed a National Parks Bill to strengthen their administration and funding, better protect their natural and cultural assets, provide stronger control over damaging developments (quarrying, military training, intensive agriculture and forestry) and to secure better representation of National Parks on the national and international stage. We also recommended a new National Park, the New Forest (the Broads having been added to the family in 1988) and we asked the Countryside Commission to review the case for other areas.

These recommendations finally tipped the National Parks into being the success stories they deserved, and needed, to be. They were implemented in the Environment Act 1995, after which the Park Authorities finally became independent of local authorities and started to attract the recognition and resources worthy of their ambitions. In 1990 the Parks had been spending £23 million per annum (from a mix of national and local authority grants and locally generated income) and although Edwards calculated that an increase of £8–10 million was needed, by 2010 spending on National Parks had risen to nearly £50 million on a like-for-like basis. Income for all the National Parks, including new ones, reached a high point of £83 million in 2011–12. This made a huge difference to what the Parks could do but are tiny sums for the benefits they bring: all the National Parks together cost the nation less than £1 per person per year. And for that small sum great things are achieved.

The National Parks have launched new programmes for land-scape-scale conservation, restoring eroded footpaths and ancient woodlands, promoting sustainable tourism and local businesses, and embracing the challenges posed by climate change. Confidence in and about what the Parks have achieved was also boosted when the status of British National Parks was critically reviewed by IUCN to establish whether or not they met the higher standards which IUCN set in 2008 for recognition as a 'protected area': they did.

Many ambitious conservation projects are now run from or in National Parks, showing how an approach founded on beauty can be a galvanising force for success. The conflicts of the 1980s have been turned into positive partnerships, including with water companies, to implement catchment management programmes that are restoring moorland's nature conservation value, safeguarding peat and providing clean water to customers. The Peak District's *Moors for the Future* Programme is restoring the degraded peat of the Pennines, helped by partnerships with the National Trust and other landowners, for the benefit of wildlife, landscape and public access, while supporting low-impact farming. The wetlands of the Broads, the mountains of the Lake District, the chalk sheepwalks of the South Downs and the traditional dairy industries of the Yorkshire Dales are moving towards sustainable management, generating local food products that command a premium in the market while protecting the landscapes that make the Parks so popular. Re-wilding initiatives, which encourage nature to take the lead, such as at Ennerdale in the Lake District, in partnership with the National Trust, are turning once monocultures of conifers and bare grazed hillsides into diverse and beautiful habitats. The parks also demonstrate how local businesses and people can earn a sustainable income, especially from tourism, in ways that are compatible with conservation aims.

These successes have been won from diligent work and by building good relationships. Since achieving independence every National Park has conducted a State of the Park Review, highlighting the parks' strengths and weaknesses and clarifying what needs to be done to fulfil their purposes. All have a vision for the next twenty to twenty-five years, to secure long-term objectives. Each park has a management plan that prescribes the action it will take for every element of its area: the management and improvement of habitats, mitigation and adaptation to climate change, the protection and management of valued landscapes, appropriate levels of recreational use and tourism, the future of farming and other economic activities, and the needs of the local community. All these plans have been the subject of extensive consultation and the parks have worked hard to secure the support of local communities. There are still, of course, periodic arguments about beauty and the 2015 decision to approve the largest potash mine in Britain in the North York Moors National Park was undoubtedly a setback. But overall the parks have more than proved their worth. Their approach has also been endorsed by the European Landscape Convention, which commends the British approach to National Parks, and their experience has given many others, at home and abroad, a positive role-model of how to achieve the protection and sustenance of lived-in, working landscapes.

Given the evocative purposes of National Parks and their now steady progress, it is not surprising that enthusiasm for new National Parks has mounted steadily. The first addition to the family was the Broads, in 1988, when an administrative solution was found that respected the Broads' peculiarities in needing to manage navigation rights in the labyrinth of its wetlands as well as land-based conservation and access. This administrative mould-breaking enabled two more National Parks, the New Forest and the South Downs, each tailored to meet their special requirements, to be designated in relatively quick succession in 2005 and 2009. Following Scottish devolution and the adoption of national parks legislation for Scotland in 2000, Loch Lomond and the Trossachs was made a National Park in 2002 and the Cairngorms in 2003. In 2015 the government approved the extension of the Yorkshire Dales and Lake District National Parks, adding another 188 square miles including the Howgill Fells to these celebrated Parks.

Now, enthusiasm for new National Parks is bubbling up all over. A group in Dorset and east Devon is promoting the case for the Jurassic Coast (a World Heritage Site) and the Dorset and east Devon AONBs to become a National Park; and the county of Herefordshire has debated the possibility of its entire area being designated. Even more ambitiously, campaign groups in London and Glasgow have launched the idea of 'National Park Cities'. The London campaign believes that London's four World Heritage

Sites (Tower Bridge, Maritime Greenwich, Westminster's Palace and Abbey, and Kew Gardens), three hundred farms, thirty-seven SSSIs and two National Nature Reserves, 850 km of streams, rivers and canals, and 8.3 million trees, not to mention its 8.6 million people, would all benefit from being embraced within the National Park ideal. Glasgow's ideas draw on the legacy of Patrick Geddes, born in the city, and the benefits National Park designation could bring to the health and well-being of its residents, the quality of its urban environment and its ninety-one parks. Glasgow and London have made an impressive case for applying the successes of National Parks to new, urban circumstances.

These ideas, and the achievements of the National Parks in the past fifteen years, throw new possibilities into play. First, whether or not the National Park City idea flies, it is time for the Parks to build closer links with all the cities of Britain to renew the promise of National Parks made by Lewis Silkin to refresh a stressed nation and improve the well-being of its citizens. As the Northern Powerhouse takes shape, why not match the focus on the engine of the economy with an equal plan to enhance the beauty of the North? With four existing National Parks (the Peak District, Yorkshire Dales, Lake District and North York Moors) and five AONBs already, there are enormous opportunities for the beautiful landscapes of the North to do more for the health and well-being of millions of people.

Perhaps even more ambitiously, National Parks are now well-placed to be the model for managing all of our beautiful, lightly populated rural areas. They have proved their ability to protect sensitive landscapes, sustain healthy soils, improve wildlife, ensure appropriate and viable economic activity, and offer inspiration and refreshment to millions. The tiny public investment in them is paid back many times by the value they deliver for people, the health benefits that flow to their users, and their contribution to protecting our natural resources. At the very least, AONBs, equal in landscape quality to the National Parks, should be given the same status and support.

Though the journey to demonstrate the power of beauty has been long and convoluted, National Parks have shown that it is a compelling force for good, offering a multiplicity of benefits that vastly outweighs their minimal cost. Their value is immense, yet under-realised. Protecting beauty can achieve so much more.

4

How nature and the wider countryside lost out

'It's a nature reserve in a plastic bag,' said Adrian Colston, the National Trust's Property Manager for Wicken Fen, to me in late 2000, 'and I can't contain the species loss without doing something radically different.' Adrian and I were standing in front of the wooden windmill at Wicken Fen, the landscape around us picturesque as the water-filled lodes dappled in the low light of a sunny October day, and the reeds waved gently in the breeze. A flat-bottomed fen boat was moored nearby and a group of visitors were admiring the preserved fen cottage, their heads nearly touching the lintel and its low thatched roof. 'The reserve may look good,' he went on, 'but it's dying on its feet. The only answer is to make it bigger, much bigger.' Adrian took me along the boardwalk into the fen. He told me how the swallowtail butterfly had become extinct here in the 1950s, and how attempts to reintroduce it had failed. Many insect and plant species were struggling as the fen dried out and the land around Wicken, intensively farmed for cereals, sucked more moisture out of the peat soils. Water levels within the fen were artificially maintained but it was becoming harder to hold the water in. He wanted to show me, the Trust's new Director-General, his plans to buy Burwell Farm, next door to Wicken. Its exhausted peaty soil was ripe for re-flooding to re-create a wetland habitat, and it would also be the saviour of Wicken Fen, the Trust's first nature reserve. His long-term vision was bigger still, but this was the first step of a landscape-scale project for nature. Just a few months later the Trust's Committees approved the purchase. The Wicken Vision had taken its first step forward.

Adrian's vision epitomised the challenge that faced conservation in the wider countryside in the second half of the twentieth century. Even places defined and designated for their nature conservation value – and Wicken Fen is a National Nature Reserve, one of the country's best protected sites – have become isolated, battered and compromised by what has happened around them, leaving wildlife and beauty vastly the poorer.

The fights for nature protection and for the beauty of our wider countryside are inextricably interlinked. In the latter part of the last century what we learned is exactly what Adrian showed me: that we cannot protect island sites. Nature has suffered serious losses throughout the country and we need – in Professor Bill Adams' words – to 'think big for nature' – at least at a whole catchment level – if we are to have a chance of recovering from the devastating damage to wildlife that has taken place over the last two centuries. If we can achieve it, the process of recovery will be good for beauty too, because as well as the rare and common species that have vanished from our day-to-day experience of nature, we have also lost much of what made our so-called 'ordinary' countryside special: field boundaries, trees and copses, ponds and meandering streams, as well as the barns and gates, odd corners and quirky elements that give character to a place.

These elements of our landscape may all seem inseparable, but in the 1930s a decision was taken which had profound conse-quences: the landscape and wildlife bodies agreed to take separate routes in seeking legislation and protection. While pragmatically

We need to 'think big' for nature if we are to restore the losses caused by over-intensive farming and environmental damage in the past. Much of the Pennines, including the plateau of Kinder Scout, has degraded peat soil and is urgently in need of restoration. (Courtesy of the National Trust/Joe Cornish)

sensible at the time, this inevitably channelled energies in different directions and fragmented the arguments. This chapter will show how the fight for nature and the fight for beauty were separated, have inched towards reunion and now need fully to join together to deliver, across our country, the protection that nature and the wider countryside so urgently need.

The split was surprising, because the origins of the nature and landscape protection movements were similar. Both were born of a simple love of and fascination for the natural world, and a desire to explore it; though in the case of nature there was always a conscious underpinning of scientific curiosity. Many people's interest was sparked by what they could see around them, and Gilbert White's *Natural History of Selborne*, first published in 1788, was both one of the first local celebrations of nature and remains one of the best loved. White, a clergyman, was not an outspoken advocate but a quiet observer of a place he loved and knew intimately. His discoveries, for example of new species of bird, bat and mouse; and of the feeding, nesting and migration habits of many mammals and birds, were born of careful observation. His prose has a poetic pragmatism about it: 'This morning I saw the golden-crowned wren, whose crown glitters like burnished gold. It often hangs like a titmouse, with its back downward.'

But while the amenity movement began publicly to grapple with threats to the beauty of the Lake District from the early nineteenth century, there was little outcry about nature at risk in Britain until that century's end. That did not mean, though, that there was nothing to shout about. In fact a combination of pressures – land-use change, sport and collecting – were ravaging Britain's wildlife.

A staggering one thousand square kilometres of wetland were drained each year between 1840 and 1880 and the process destroyed the breeding grounds of the bittern, spoonbill, greylag goose, marsh harrier, ruff, black-tailed godwit, avocet, black tern and Savi's warbler. The native large copper butterfly was last recorded in the fens in the 1840s. The extinction of the great bustard in Britain, a bird which needs huge areas of undisturbed grassland to breed successfully, can be traced through the records of its last sightings, in Suffolk (1812), Wiltshire (1820), Yorkshire (1830) and finally Norfolk in 1838.

While historically nearly everyone (including Gilbert White) shot animals for food or sport, the improved firearms of the nineteenth century and increasing organisation of the sport accelerated the damage to wildlife. And there was a difference between taking a rabbit for the pot and devoting large areas of the countryside to grouse-shooting and hunting. Frank Perring concluded that 'from the mid-1800s until the Second World War the survival or otherwise of Britain's fauna was determined predominantly by the landed proprietors and their gamekeepers.' Birds of prey were worst affected: the osprey and the white-tailed sea eagle were extinct by 1916; the golden eagle was driven out of England and Wales and the buzzard reduced to a remnant population by 1915. The red kite was gone from England by 1870 with only a few breeding pairs left in remote mid-Wales. Marsh, hen and Montagu's harriers, the goshawk and the sparrowhawk joined the list of birds reduced to the edge of survival.

The story was similar for mammals. Wolves had been hunted out by the 1680s, but the pine marten was driven out of lowland England by 1850; the wild cat out of England and Wales by the end of the nineteenth century, though a small remnant population hung on in Scotland; and polecats reached a record low by 1900 as a result of hunting and persecution.

A third threat came from collecting, with cabinets of birds' eggs and stuffed carcasses gracing many respectable as well as stately homes: Calke Abbey's ten thousand or so stuffed birds, mammals, shells and eggs in an extraordinary collection probably sets a record. Egg collecting was both highly popular and damaging: in 1884 alone 130,000 guillemot eggs were taken from Bempton Cliffs in east Yorkshire, now an RSPB reserve. The rarer the bird the more eager collectors were to own a dead one, and so the great auk's extinction by 1844 was hastened by its collectors. The fashion for trapping and caging live songbirds led to a collapse in the wheatear, goldfinch, bearded reedling and woodlark. And that for feathered decorations in women's hats caused devastation. In the 1790s fishermen at Clovelly in Devon collected a staggering nine thousand kittiwake wings in a fortnight, and soon feathers from overseas birds – especially egrets, hummingbirds and birds of paradise – were much in demand.

The first campaigns for wildlife focused on birds, and the first legislation passed was the Sea Birds Preservation Act 1869 and the Wild Birds Protection Act 1875. These introduced a close season (when birds could not be killed) and the first lists of protected species. Birds' eggs were first protected in 1894. The RSPB was set up in 1889, initially as the Fur and Feather Group to stop feather collection and cruelty, though it also had a Watchers' Committee to oversee vulnerable breeding birds and promote garden-bird feeding.

But there was little interest in the conservation of habitats until the early twentieth century, when Charles Rothschild, scion of the banking family and a leading amateur entomologist, set up the Society for the Promotion of Nature Reserves (SPNR) in 1912. He and a small group of eminent naturalists set about collating and collecting information on sites worthy of protection, with the aim of establishing them as nature reserves and educating the public about nature.

And here the movements were aligned, at least for a while, for at first the SPNR's plan was to acquire important sites and hand them to the National Trust. In fact Rothschild bought part of Wicken Fen in 1899, the place to which Adrian Colston took me all those years later, and donated it to the Trust in 1901. It was one of the last surviving un-drained remnants of the fens. In 1912 a public appeal organised by Professor Frank Oliver – an enthusiastic member of both the SPNR and the National Trust – secured Blakeney Point in Norfolk, renowned for its seals and seabird colonies, for the Trust. But to SPNR's disappointment the Trust declined to take on Woodwalton Fen in Cambridgeshire because of the high management costs it had incurred at Wicken Fen, confirming its interest in buildings and landscapes rather than habitats for wildlife.

By 1914 SPNR had identified ninety-eight sites worthy of protection as nature reserves, but with the imminence of war and growing pressures to step up home-grown farm production they hurried to do more. In 1915 they submitted a schedule of 284 sites to the Board of Agriculture together with a plea that they should not be 'improved' by drainage or ploughing in the war-time food production effort.

But then the campaign went quiet. The government, no doubt weighed down by the pressure of wartime matters, did not respond to the list; and Charles Rothschild, already plagued by depression and illness, took his own life in 1923. SPNR's progress stalled.

The main legislative progress made in the 1920s and 1930s was, again, for birds. The RSPB finally won its founders' campaign when the 1921 Importation of Plumage (Prohibition) Act was passed, and Wild Birds Acts in 1925 and 1933 attempted to simplify the tortuously complicated earlier legislation. But in the decades between the wars official attention was distracted by economic depression, social unrest and concerns about poverty.

As we saw in chapter two, though, plans were being developed for comprehensive legislation as part of the post-war reconstruction programme. But by common consent, in the late 1930s, the nature and National Parks movements reached a historic decision when they decided to present their cases to government separately. The Standing Committee on National Parks had, in its *Case for National Parks* of 1938, concluded that 'the establishment and control of Nature Reserves requires separate and distinct measures, which the National Park movement should do all it can to assist, but for which it cannot be wholly responsible.'

This stance, with which the SPNR and RSPB agreed, led to one of the most significant decisions of the movement in the twentieth century: to separate protection for nature and landscape. It would be decades before steps towards reunion would be taken. But at the time the arguments seemed clear, and the 1941 SPNR *Conference on Nature Preservation in Post-war Reconstruction* concluded that nature protection would stand more chance of success if it was not harnessed to the growing but politically insecure movement for National Parks. They decided to concentrate on the scientific aspects of nature conservation and their strategy worked, giving them stronger legislation in the 1949 Act for nature than the landscape and access movement achieved.

The nature bodies were diligent in preparing for the legislation. In 1942 William Jowitt, who had succeeded Lord Reith as Chairman of the Reconstruction Committee, invited the SPNR to set up a Nature Reserves Investigation Committee which, with the British Ecological Society, examined the state of ecological research and the role of nature conservation. In 1943 they published an influential memorandum *Nature Conservation in Great Britain* which listed the sixty-one reserves by then in existence and outlined a process for establishing more, covering the full range of habitat types in the UK.

In the same year Arthur Hobhouse (the author of the final National Parks report) set up a Wildlife Conservation Special Committee chaired by Julian Huxley. It reported in 1947, proposing seventy-three national nature reserves covering around 28,000 hectares 'to preserve wild species of flora and fauna and provide opportunities for research and experiment'. It also added a further, much larger, category of 'scientific areas' covering around one million hectares to be notified to local authorities, enabling them to consider the impact of damaging developments; these would become the Sites of Special Scientific Interest (SSSIs). The report also proposed that a biological research service, the Nature Conservancy, should be established by Royal Charter to oversee this process.

Huxley cleverly positioned these proposals as scientific, inexpensive and undisruptive so that unlike the lobbying, compromise and weakening which surrounded the designation of National Parks there was little adverse comment when the Nature Conservancy was established and began its work. Its role was to provide scientific advice on conservation matters, establish and manage nature reserves and carry out research. And unlike the thousands of square miles to be designated as National Parks the proposals for nature reserves amounted to relatively small areas of land, much of little economic value, and the plan was expected to cost as little as £500,000. The functions of the Nature Conservancy, though stronger than the National Parks Commission, were not felt to be in conflict with other bodies.

Once established, the Nature Conservancy followed the lead given by Huxley, aiming to protect a representative sample of Britain's natural and semi-natural habitats, including the most rare or vulnerable species. It set out to designate 150 nature reserves and forty geological sites in England, Wales and Scotland. It did not expect to purchase the sites but to enter instead into agreements with landowners, encouraging them to continue any system of land management (e.g. grazing) that had led to the site's value for nature. Separately, it would notify local planning authorities of SSSIs in their localities and local authorities could set up local nature reserves.

And again unlike the National Parks, where implementation stumbled from the beginning, the Nature Conservancy got off to a good start. In its first decade it designated eighty National Nature Reserves, covering over fifty-five thousand hectares, nearly double the area predicted. The first, in 1951, were Beinn Eighe in Wester Ross, Yarner Wood in Devon and Moor House in the Lake District.

Already, though, it was becoming clear that outside National Nature Reserves the prospects for nature were bleak. There were no tools to protect nature in the wider countryside, including in the important SSSIs. It was also soon apparent that the activities which most threatened nature were not development under the Town and Country Planning Acts (housing developments and so forth) but agricultural intensification and forestry. And as we have seen there were no controls over these activities, even though agricultural technology was developing rapidly, with new, larger and more powerful farm machinery and increasing use of pesticides and agricultural chemicals. All the Conservancy could do was conduct research, though it used this facility well. When Derek Ratcliffe (later its Chief Scientist) looked at the effect of pesticides on birds of prey he found evidence of eggshell thinning, a fact which proved a breakthrough in connecting the decline of bird populations with specific poisons.

Between them, pesticides and pollution were to have a huge and irrecoverable impact on Britain's nature. In the first half of the 1950s oil pollution was responsible for the deaths of between 50,000 and 250,000 seabirds annually, and attempts to address it were ineffectual. It took the *Torrey Canyon*, which ran aground off the Isles of Scilly in 1967, for public outrage about the sight of drowning, oiled sea birds to persuade governments to ban the dumping of waste oil at sea. River pollution too reached appalling levels. In 1951 a 72 km stretch of the River Thames was declared entirely devoid of oxygen and river life, and salmon disappeared from the whole length of the Thames. Following the introduction of organochlorine pesticides in 1955 otters declined in many rivers. Factory and farm waste was discharged directly, without control, into rivers and estuaries.

The Rivers (Prevention of Pollution) Act of 1951 began the process of managing discharges into rivers and tidal waters but progress was tentative and painfully slow. Air pollution, caused by domestic fires and industrial discharges, reached dire levels with the London smog of 1952 claiming four thousand lives. The Clean Air Act of 1956 took the first steps to clean up urban skies but still, in 1962, 750 people in London died as a result of smog.

Rachel Carson's *Silent Spring* blew the whistle on the grip held by the chemicals industry in the USA, and a year later (1963) it was published in the UK. Her book evoked a fabled town in

America, transformed from a place where 'all life seemed to live in harmony with its surroundings' to one where 'only silence lay over the fields and woods and marsh'. Her analysis of the devastating impact of pesticides on plant, animal and human health sparked a fierce row on both sides of the Atlantic during which the pesticides industry tried to discredit her. Yet her analysis held up and slowly the government responded, banning the most damaging organochlorine pesticides including aldrin and dieldrin by the 1980s.

But the damage was done. By then insect, bird and butterfly populations had fallen by as much as half and the abundance of much common wildlife was gone, never to recover.

By now, though, public concerns about pollution were driving improvements. In fact one of the most effective environmentalists of the 1970s and 1980s was the European Community. Britain had joined the Common Market in 1973 primarily for the benefits of free trade. What no-one then anticipated was that the member states of the EU would promote a significant programme of legislation for cleaner air and cleaner water, to stop acid rain, introduce better protection for birds and habitats and, working internationally through UNEP, solve the ozone problem.

The voluntary bodies became more ambitious and effective too, our work attracting ever greater public support. The RSPB grew from 25,000 members in 1964 to 300,000 by 1979, to over a million today. The SPNR (now The Wildlife Trusts, whose membership is disaggregated among local Trusts) grew from 3,000 to 55,000 in the 1960s, to 145,000 by 1982 to more than 800,000 now. Moreover many new trusts were created, including in Ulster (1978), Avon (1980) and London (1981) to reach the urban population. After its shaky start, the National Trust became a nature conservation body too: its membership reached half a million in 1975, a million in 1981, and four million in 2011; its coast and countryside acquisitions as much about nature conservation as landscape, and nearly all open for public access.

While the public was enthusiastic about wildlife and the beauty of the countryside, by the 1960s the problems both faced were all too apparent. These ranged from wildlife losses and pollution to the overcrowding of beauty spots and damage from poor quality development. The Council of Europe declared 1970 European Conservation Year and in anticipation, in 1963, HRH The Duke of Edinburgh chaired the first of three *Countryside in 1970* conferences convened by the Council of Nature, Nature Conservancy and the Royal Society of Arts. Their question was 'what sort of countryside do we all want to see in 1970?' The process of debate and consultation was an attempt to bring together everyone with an interest in the countryside, and where possible reconcile tensions. Though this was an ambitious goal, it encouraged the government to take the needs of the wider countryside more seriously. It established the Countryside Commission from the National Parks Commission (a decision implemented in the 1968 Countryside Act) with powers to protect the wider countryside and provide facilities, such as Country Parks, for people to enjoy it. And it also awoke the government's conscience on nature protection: in 1973, soon after the conference, in some embarrassment it was forced to re-establish the Nature Conservancy as the Nature Conservancy Council, following its ignominious swallowing up by the Natural Environment Research Council in 1965.

The 'new' NCC's highest priority was a massive *Nature Conservation Review*, pursuing Julian Huxley's still elusive ambitions for protecting a representative sample of Britain's wildlife. It was clear that earlier efforts had been too meagre. This time 735 sites, covering 950,000 hectares or four per cent of the land area of Britain, were declared the bare minimum needed to protect the full range of British habitats and wildlife, including SSSIs for which there were high hopes. But again implementation lagged behind, and by 1977 only 153 NNRs had been designated covering 120,000 hectares.

Yet the biggest challenge for the wider countryside was still to come, for the new agricultural revolution was now gearing up. Farm intensification fuelled by subsidies, and government incentives to farmers to intensify production and feed more people from domestic production, had been going on since the war. But the 1970s was the decade in which intensive agriculture's devastating impacts on the so-called 'ordinary' countryside were fully exposed.

The main victims were the semi-natural habitats that represented old-style farming, before massive machinery demanded big fields and pesticides stripped the countryside of permanent pasture and flower-rich fields, leaving only a few messy corners and edges for the birds, butterflies and bees. Hedgerows were among the most visible losses, with 300,000 km grubbed out between 1947 and 1987. And as farm animals' feed switched to silage, hay-making collapsed and flower-rich lowland meadows declined by ninety-seven per cent between the 1930s and 1984. Lowland heath, with its displays of gorse and heather, swarming with wildlife, was transformed to grassland: eighty per cent of the lowland heath that had existed in 1800 had gone by the 1970s. Coppiced woodland, with its light and shade, bluebells and wood anemone, declined by ninety per cent between 1900 and 1970. Wet bogs were drained to make more efficient use of land: ninety-four per cent of lowland mires were lost between 1800 and 1978, and in Scotland upland bogs declined by nearly half between the 1940s and the 1980s.

And yet by the late 1970s, as Exmoor's moorland was being ploughed up, there were still no legal powers to protect either nature sites or landscapes. Thus the scene was set for the Wildlife and Countryside Bill's introduction into the House of Lords.

In fact nature protection was a bigger driver for this Bill than landscape concerns, because the government was obliged to bring the UK's policies for nature protection in line with the European Birds Directive, which relied on habitat as well as species protection and which had been agreed in 1979. But the Bill presented to the House of Lords was as pitifully weak for nature protection as it was for landscape, and the voluntary bodies were determined to improve it. Under the leadership of Lord Melchett all the voluntary bodies with an interest in nature (including some of the landscape bodies; I was then at CNP) banded together in a special committee to co-ordinate efforts and present a united face to legislators. In 1982 it was launched as a new organisation, Wildlife Link. In all over 2,300 amendments were moved during the Bill's long passage through Parliament, many of them promoted by Wildlife Link, and some succeeded.

The Bill's debates ranged from the strategic and visionary to the pedantic: it was not unusual for the House of Lords to be entertained by late night sessions on the breeding habits of the redshank, the history of moorland ploughing on Exmoor, or why the swallowtail butterfly should be included in this or that schedule, while a campaigner (sometimes it was me) sat sleepily below the Bar, waiting to answer questions or provide another snippet of useful (or merely distracting) information.

The Wildlife and Countryside Bill is said to have been one of the most time-consuming and controversial ever placed before Parliament. It provided the stage where the rows about beauty, nature and farming were played out. But by the end of its passage there were still few actual powers of protection. As with National Parks, the only safeguard was that farmers in National Nature Reserves and SSSIs should tell the Nature Conservancy Council if they wanted to carry out potentially damaging operations, and the NCC would have to pay profits-foregone compensation if they persuaded the farmer not to go ahead. But the NCC's paltry budget (in 1978 £7 million against MAFF's improvement grant budget of £154 million) meant this was not feasible. The worst to suffer were SSSIs, that 'bare minimum' of nature sites. In 1983–84 156 SSSIs and potential SSSIs (some were still in the process of being designated) were damaged, sixty-seven of them seriously. The following year 255 sites were damaged, ninety-four of them seriously. And if sites no longer deserved SSSI status the NCC had to de-notify them; by 1985 it expected to de-notify a staggering ten per cent of the total. And outside SSSIs there was no defence for nature at all.

Then, without warning, another threat appeared, this time reviving the risks of development in the wider countryside. In 1986 the Department of the Environment issued a draft guidance document: *Development Involving Agricultural Land*, suggesting that the long-established presumption against the development of farmland should be dropped. At one level this was not a surprising development. Farm subsidies had led to embarrassing surpluses of cereal, butter mountains, and milk and (outside the UK) wine lakes, provoking questions about over-production. But at a stroke the new policy would have removed one of the central planks of countryside protection, and all of us were concerned about the loss of more land to development. Led by its Director Robin Grove-White, CPRE threw its entire campaigning weight at it, running a major press campaign, holding an Extraordinary General Meeting and drawing together an alliance of a formidable array of organisations, including farmers. In March 1987, just as I joined CPRE's staff, the Countryside Minister William (now Lord) Waldegrave conceded the point, announcing in a government Circular (16/87) a new and welcome planning principle: 'the continuing need to protect the countryside *for its own sake* [my emphasis] rather than primarily for the productive value of the land'.

Helpful though these new words were, the campaign, combined with our experience of lobbying on the Wildlife and Countryside Bill, brought into sharp relief the risks to any land or feature that was not specifically protected, designated or recognised. All of us knew that it was not just protected areas that people cared about, but the disappearance of the local features that make a place special: the old stone walls or field boundaries, the unpredictable curve of a rural lane, the patch of wild flowers near the village green or the pond in the corner of the field. These were the features that were disappearing, often from under our noses, as farm improvements, new houses, lamp posts and kerbs suburbanised the rural scene, removing idiosyncratic local features and odd scruffy corners, the elements E. M. Forster described in *Havoc* as 'oddments and trifles, which decline to be scheduled, the crow flying into the wood, here a bush and there a sheep, the England of Cowper and Crabbe, Tennyson and Housman'.

To speak up for the wider countryside a new charity, Common Ground, was set up in 1983. Common Ground's first publications were an action guide to local conservation, *Holding your Ground*, designed to help people identify and protect what they cared about locally; and *Second Nature*, edited by Richard Mabey, a beautiful evocation of the value of Britain's dwindling wildlife and countryside by poets, writers and artists. Its first campaign was to protect milestones, those too-often forgotten features of the landscape, often carved from local stone and evoking a time of slower, more reflective travel. Its second was to promote British varieties of apples, then almost impossible to find in supermarkets. Common Ground invented 'Apple Day' which is now widely celebrated every autumn, reviving interest in orchards and local apples, and more recently published *England in Particular*, to celebrate 'the commonplace, the local, the vernacular and the distinctive'.

Once again the Countryside Commission showed leadership with the Countryside Character Programme, a process which captured the distinctive character of different parts of England, drawing on local geology, geography, natural history, patterns of land use and farming types, field boundaries, building materials and architectural styles. The National Character Areas describe what is special about each type of scenery and encourage local authorities to try and protect, and local people to explore and treasure, what is on their doorsteps.

All these initiatives were helpful, but it was impossible to ignore the fact that the cause of all the damage was government policy and particularly subsidies that encouraged the intensification of agriculture. And not just agriculture. In 1987 another fight erupted, this time in the far north of Scotland, and this time about trees. For largely out of the public eye great swathes of the Sutherland Flow Country – a unique and internationally important blanket-bog habitat – were being systematically planted with conifers by private individuals and companies, lured by generous tax breaks, again thanks to the government.

As chapter six describes, once the alarm was raised by the Nature Conservancy Council the campaign united the entire conservation movement in a bid to save the Flow Country. Chancellor Nigel Lawson's decision to stop the generous tax concessions in his 1988 Budget effectively achieved that, and forced the Forestry Commission to re-evaluate its priorities and how it handled landscape and wildlife conflicts.

The unexpected outcome of this victory, however, was a fierce backlash against the NCC, which triggered another fight for nature protection. Resentment had built up in Scotland because the Flow Country was an area of high unemployment and forestry provided an injection of money and jobs. Within a year of the row, the Department of the Environment published proposals to break up the NCC, and create new bodies in England, Wales and Scotland combining nature functions with those for landscape and access (and in Scotland, also heritage). There was general dismay, for whatever the intellectual cases for merger and devolution, proposals born out of such conflict left a sour taste in the mouth.

When the Environment Act 1990 was passed the NCC was indeed broken up but not as the government had proposed. Integrated organisations (Scottish Natural Heritage and the Countryside Council for Wales) were set up in Scotland and Wales but in England separate bodies, English Nature and the Countryside Commission, remained. A powerful group in the House of Lords also succeeded in insisting that a Joint Nature Conservation Committee be established to speak for Britain at European and international levels and to maintain a UK-wide overview of the state of Britain's nature. Their arguments were buttressed by the knowledge that a European Habitats Directive was in preparation (it was agreed in 1992) establishing objectives for nature for which the UK government as a whole would be held accountable.

While the reasons behind these proposals were deeply unpalatable, in reality there was growing convergence in thinking and practice between the landscape and nature movements. The decision to take separate routes in the 1930s was beginning to look unwise. The exercise of working together, through Wildlife Link on the Wildlife and Countryside Bill, had confirmed that we had a lot in common. All of us wanted special sites for landscape and wildlife to be protected but we were also increasingly concerned about the state of the wider countryside; and we were by then beginning to engage in the climate change debate, brought to prominence by preparations for the 1992 Rio Earth Summit. Many of the places and habitats we cared about mattered for nature, landscape *and* access reasons. As a movement, we could see that it was a mistake to be divided over details when we should be united to face bigger challenges. In fact in 1993 we merged our own co-ordinating organisations, Countryside Link (which I had helped set up in 1982, while at CNP) with Wildlife Link to form Wildlife and Countryside Link.

Thus we acquiesced when, after a further review of rural policy and rural bodies, the government decided first to merge the Countryside Commission with the Rural Development Commission to become the Countryside Agency, and then in 2006 to form a single body, Natural England, from English Nature, the Countryside Agency and the Rural Development Service functions of the Department of the Environment. It helped that Natural England's first Chairman, Sir Martin Doughty, was a passionate rambler and a former Chairman of both the Peak District National Park and English Nature and was therefore uniquely qualified – and trusted – to bring this new organisation together. His untimely death in 2009 coincided with the beginnings of a deeper threat: the loss of Natural England's 'voice' as the government instructed its public bodies not to air their views in public. The days of the Countryside Commission and Nature Conservancy Council as champions for beauty and nature were over: this marked the start of the loss of independence and voice for nature and the countryside that these organisations had provided since 1949.

But now another transformation was in the making. Just as in the early twentieth century there had been a shift from species protection to site protection, by the early 2000s the limitations of a site-based approach to nature protection were becoming clear to everyone. As Adrian Colston had shown me, efforts put into protecting 'island' sites were being undermined as the landscape around became ever more diminished and degraded. Now, with the additional threat of climate change, the risks to species isolated on individual sites were clear. We needed, as by now many people were warning, to think bigger.

Adding to the urgency was a series of global reviews which demonstrated just how parlous the state of nature had become. Since the 1940s the bodies charged with looking after nature at the global level, the International Union for Conservation of Nature (IUCN, set up by UNESCO, headed by Julian Huxley, in 1948) and the United Nations Environment Programme (UNEP, set up in 1972) had gone through the same thinking processes, from species to sites to a bigger vision. As the millennium approached they too were exploring the need for a more radical approach.

In 2000 Kofi Annan, then Secretary-General of the United Nations, commissioned the Millennium Ecosystem Assessment. This was the first international review of its kind and it coined the phrase 'ecosystem services' to describe the services nature provides for people, including health and well-being, food and clean water. While its work was in progress, UNEP's 2002 Convention on Biological Diversity was agreed, committing its members to achieve by 2010 a significant reduction of the current rate of biodiversity loss at the global, regional and national level, as a contribution to poverty alleviation and to the benefit of the Earth's ecology. But from the outset it was clear that this goal would not be met.

The reasons why were confirmed when in 2005 the Millennium Ecosystem Assessment was published. It made deeply uncomfortable reading. Over the past fifty years, it reported, humans had changed ecosystems more rapidly and extensively than ever before, with our demands for food, water, timber, fibre and fuel causing a substantial and irreversible loss in the diversity of life on Earth. Though we had benefited economically from exploiting nature, this had been at the cost of degrading many ecosystem services, irreversible declines in natural resources and species, and increased poverty for some. It offered no comfort for the future, concluding that the degradation was continuing and could become much worse; and while it was theoretically possible to reverse it there was no evidence that there was the political will to do so.

Of the twenty-four ecosystem services it examined, fifteen were degraded or being used unsustainably, including fresh water, fisheries, air and water; and species extinction was running at more than a thousand times higher than the fossil record suggested it should. The adverse impacts included damage to human health, desertification and dust clouds, eutrophication of water systems, drought and flood. While these consequences were most severe in the poorest parts of the world, they were increasingly affecting richer countries. This shook the developed nations and triggered the UK government to commission its own review.

The UK's National Ecosystem Assessment, published in 2009, was equally frank. While some UK ecosystems were delivering services well, others were in long-term decline. Of eight aquatic and terrestrial habitat types, a third were declining and most were in a reduced or degraded state. The most seriously affected were marine fisheries, wild species and soils: resources on which we critically depend.

Lobbied by The Wildlife Trusts and others, the Secretary of State for the Environment, Hilary Benn, commissioned Professor John Lawton to review the state of Britain's ecology. And in setting out to answer the question, initially posed in the 1930s, as to what would make a coherent and effective ecological network of sites in the UK, Lawton's report *Making Space for Nature* did not mince words: what we had done so far had failed.

Lawton explained why it was no longer credible to think of sustaining Britain's wildlife through discrete sites. The losses endured by years of attrition meant that Britain's remaining semi-natural habitats were now too small, too poorly protected and not managed well enough to sustain enough biodiversity. To thrive, especially under pressure, wildlife needs corridors, connections and links; species need to be able to move between sites and above all larger sites are needed. Much larger. Species holding on by their fingertips would not last for long.

Lawton's message was summed up in four words: 'more, better, bigger, joined'. Clearly things had to change if nature losses were to be stemmed and the services provided by nature sustained, and he recommended a clear way forward. But it required nature to be taken much more seriously.

In fact one of the first steps taken by the coalition government in 2011 was to honour its predecessor's commitment to produce a Natural Environment White Paper in which exactly such a serious commitment was made. *The Natural Choice: Securing the Value of Nature* ambitiously committed the government to be 'the first generation to leave the natural environment of England in a better state than it inherited'. It endorsed Lawton's recommendations, promising 'to improve the health of ecosystems, promoting an integrated approach to managing the natural environment, particularly at the landscape scale'. It established a Natural Capital Committee to 'put the value of England's natural capital at the heart of our economic thinking', and to design mechanisms to support new markets for green goods and services, promising a new approach to valuing nature. It introduced Nature Improvement Areas, as recommended by Lawton, to reverse habitat decline, and Local Nature Partnerships, mirroring Local Economic Partnerships, to co-ordinate action locally. And it set out the material benefits of nature too: wetlands that prevent flooding, resilient habitats that absorb the adverse impacts of extreme events, and sustainable farming systems that protect the soil and help us adapt to climate change. Moreover at EU level the government agreed a new Biodiversity Strategy with the objective of halting biodiversity loss by 2020; and the 2015 Conservative manifesto promised a '25-year plan to restore the UK's biodiversity'.

Though these commitments are enormously welcome they have not yet brought about the sea-change in attitudes and actions they seemed to promise. Some practical steps have been taken. In the first twelve Nature Improvement Areas, including Morecambe Bay's limestones and wetlands, the meres and mosses of north Shropshire, the Peak District's degraded peatlands, and the Purbeck heath and coast, there are new management regimes, with trees cleared or planted, drainage ditches blocked, rhododendron cut back, reed harvesting re-established and grazing reintroduced. And the Natural Capital Committee has done some important work setting out the ground rules needed if we are to take ecosystem services seriously.

But nature protection remains weak. Local Enterprise Partnerships, sponsored by the Business department, are where the energy and resources are to be found; while many Local Nature Partnerships have struggled to gain purchase on local decision-making. We continue to hear from government that economic growth is the priority and rather than measures to strengthen nature protection, the emphasis has been on how to reduce its bureaucracy. Amid claims that nature protection is 'gold-plated' and imposes 'unnecessary burdens on business', the government launched a review of the implementation of the Birds and Habitats Directives in England in 2011. While anecdotal complaints about over-zealous protection for newts and bats abounded, the reviews found no evidence that conservation policies were over-egged, and indeed recognised that many sites are still at risk. And while the commitment to a twenty-five year plan for nature is exciting, the promise to create it sits alongside another manifesto commitment, to prepare a twenty-five year plan for farming and food. The latter's objectives, to 'grow more, buy more and sell more British food', contain worrying echoes of the single-minded food production focus of the past and are hard to reconcile with a determination to restore nature's health.

For still nature's decline continues. The *State of Nature* report, commissioned by the RSPB and twenty-four other conservation charities, was published in 2013. It examines over three thousand species (five per cent of the total in the UK) and their habitats, and its conclusions are stark. In spite of all our efforts for nature, more than sixty per cent of the species examined were in decline, and those that were not have only been safeguarded by specific, focused conservation measures. Our everyday, much loved wildlife is most at risk: once common farmland birds such as the starling and the grey partridge, the lapwing, skylark and turtle dove declined rapidly in the 1970s and 1980s, and by 2000 their number was just half what it had been in 1970. The 2020 target of a halt in biodiversity loss cannot be achieved on current trends.

A further international study has provided another jolt. In June 2015 the University of Mexico produced confirmation of the sixth mass extinction in the history of the world, the first to be caused by humans. Rather than the loss of nine species that in normal geological circumstances would have been expected, 468 species have been lost, spread among mammals, birds, reptiles, amphibians and fish. Looking at mammals alone, a University of Manitoba study reported that humans now control between twenty-five per cent and forty per cent of primary productivity on Earth, that humans now make up a third of land vertebrates, with the animals we breed for eating constituting most of the other two-thirds. Wild animals are now less than five per cent by mass, a sign of how far they have been pushed to the fringes. In what is becoming known as The Great Acceleration, human domination of the planet is on an ever more cataclysmic journey.

Yet scientists still think we can avert disaster, and there is room for some optimism. Research shows that it is possible to reverse some nature losses and that habitats can be improved. It takes effort, expertise and focus; attributes possessed by the conservation organisations in this country. It also takes money, often in shorter supply; and it requires control and collaboration. But it can be done.

Thanks to well-organised conservation programmes the red kite has been successfully reintroduced, starting in the Chilterns, and is spreading throughout England. Peregrine falcons now nest in every county of England and the buzzard is once again a common bird. The otter is back in many English rivers, due to cleaner water, the banning of otter hunting and habitat protection; and the large blue butterfly has been reintroduced at several sites, including Collard Hill in Somerset by the National Trust and Daneway near Stroud by the Gloucestershire Wildlife Trust. The bittern booms again at Slimbridge, Minsmere and – improbably – Barnes, where the Wildfowl and Wetlands Trust has set up a successful urban wetland centre; and there are many more brown hares and greater horse-shoe bats than twenty years ago. The corncrake and the stone curlew have been retrieved from the brink of extinction through expert management of their specialised habitats, and an eastern European relative of our great bustard now thrives in remote parts of Salisbury Plain. The beaver has been successfully introduced in Devon and produced young in 2015. Due to impressive improve-ments in water quality and habitat management the populations of seventy-four per cent of freshwater and wetland birds are now increasing. Wicken Fen's vision is being realised: after Burwell Farm more land has been acquired and the regeneration of grazing marsh and fenland is under way. An inspiring partnership, the Great Fen Project, has similar goals for creating three thousand hectares of fenland habitat near Peterborough. The Wildlife Trusts have a *Living Landscapes* recovery plan for nature involving 150 projects around Britain.

But we have also made our task more difficult by introducing species, often accidentally, which compete devastatingly success-fully with their native counterparts. Some were introduced so long

ago that we have accommodated them: the beech tree was introduced by the Romans, and the rabbit by the Normans. But in our
lifetimes the grey squirrel has forced the retreat of the native red
squirrel to the extremities of England and Wales, the signal crayfish
has displaced the native white-clawed crayfish in many lowland
streams, and the harlequin ladybird is out-competing the common
British ladybird. The government's non-native species secretariat
currently has alerts out for the quagga mussel, the Asian hornet,
the water primrose and the carpet sea-squirt. Japanese knotweed
and Himalayan balsam have long been recognised for their ability
to choke wetland areas but the charity Plantlife now warns in addition of the risks of floating pennywort, water fern, New Zealand
pigmy weed and parrot's feather.

The uncomfortable, unavoidable conclusion is that nature, and
the beauty and diversity of the wider countryside, are in a worse
state than when the conservation movement set out to protect
them. Despite the promising start in 1949, with a strong Nature
Conservancy and plans to protect a representative sample of our
natural habitats and species, nature has declined.

So why have National Parks (eventually) begun to succeed
while our attempts to protect nature and the wider countryside
have proved so difficult? The answer in part is because their goals
are different: the National Parks have multiple objectives and their
recent strengthening has allowed them to adopt ambitious goals
embracing nature, heritage and landscape protection. They are
also, crucially, big, and can operate at a scale that will, in time,
benefit nature as well as landscapes.

But mainly it is because we have had too many contradictory
and hostile policies, particularly those affecting the way land is
managed, to protect the nature on which our future lives will
depend. It is transparently clear that nature cannot survive in
pocket-handkerchief reserves, and so we must now adopt a more

strategic approach, covering bigger stretches of countryside and joining up our efforts more successfully. The divide between nature and beauty has not served us well: we now need to work together to achieve their protection.

To truly succeed we need to think and act at a landscape scale, and to crack the conundrum, addressed by the next two chapters, that farming has both created and destroyed the beauty of Britain, and that trees can do the same. Until these policies are aligned with the protection of beauty and nature the conflicts will continue. The fight for beauty must go on.

5

How farming made and destroyed beauty

On a warm, scent-filled morning in late spring 1981 I took a walk with Aitken Clark, the passionate and witty Scotsman who was the first person to be made officially responsible for looking after the landscape of the Norfolk Broads, supporting the first Broads Authority. The area was not yet a National Park (it would be by 1988), though it had been on John Dower's 1945 reserve list.

The Broads could not have offered a sharper contrast to the earlier-designated upland and coastal National Parks: most of its landscape is at or below sea level and it was only in the 1950s that it was understood as a man-made landscape, created by deep peat-diggings (for fuel) from the twelfth century onwards. The process of peat extraction initially created deep, open pits, but by the fourteenth century the holes had flooded, leaving lakes and broads interspersed with reedbeds and wide expanses of marshland over which the lone cry of the curlew was often the only sound. For another three hundred years the water channels provided invaluable transport routes with sail-powered Norfolk wherries plying between the coast and Norwich. In the twentieth century the area was discovered for tourism, becoming a magnet for sailing holidays.

Our walk was not simply to enjoy the magical quality of the

landscape, though we did: it was undeniably beautiful. Butterflies and birds swirled around us, and across the fields the bizarre sight of an apparently land-borne sail moving through the marshes indicated one of the last wherries still in operation. A wooden windmill's blades turned lazily in the breeze. Aitken was taking me to Halvergate Marshes, the site of an enormous row between, on one side, the Internal Drainage Board and the farmers; and the other the penniless but passionate Broads Authority. He was looking for support and I was about to give it.

The row at Halvergate epitomised the clash between beauty and money, and between productive agriculture and conservation for both landscape and nature. The Internal Drainage Board (controlled by agricultural interests) wanted to drain the land to grow arable crops; the Broads Authority wanted to save from irreversible destruction one of the last traditional grazing marshes with its big skies and cud-chewing cattle, flower-studded grassland and deep, clear drainage ditches. A man-made landscape was about to become so man-dominated that it would lose without trace the landscape characteristics, wildlife value and cultural distinctiveness that had taken hundreds of years to evolve.

When W. G. Hoskins wrote *The Making of the English Landscape* in 1955 the whole of Britain was teetering on the brink of this transformation. Then, much of the countryside was still recognisably that of centuries earlier and its apparently timeless nature evoked a strong sense of patriotic loyalty and affection. This was what CPRE had been formed to protect and this was what the war-time posters had invoked to motivate the troops: *Your Britain, Fight for it Now*. Hoskins guided his readers through the story of landscape evolution, pointing to the distinctive soils, building materials, field boundaries and agricultural practices and techniques that made the landscape of Suffolk instantly recognisable and different from that of its neighbour, Norfolk; and the

Cumbrian valleys, each with their own pattern of stone walls utterly distinct from the deep hedge-banks and clustered farm settlements of Cornwall or the defensive farmsteads of Northumberland. Though he believed that the ancient farmers 'had no eye for scenery, any more than other hard-working farmers of later centuries' he showed how the cumulative impact of their activity on the geomorphologically diverse bones of Britain created a symbiosis between the landscape and man's occupation of it that was unquestionably beautiful to contemporary eyes. Alongside food, the landscape produced beauty, nature and the story of our rich cultural heritage.

In the 1950s Hoskins' work was new and inspiring. Combining geography with history, politics with economics, geology with botany and injected through with social and historical narrative, he established the completely new discipline of landscape history. He explained why and how our landscape has evolved, and to a generation battered by the Second World War and the strained patriotism of hardship and loss his book was a refuge, a homecoming, and a confirmation of the value of what people had been fighting for. Those posters with their atmospheric rural images. Our landscape, our history, the places people love.

So Hoskins' book had an extraordinary impact, feeding people's hunger to know and understand the places whose identity, so recently under threat, had become so precious. He explained that, contrary to perceptions, in England almost no landscape was natural, even if it looked that way: the rich fenland soils having been created by the drainage of the marshes; the moorlands by centuries of burning, sheep-grazing and grouse-rearing; the 'native' woodlands (as the historical ecologist Oliver Rackham was later to elaborate) owing their structure and shape to centuries of management.

But even in the 1950s, the tensions between landscape, nature and cultural heritage and a rapidly intensifying agriculture were evident. By his final chapter Hoskins' measured narrative had turned to despair, writing 'in some parts of England such as East Anglia the bulldozer rams at the old hedges, blots them out to make fields big and vacant enough for the machines of the new ranch farming and the businessmen farmers.' The 1950s marked the turning point in the relationship between farming and beauty, and the beginning of an era in which they could no longer be assumed to be compatible.

Though it took time for the country to wake up to the conflict, the reasons were clear. The Agriculture Act of 1947, another element of the post-war reconstruction programme, was designed to pull British agriculture out of recession, step up production to reduce the country's reliance on imports, and feed more people from home-grown food. This plan was encouraged by the 1942 Scott Committee into Rural Land Utilisation which, as we have seen, wanted to address rural poverty and assumed that a prosperous agriculture would pose no threat to all that was loved about the countryside. Thus money was pumped into farm mechanisation and improvement, subsidies guaranteed farmers a minimum price for what they produced, and capital grants incentivised production. What was not anticipated was that the net result of grassland improvement, increased stocking densities and the ploughing of semi-natural habitats would have such devastating impacts on beauty, nature and our cultural landscapes. And this was not just a short-term phenomenon: Britain's entry into the European Common Market in 1973, followed by our full participation in the Common Agricultural Policy, intensified the trends, particularly by sustaining high prices for cereals. And in 1975 a British government White Paper *Food from Our Own Resources* concluded that 'a continuing expansion of food production in Britain will be in the national interest'. Though an understandable reaction to wartime food shortages, nowhere did it acknowledge the possibility that it might create new conflicts with other government objectives.

The benefits of the new policies for farming were obvious: more, cheaper, home-grown food and a guaranteed income for farmers, many of whom were desperately poor, especially in the hills and remote areas. But the costs to rural landscapes and wildlife were cataclysmic: ninety-seven per cent of hay meadows were lost between 1945 and 1984; twenty-seven per cent of heather moorland between 1947 and 1980; and a net loss of twenty-one per cent of hedgerows, those classic features of the English landscape, between 1984 and 1990 alone.

This was the heart of the clash between farming and beauty, and it is not over yet. It is not a matter of whether to farm or not: the landscape of Britain depends on farming and has always done so. Moreover it has always changed. Farming can sustain the beauty and diversity of the countryside, but the extent and intensity of the changes that took place in the second half of the twentieth century strained that possibility, sometimes to the limit.

The first farmers were those who settled here, marking the evolution from the early hunter-gatherers, to the Mesolithic people's use of fire to clear land, to the establishment of settled Neolithic communities. These events may seem lost in time, but some of the earliest farmers left the most enduring signs of their occupation. In the Bronze Age the climate was milder than it is today, allowing cultivation to reach heights that have not been re-visited; there are hut circles and crop marks on Dartmoor, and evidence of early ploughing on the chalk downlands of southern England and the Yorkshire Wolds. Generations of later settlers – the Romans, Danes, Anglo-Saxons and Normans – came to Britain because of its deep, rich soils and plentiful food supplies; and each left their mark in distinctive settlement patterns, farming traditions and place names. Bede's description in his eighth-century *Ecclesiastical History* explains why Britain was so attractive:

> Britain is rich in grain and trees, and is well adapted for feeding cattle and beasts of burden. It also produces vines in some places, and has plenty of land and water fowl of divers sorts; it is remarkable also for rivers abounding in fish, and plentiful springs. It has the greatest plenty of salmon and eels; seals are also frequently taken, and dolphins, as also whales, besides many sorts of shell-fish.

By the time of the Domesday survey in 1086 the settlement pattern of rural England was more or less established, with many of the villages existing today already in place. It describes an occupied, bustling countryside of a thousand years ago. And though much has changed, there is a remarkable sense of continuity through which we can trace the landscape, wildlife and human story of our countryside.

For the areas it covered (all England except its four most northern counties), the Domesday survey recorded the amount of land in cultivation, the number of plough teams, meadow land (the source of hay, a precious commodity), pasture and fisheries. While scholars argue about how literally the Domesday record can be taken, it provides us with more than a glimpse of the early English landscape.

And already there were regional differences. The most intensively farmed areas were on the coastal plain of Sussex, the eastern fringes of East Anglia, the richest soils of the Midlands (the 'red lands' of north Oxfordshire, the Vale of Evesham and south east Herefordshire) and the lower Exe Valley in Devon. The least farmed areas were the tougher heath and breckland areas of the

Weald, New Forest, Dorset and Surrey, and large parts of northern England, which were often described as 'waste': a value judgement, of course, then as now.

Fish were clearly very important, for fisheries and mill ponds figure prominently, especially eels (for which Ely was named), and salmon along the Severn, Dee and Dart rivers. In fact eels dominate the records of north Cambridgeshire and the fens, where the vills returned tens of thousands of eels each year to their lords. Fishing enterprises (boats, nets, fish traps etc.) were often associated with the great monasteries, and vineyards were common in the south, with Ely the most northerly location.

The main development by the fourteenth century was the system of open-field farming that dominated middle England. The usual arrangement was strips, allocated to individuals, within two or three large open fields, around which a three-course rotation (first winter wheat/rye; then spring barley/oats/legumes; then fallow) was practised. The system depended on animals to fertilise the soil and, within each field, strips were grouped into furlongs enabling subdivisions between crops.

Open-field farming underpinned the social as well as economic structure of the countryside. It represented an impressive and largely successful co-operation between the workers, who belonged (in more senses than one) to the manorial lord, and both fed and provided a living to the largely rural population. There are still parts of the Midlands where, when the light is low, the fossilised remains of strip farming can be seen, creating gently undulating waves in the landscape.

Outside this Midland belt pasture was dominant. Sheep were very important in mediaeval England: it has been estimated that there may have been eight million sheep in England in the early fourteenth century (there are around fourteen million today), many associated with the powerful Cistercian monasteries whose enormous Pennine flocks fuelled the wool trade and mediaeval England's prosperity. Cattle are recorded as grazing Romney Marsh, the Isle of Thanet and the Fens; as well as in Nidderdale and Wensleydale associated with the abbeys of Fountains and Jervaulx. For many centuries the church was an agricultural pioneer, draining marshland, improving grazing and setting up markets.

'High' mediaeval farming was well organised, efficient and innovative, producing surpluses of wool and food to sell domestically and overseas. But it collapsed after the Black Death of 1348, which was the worst of a series of cataclysmic events brought about by bad weather, failed harvests and plague. In what would be a recurring theme, as farming prosperity fell arable land reverted to grassland.

After the Black Death many large estates, including monastic lands, were broken into smaller units and the more egalitarian aspects of the open-field system began to fail, with a richer landowning peasant class winning out over a landless labouring group. The Black Death also contributed to the abandonment of as many as two thousand villages as the population shrank and moved away from the sites of plague and sickness. Enclosure of some open fields began then, often to contain livestock as meat and wool were more valuable than grain. From the beginning enclosure was unpopular, depriving agricultural workers of their small stake in the land.

Between 1600 and 1800 stronger regional trends emerged. The uplands were still largely pastoral, with breeding and grazing dependent on transhumance, the movement of animals to summer pastures to fatten stock for sale. We can still see some of the early wall-lined drove roads that were built across the hills to walk animals between winter and summer grazing and to markets. The lowlands were divided between enclosed, usually hedged, fields in a mixed farming system combining arable and pasture, and the remains of the open fields.

Specialisms we would recognise today were already present: dairying in the valleys, cheese production in Dorset, Somerset and Cheshire, apples and pears in the Welsh Borders and Devon. In the South East, London's demands encouraged market gardening in Lambeth, Fulham, Putney, Whitechapel, Stepney and Greenwich, and there were sheepwalks on Blackheath and in Hounslow.

There were many innovations in the seventeenth and eighteenth centuries, led by the introduction of 'ley' farming, where pasture was ploughed for arable, then 'rested' under grass with grazing animals before being ploughed again, sustaining soil fertility. It worked best in enclosed fields, triggering more enclosure and creating large areas of mixed farming: a tradition that lasts today. New crops, especially root crops, clover and grasses, were introduced to improve fertility, and since the open fields were dominated by grain production, the spread of potatoes (introduced from South America in the late sixteenth century), carrots and turnips gave a further push towards enclosure. Clay marl was applied to improve sandy soils, and lime to lighten heavy soils; and selective livestock breeding began with rams and bulls imported to improve the quality of the stock. Many of the distinctive breeds of sheep and cattle with which we associate different parts of the country stem from the animal-breeding enthusiasts of this time.

More radical change was brought about by the widespread drainage of the Fens, allowed by the General Drainage Act of 1600. Until then incremental experiments had been the norm, but now landowners could embark on landscape-scale change. In 1630 the Fourth Earl of Bedford together with thirteen 'co-adventurers' contracted Cornelius Vermuyden, a Dutch engineer, to drain the entire southern fenland between Cambridge and the Wash. He created the two Bedford Rivers which drain the Bedford Level and established farming on an unprecedented scale. The landscape it created is like no other in Britain: huge, flat fields, with black peat soils criss-crossed by ruler-straight drainage ditches.

Vermuyden did not foresee, though, the extent to which the peat would dry out and shrink. Disastrous flooding occurred by 1700, which was remedied by the installation of hundreds of windmills to pump the water uphill into the rivers. But this only provided a temporary solution as the peat shrank further, and the situation was only retrieved by the introduction of steam pumps in 1820. The process of shrinkage goes on: the famous Holme posts, which were driven into the peat in the low-lying village of Holme near Peterborough in 1851 are now four metres above the ground, showing the degree of shrinkage since then. Today the fenland rivers and drains flow high above the level of the soil, which continues to dry and blow in the wind.

The eighteenth century was a time of taming, order and structure. Farm buildings were renewed and improved; new varieties of corn, barley and wheat meant that crops became stronger and less weedy; fields were tidier and new rotations brought new crops, especially rape-seed and flax. Field drains made heavy soils more manageable, and the sandy soils of Norfolk were enriched by root crops, most famously by 'Turnip' (Charles, 2nd Viscount) Townshend, politician turned farmer. He introduced the four-field crop rotation pioneered in the Waasland region of Holland, adding turnips (for fodder) and clover (for nitrate enrichment) to the traditional rotation. Norfolk's soils appealed to the experimentalists, and the innovations developed there were snapped up by farmers on the chalky soils of south Cambridgeshire, Lincolnshire, Gloucestershire, northern Shropshire and the sandstone outcrops of the Midlands. Jethro Tull invented the seed drill in 1703 and it was followed by the Norfolk plough, threshing machines, lighter harrows, and mowing and hay-making devices. When iron, with its sharper edges and more powerful leverage, was added to ploughs and other farm implements in the early nineteenth century productivity leapt up. But for all these advances in 1800 for every acre of arable there was still one-and-a-half acres of grass; the crop that cool, rainy Britain produces so well.

When Daniel Defoe published his *A Tour through the Whole Island of Great Britain* between 1724 and 1727, he admired the spread of turnips and the drainage of the fens, but described the uplands as wild and barren. Even here, though, the hand of the improver was at work, building thousands of miles of drystone walls to enclose and improve grazing. But just as the limit to improving these wild and rugged uplands was being realised they began to acquire a new aesthetic significance in the eyes of artists and poets.

In spite of all the efforts focused on agricultural improvements, Arthur Young's record of farming and rural life in the 1760s describes many areas where farming was primitive and the land abandoned or exhausted. In *Rural Rides* (1821–26) William Cobbett expresses outrage at the poverty of many farm workers, living in hovels on a diet of potatoes and tea. In Hammersmith and Hounslow, west of London, he notes 'the soil is a nasty stony dirt upon a bed of gravel . . . a sample of all that is bad in soil and villainous in look. Yet this is now <u>enclosed</u>, and what they call "<u>cultivated</u>" [his emphasis].' In the Isle of Thanet he observes good soil but desperate inequality:

> Invariably have I observed, that the richer the soil, and the more destitute of woods; that is to say, the more purely a corn country, the more miserable the labourers. The cause is this, the great, the big bull frog grasps all. In this beautiful island, every inch of land is appropriated by the rich. No hedges, no ditches, no commons, no grassy lanes.

Yet near Winchester he is driven to hyperbole by the beauty of the landscape: 'There are not many finer spots in England . . . Here are hill, dell, water, meadows, woods, cornfields, downs; and all of them very fine and very beautifully disposed.'

It was to address the problems identified by Young, Cobbett and other commentators that the government decided to force the enclosure of the remaining open fields. The General Enclosure Act of 1801 ended the previously ad hoc local processes of change in favour of systematic enclosure. Its purpose was to improve production and it did: Samuel Jonas wrote of Cambridgeshire in 1846 that 'few counties, if any, have improved more in cultivation . . . all the common fields have been enclosed with the exception of five or six parishes.' Its most visible result was new boundaries and ditches around the new, smaller fields: as required by the Acts these were hedgerows made by planting 'quick' or live cuttings of hawthorn; or stone, in areas like the Cotswolds or Purbeck.

But the social and cultural impacts of enclosure ran much deeper. Resentment had been running against it since the early seventeenth century, when there were riots in the Midlands protesting against the way open-field workers were thrown off the land. But the most articulate narrative came from John Clare, country boy turned poet, anguished by the enforced enclosure of his native village, Helpston, in Northamptonshire in 1809. He mourns the loss of the open landscape:

> Moors losing from the sight, far, smooth and blea
> Where swopt the plover in its pleasure free
> Are vanished now with commons wild and gay
> As poets' visions of life's early day . . .
> Fence now meets fence in owners' little bounds
> Of field and meadow, large as garden grounds

In little parcels little minds to please
With men and flocks imprisoned, ill at ease . . .
(John Clare, 'The Moors',
from *The Shepherd's Calendar*, 1827)

Clare had been observing the nature of his locality since his childhood and he was dismayed by the transformation wrought by enclosure. It was not just the loss of the open fields but the new roads, diverted footpaths, fences, 'No Trespassing' signs and barred gates that turned a landscape which had belonged to everyone into one where a few people held both the land and the power. Enclosure drove a wedge between people who had lived and worked co-operatively, dependent on each other; and it sowed the seeds of greed and exploitation. His anger spills out, but he is impotent. Clare ended his days in a lunatic asylum, his life destroyed as well as the place he loved:

By Langley Bush I roam, but the bush hath left its hill
On Cowper Hill I stray, 'tis a desert strange and chill
And spreading Lea Close Oak, ere decay had penned its
    will
To the axe of the spoiler and self-interest fell a prey
And Crossberry Way and old Round Oak's narrow lane
With its hollow trees like pulpits, I shall never see again
Inclosure like a Bonaparte let not a thing remain
It levelled every bush and tree and levelled every hill
And hung the moles for traitors – though the brook is
    running still
It runs a naked stream, cold and chill.
(John Clare, 'Remembrances',
from *The Midsummer Cushion*, 1832)

More than three thousand Enclosure Acts were passed between 1800 and 1900. They turned middle England, where open fields had shaped the countryside and its social organisation for centuries, into a structured, contained and corralled landscape. Their only remnants are the fossilised ridges and furrows that have survived ploughing, and a handful of open field systems that were never enclosed. The last significant survival is at Laxton in Nottinghamshire, now owned by the Crown Estate yet vulnerable to the increasing commercial pressures of a system which cannot, alone, sustain its tenants. Ironically, today we value the enclosure landscape with its hedged fields as much as any other; a reminder of Hoskins' determination that we should understand why and how the landscape evolved.

Thus the chalk downlands that sweep across Yorkshire, Wiltshire, Kent, Hampshire and Dorset with their precious flower-rich sward, abundant in plant and insect species, were created by a regime of day-time grazing, which reduced their fertility and increased their wildlife value; while night-time dunging of the lowland fields made these more productive. Cattle and sheep breeds evolved to meet local conditions: the wiry Norfolk sheep (bred for heathland) giving way to the fatter South Down and Hampshire breeds, while the shorthorn cattle had displaced the ancient longhorn breeds from Westmorland and Lancashire by the 1840s.

Technology continued to drive farm improvements, for example field drainage became more effective from the 1840s when clay drainage-tiles could be mass-produced at an affordable cost. It was less welcome to the workers, though: the Swing Riots in Kent, the Rebecca Riots in South Wales and the trade-union-like behaviour of the Tolpuddle Martyrs in Dorset in the 1830s reflected rural workers' unhappiness at being overtaken by machines. But there was little sympathy for them: agriculture's grip on the economy was fading as industrialisation and urbanisation took hold. It would not be long before the numbers (and the problems) swung Britain into being an urban nation. Yet in 1851 more people were still employed in agriculture (a quarter of employed males in the country) than in most manufacturing industries, and in rural areas of East Anglia, the South and South West it was nearly two-thirds.

Agriculture was now entering its golden age. Reflecting its increasing professionalism the Royal Agricultural Society of England (RASE) was founded in 1838 and conducted surveys of the country, reporting increasing prosperity and productivity. It divided England's agricultural land into five categories: the sandlands (in the East, centred on Norfolk), the fens, the South East chalk and limestone areas, the claylands and the uplands. These are landscapes whose character we can trace today, even though most have been 'improved' since.

The sandlands were the most prosperous, with the Norfolk farmer still regarded as without equal. James Caird, who surveyed for RASE in the 1850s described the 'large, open, well cultivated fields, divided from each other by straight lines of closely trimmed thorn hedges, and tilled with garden-like precision and cleanliness'.

The fenlands had come through intense improvement followed by setbacks to reach a state described by Samuel Jonas as 'a wonderfully fine district, and one in which more improvement had taken place within a few years than any other'. Their fertility was becoming an agricultural legend with their black peat soils producing exceptional yields of grain, potatoes and vegetables.

Many chalk and limestone downlands were still unploughed with extensive sheepwalks, water meadows and large farms built of chalk and flint. The Yorkshire Downs were enclosed and improved, but the flower-rich grasslands of the North and South Downs, and the downlands of Hampshire, Wiltshire, Dorset and Berkshire were ideal sheep country. By now the limestone uplands of the

Cotswolds, Oxfordshire and Northamptonshire had been enclosed and converted to an economy combining grain and sheep production, the fields divided by stone walls.

Mixed among these higher, lighter soils were the claylands, typically enclosed for much longer, forming a close-knit countryside of small fields and high hedgerows, stocked with trees, giving the impression of a deeply wooded landscape. The dense hedgerows were already irritating the agricultural improvers, though, as Caird reported: 'the luxuriant foliage of summer ... must overshadow the surface, and draw from the soil much of that nutrient which fields would otherwise yield to the farmer's stock.' The fields were tiny: in Devon ten parishes of 36,976 acres contained 7,997 fields with 1,651 miles of hedge.

In the mountains and moorlands of the North, North West and South West, attempts to improve farming struggled. They were predominantly grazed: oats were the crop most tolerant of height but could not be grown above 800 feet. Though people tried, it proved hard to convert moorland to grassland in places like Exmoor. Yet soon other demands would be made of the hills, to store water, rear grouse, to protect beauty and to walk. And as we have seen, what frustrated the nineteenth-century improvers would be overcome by twentieth-century technology.

The mid-1800s were the high summer of English farming, and its landscapes the ones we came to love in the twentieth century. Farming, though prosperous, had not stripped out all character and personality, as George Eliot writes in *Middlemarch*:

> The pool in the corner where the grasses were dank and trees leaned whisperingly; the great oak shadowing a bare place mid pasture; the high bank where the ash-trees grew; the sudden slope of the old marl-pit making a red background for the burdock; the huddled roofs and ricks

of the homestead . . . These are the things that make up the gamut of joy in landscape to midland-bred souls.

Thomas Hardy's description of Egdon Heath in *The Return of the Native* similarly reminds us of a landscape not yet subjugated to efficiency: 'majestic without severity, impressive without showiness, emphatic in its admonitions, grand in its simplicity . . . a sublimity in which spots renowned for beauty of the accepted kind are utterly wanting'.

But falling grain prices in the 1870s–90s and the build up to the First World War shattered the prosperity of farmers and landowners. The depression was exacerbated by bad harvests in the late 1870s and imports of wheat to feed the rapidly expanding urban population: the proportion of foreign wheat in the nation's bread rose from a quarter in 1850 to three-quarters in 1894. The controversial Corn Laws, introduced in 1815, had been urged on the government by landowners in an attempt to support domestic production and protect the price of home-grown corn; but manufacturers wanted cheap bread for their workers and were against intervention. The government, committed to free trade, was happy to rely on cheap imports so repealed the Corn Laws in 1846. The effect was a collapse in grain prices and a dramatic shrinkage of the arable area, resulting – again – in the widespread reversion of arable fields to pasture: at least two million acres between 1875 and 1900, and a further half a million by 1914; a fall in grain crops of forty per cent and an increase in grassland of nearly a third. Farm incomes collapsed and rural poverty escalated, fuelling a further exodus of rural workers into the cities.

The agricultural depression lasted until the end of the Second World War, with only marginal increases in home-grown demand providing a boost during the First World War. As we shall see, timber shortages were of more concern to the government than food supplies, though blockades always posed a risk. The government established milk and egg marketing boards in the 1920s, but seemed content that cheap imports would undercut most other domestic products.

These were hard times, parodied by Stella Gibbons in *Cold Comfort Farm* but evocatively described in Vita Sackville-West's epic poem *The Land* which captures the lifelong, intimate relationship between farmers and their land and stock: 'There is a bond between the men who go / From youth about the business of the earth, / And the earth they serve, their cradle and their grave; / Stars with the seasons alter.'

Those who flourished most in these lean times were those supplying fruit, vegetables and dairy products to urban markets. The railway encouraged dairying to expand to new areas and by the 1890s over four-fifths of London's milk was coming by rail from as far away as Dorset, Wiltshire and Berkshire: the Great Western Railway would carry milk for up to 130 miles. Cornwall and the Isles of Scilly produced the first flowers and new potatoes of the season and used the new railways to get them, still fresh, to London.

By the 1920s farming was a much less important industry to Britain. Agriculture's share of GDP fell from 18.4% in 1859 to 6.4% in 1913, though it still employed 11% of the workforce (by 1950 this had declined to 6% and by 1973 to 3%). Governments seemed content to take a *laissez-faire* view of farming; they had many other priorities. But with rural poverty mounting they were coming under pressure to lift it out of its state of social and economic collapse and they knew this would require intervention: the emphasis on free trade and cheap imports had been disastrous for rural England.

In *Labour and the Nation* (1928) the new Labour Party pressed for:

the emancipation of agricultural land from the hampering restrictions of private ownership, the establishment of equitable and humane conditions of life and employment for all rural workers, and the creation of the largest possible measure of security against the catastrophic changes in market conditions which are the curse of the industry today.

Though the Conservative and Liberal Parties were ideologically opposed to nationalisation, they recognised that market intervention and investment were needed for agriculture to recover, and the newly powerful National Farmers' Union (NFU) also began to lobby for state intervention.

The trigger for action, however, was provided by the Second World War, when German U-boats sank supply ships, leading to rationing and fears of serious food shortages. It was not just the reliance on specific food imports that exposed Britain's vulnerability but risks to the whole food-supply chain. The case for state intervention and control was made.

Clement Attlee's government acted. The 1947 Agriculture Act, part of the post-war reconstruction package, was motivated by the need to help farmers and stimulate the economy of rural areas, but by now the government also wanted to secure a positive balance of payments, and to reduce food imports into Britain. The Act therefore gave farmers an assured market and guaranteed prices for their produce 'to promote a healthy and efficient agriculture capable of producing that part of the nation's food which is required from home sources at the lowest price consistent with the provision of adequate remuneration and decent living conditions for farmers and workers, with a reasonable return on capital invested'.

In those terms the Act was an unqualified success. In 1938–39 agricultural output in Britain had been valued at £2.5 million (of which £1.4 million was exports); by 1951 it had reached over £1 billion, half of which was exported. The legislation gave farmers the prosperity and security they had not known for a hundred years. And guaranteed markets brought agriculture within the government's economic planning system.

The situation observed by Hoskins in the mid-1950s, then, was a countryside and agriculture on the brink of massive change. The changes were well intentioned, but the consequences were not anticipated. It was these that triggered the renewed fight for beauty.

But for more than twenty years after the 1947 Agriculture Act little was said or done to question the focus on ramping up farm production. There was, after all, little doubt that agriculture had been in a ruinous state and people accepted that the country needed to grow more food; rationing was still a recent memory. The words of the Scott Committee lingered on: 'a radical alteration in the types of farming is not probable and no striking change in the pattern of the open countryside is to be expected.' Moreover many of the leading figures in the voluntary conservation bodies including CPRE, the National Trust, RSPB and The Wildlife Trusts were landowners. Beneficiaries of the new farm policy, they were unlikely to question it. But by the late 1960s the tensions were impossible to ignore: the question was what to do about it.

Once again the Countryside Commission took the lead. In 1971 it commissioned a study, *New Agricultural Landscapes*, to quantify the changes that had taken place across lowland rural England. Its study of seven different areas exposed shocking losses, especially in East Anglia: the removal of field boundaries and landscape features as enormous fields were created, hedgerows replaced by barbed-wire fences, the disappearance of trees and patches of marshy land, the arrival of ugly new farm buildings and the loss of local character from the countryside through the ubiquity of modern materials and standard designs. Here was tangible evidence for those wanting to protect the countryside, but the study put the cat among the pigeons by suggesting that instead of regretting what had been lost (and by implication saving what was left), effort should be put into making new landscapes. It appeared judgemental about conservationists, saying 'Unfortunately, vivid impressions of the countryside during childhood often dominate preferences in adults and can lead to a sentimental and preservationist approach to landscape appreciation.'

The voluntary bodies were incensed. In *Landscape – The Need for a Public Voice* (1975) CPRE accused the authors of 'patronis[ing] those who value the existing landscape of lowland Britain', and said it 'would have done better to recognise the force of popular liking for the traditional landscape'. CPRE argued that farmers did not have the right to do as they wished on their land, because they were receiving public money and protection under the newly-joined European Community's Common Agricultural Policy (CAP). But it also refused to accept that all farmers wanted to destroy the landscape, and argued that those who wished to sustain the beauty of the countryside should be helped to do so. CPRE suggested that farmers should give their planning authority six months' notice of their intention to remove a hedgerow, stone wall or tract of down or heath; that those who managed their land beneficially for landscape and wildlife should receive tax concessions; that capital grants should have landscape conditions attached; that the Countryside Commission should launch a grant scheme to support the retention and management of landscape features; and that existing legislation to protect trees, woods and ancient monuments should be extended to other landscape features.

This document cut little ice with the Ministry of Agriculture, Fisheries and Food (MAFF), although the same ideas were to recur repeatedly over the next thirty years and in some form most were eventually implemented. But for a further decade the establishment refused to acknowledge the problem, and it took two highly charged polemics before the strength of feeling penetrated the Ministry and change was contemplated.

The first was Marion Shoard's *The Theft of the Countryside*, published in 1980. As we have seen, she pointed the finger of blame firmly at the farmer and picked apart, thread by thread, the way in which post-war agricultural policy had systematically destroyed much that people cared about in the countryside for increasingly dubious benefits. The second, Conservative MP Richard Body's 1982 *Agriculture: The Triumph and the Shame*, perhaps because it came from an unexpected source, finally did as he intended and shamed the government into action. Body showed that far from helping small farmers and reviving the rural economy, taxpayers' money had gone into ever fewer and deeper pockets, accelerating the exodus of small farmers (whose plight was at the heart of the original rationale for intervention) and – as well as destroying the countryside – was now dumping high-cost food on world markets. Post-war agriculture had been so successful that it had catapulted a nation focused on food shortages and rationing into an era of unjustifiable surpluses and damage to beauty and nature.

By now the voluntary bodies were more than ready to campaign. At CNP we were clear that the cause of most damage to National Parks was the intensification of agriculture. Here were the visible consequences of the Scott Committee's failure to anticipate the damage that would be imposed by ramping up farming and forestry production. By the 1980s a quarter of the moorland in the Exmoor National Park and a fifth of that in the North York Moors had been lost to intensification and improvement; and other semi-natural habitats, especially flower-rich hay meadows, ancient woodlands and hedgerows, were rapidly diminishing.

Our main preoccupation was with the hills, since the majority of the British National Parks are upland landscapes. Into the ferment, still continuing over Exmoor, we pitched *New Life for the Hills* (1984), an attack on the hill livestock allowances which paid farmers an amount per sheep, encouraging them to increase their flocks. Under this policy breeding-ewe numbers had more than doubled between the 1950s and 1980s from 3 million to 6.5 million, and their intensive grazing destroyed large areas of rich semi-natural vegetation, turning extensive parts of the hills of Britain, including National Parks and Areas of Outstanding Natural Beauty, into smooth, tightly nibbled, soulless landscapes. Farming was tough in these remote landscapes and we passionately wanted to keep farmers in the hills, but we were convinced there was a better way of supporting them. So we advocated paying farmers per acre rather than per head of sheep, with limits to stop over-grazing. The biggest hill farmers and the NFU initially fought these proposals, but that's what was eventually agreed, along with payments to farmers to look after the countryside as well as produce food.

A parallel campaign, led by CPRE, was to lobby to stop the capital grants paid to farmers to improve production. Farmers could get grants to cover three-quarters of the cost of removing and filling farm ponds, digging out ditches, replacing field boundaries of hedgerows and stone walls with wire fencing, removing small woodlands, improving meadows and rough grassland and building farm roads. In 1979–80 a staggering £171 million was paid in such grants.

Our campaign was directed at both the Ministry of Agriculture and the Agricultural Directorate in Brussels, where the European Commission was waking up to its environmental responsibilities. And our success was won there, when a new Agricultural Structures Regulation was issued in 1985, switching off the funding to farmers to remove landscape and wildlife features. However there were still no sanctions against farmers who decided to remove them anyway; and since the subsidy regime remained unchanged it was often worth removing landscape features without a grant because the extra income outweighed the cost of doing so.

These arguments all came to a head on Halvergate Marshes in the Norfolk Broads. As Aitken Clark had showed me, one of the last remaining expanses of lowland grazing marsh was to be turned into a cornfield.

The controversy had begun when the Lower Bure Internal Drainage Board, the authority responsible for managing the Broads' water levels and drainage system, decided that the Halvergate pumps needed replacing. But they would only pay their half of the cost (a massive £2.3 million) if it earned a return on their investment, so bigger pumps were proposed with the objective of turning four thousand hectares of grazing marsh into arable land. MAFF was ready to contribute the other half, but the Broads Authority (established in 1978 as the first, tentative, step towards their designation as a National Park) objected. Under the rules at the time, imposed by the compensation provisions of the Wildlife and Countryside Act, it would have had to find a staggering £1.5 million in compensation to protect just 310 hectares for twenty years. Practically penniless, the Authority refused to pay, but also refused to consent to the drainage pumps being replaced. Stalemate. The battle raged but the Authority stood its ground, encouraged by the Countryside Commission, and campaigners at CPRE, Friends of the Earth and me, at CNP. The Authority bravely exposed the nonsense of such massive sums of money being paid to compensate landowners for doing something clearly against the public interest. And as the press weighed in, people in high places started to listen.

Eventually the Treasury and the Department of the Environment intervened, and in November 1982 MAFF was forced to back down, saying it was not prepared to contribute its share of the cost. By early 1984 a deal was being brokered by the Countryside

Commission, using its experimental powers, to pay the farmers on Halvergate Marshes much smaller sums of money annually to sustain the grazing marsh. In 1985 the British government negotiated in Brussels the ability to declare a new category of farmed landscape called Environmentally Sensitive Areas (ESAs), places of recognised landscape and nature value where a new type of subsidy would be available, to pay farmers to sustain traditional methods of farming rather than to encourage intensive production.

It was, therefore, the same Agricultural Structures Regulation that stopped capital grants for landscape damage that also made it possible for governments to support conservation farming for the first time, by designating ESAs. By 1987 the first were established and over the next ten years twenty-two were designated: the first ten in Breckland, the Broads, Clun, the North Peak, the Pennine Dales, the Somerset Levels and Moors, the South Downs, Suffolk River Valleys, Test Valley and West Penwith. A further twelve areas were added in 1993 and 1994: the Avon Valley, Exmoor, the Lake District, the North Kent Marshes, the South Wessex Downs, the South West Peak District, the Blackdown Hills, the Cotswold Hills, Dartmoor, the Essex Coast, the Shropshire Hills and the upper Thames tributaries. By 1995 ESAs covered ten per cent of the farmed area of England – an area similar to the National Parks – and at their peak 7,500 individual agreements covered 410,000 hectares that were being managed specifically for conservation. This was progress, but it still left large areas of the countryside shaped only by production subsidies.

The negotiation of these new measures exposed a philosophical split within both the farming and conservation communities that lies at the heart of the fight for beauty. Some believe that farming needs to be free to compete in international markets, as efficient and mechanised as possible; and that nature and landscape are better protected by separating them from farming. This would be achieved either by protecting nature and landscape in specially designated areas on the farm, or by establishing separate protected areas.

Those in the other camp, in which I sit, disagree. We argue, as Hoskins did, that our landscape is the product of human management and that we should find ways to enable that symbiotic relationship to continue. Thus *all* farming should be responsive to and sustain nature and a diverse landscape (though the intensity can and should vary) and conservation objectives should be integrated *into* farming, not separated from it. We believe that farming sustainably will look after the soil, maintain landscape, wildlife and cultural identity, and still produce enough food. We want farming – as it has done since the landscape was settled – to continue to produce benefits for nature and landscape alongside food.

These arguments came to a head over set-aside: the scheme launched by the European Commission in 1984 to pay farmers *not* to farm, to manage the problems of surpluses. Those were the days of butter, milk and grain mountains, and there was pressure to curtail production to avoid distorting world markets. Under the set-aside policy whole fields or field margins were left uncultivated while the remainder continued to be farmed intensively. The nature bodies were more supportive of set-aside than those concerned with landscape, because it brought demonstrable benefits to field-nesting birds and insects whose populations had crashed due to intensive farming.

In an attempt to bridge the divide, the Countryside Commission persuaded the government to fund first a Countryside Premium scheme, offering incentives to farmers in the set-aside scheme to look after landscape features and offer public access; and from 1991 a Countryside Stewardship Scheme, which provided £25 million of funding potentially applicable anywhere in England, to incentivise the protection of landscape features and wildlife.

Valuable though these schemes were, they were tiny by comparison with the scale of the set-aside programme, which reached 600,000 hectares in the UK by 1992: fifteen per cent of the arable area and larger than all the country's nature reserves put together. So in the short term the 'separatists' gained ground, since it was clearly easier to take land out of production than to reform the fundamentals of farm policy and respond to the more qualitative concerns of beauty. But we kept on trying.

In 1994 I was invited by William Waldegrave, a progressive Minister of Agriculture whose instincts were to try to reconcile the tensions, to sit on a Commission looking into the future of farming. Though he was personally sympathetic it was not a happy experience. The Commission was stuffed with conventional farmers and managed by the bullish and ferociously clever Permanent Secretary of MAFF, Richard Packer. There were three women on the Commission: me (by now Director of CPRE and expecting my third child), Bridget Bloom (the former Agriculture Correspondent of *The Financial Times*) and Helen Browning (already a leader of the organic movement). We were also the main proponents of the 'integrationist' vision and argued strongly and – we thought – relatively successfully for reform along these lines.

But in the end we were stitched up. As the Commission's work drew to a close, William Waldegrave was shuffled away from MAFF and a more hard-line replacement, Douglas Hogg, came in. Suspicious late redrafting emphasising the importance of the market and inclining towards the status quo began to appear. We were dismayed. And I was compromised because my third daughter, Olivia, was born on the day of the last meeting.

Bridget, Helen and I ended up publishing an independent commentary to the report but in the end neither it, nor the report, made much difference. It spoke of the 1990s: a decade of painfully slow, incremental reform, setbacks and small advances; a decade of passionate arguments for protecting the beauty of nature and wildlife but one in which the direction of farming and farm policy remained fundamentally unchanged.

But other pressures were mounting, in particular a growing concern about food quality. For decades food had been the invisible 'F' in MAFF's title, but that came to a shuddering end during the BSE or 'mad cow disease' crisis of the early 1990s. Bovine spongiform encephalopathy is a neurodegenerative disease caused by feeding cattle the remains of infected carcasses; it causes a spongy degeneration of the brain and spinal cord. From the moment when John Gummer famously fed a beefburger to his daughter Cordelia in 1990 to demonstrate the safety of British beef, to the slaughtering of more than 4.4 million cattle (180,000 of which were infected) in the mid-1990s, to the first human deaths from the related Creutzfeldt-Jakob Disease in 1995 and the banning of British beef exports in 1996, people began to ask ever more searching questions about where our food comes from.

The biggest trigger for change, though, came when the country was devastated by the foot and mouth crisis in 2001. That finally exposed the full extent of the disconnect between people, farming and food, revealing the truth of what was going on in parts of the food chain and in the process depriving people of access to the countryside. It also revived the fight for beauty.

Foot and mouth broke out in February 2001, six weeks after I had started as Director-General of the National Trust. Its effect was devastating. As the disease spread rapidly, unpredictably and uncontrollably, the government closed rights of way and advised countryside businesses to shut to reduce the risk of infection. Like most others we did so, cutting off many of our income sources at a stroke: in fact much of the rural economy went into free-fall as

The 2001 foot and mouth outbreak brought chaos to the countryside and forced a reappraisal of farm policy. (Courtesy of the National Trust/David Levenson)

people stopped going into the countryside. Infected (and not infected, but at risk because nearby) animals were slaughtered and burned in pyres in the fields, and people were frightened to eat British meat. The country was plunged into crisis, and we plunged into action. Our tasks ranged from negotiating with the government on the terms on which the countryside might open again, to lobbying (eventually successfully) to stop rare or vulnerable breeds of cattle and sheep from being slaughtered unnecessarily in the contiguous culls. One population we managed to save was the Herdwick sheep flock, descendants of Beatrix Potter's flocks in the Lake District. It was a fearsomely difficult time.

But it was soon clear that it could also be an opportunity. For the joy with which people streamed out into the countryside as soon as it was finally open again could not have illustrated more clearly how much the human spirit wants and needs beauty. Moreover it also showed that leisure and tourism were at least as important to the economy of rural areas as farming. When the footpaths

The descendants of Beatrix Potter's Herdwick sheep flocks were at
risk during the foot and mouth crisis, but were saved by National
Trust lobbying. (Courtesy of the National Trust/David Levenson)

reopened many farmers welcomed ramblers back with open arms
and perceptions were for ever changed.

It also presented an opportunity for a root-and-branch review of
the way farming and food were supported in this country. Though
the problems were not all related to foot and mouth and some had
been building for many years, the fear triggered by disease and the
dreadful sight of burning carcases sparked an impassioned public
debate which created the space for real change. People were
appalled by what was revealed about how some animals were kept
and fed; and by how hard it was to find out where your food came
from and what was in it. Fairly or not, supermarkets were blamed
for caring only about profits and farmers about production; neither
were seen to care sufficiently about food quality or animal welfare.

As the disease was controlled and the countryside began to get back on its feet, the government announced three reviews into the disease and its implications. Two were held into the science and management of the disease. Had the pre-emptive cull policy been right? Should farm animals be vaccinated against foot and mouth? How should movements be managed to track infected animals? These and other questions needed answers to avoid a repetition of the way the disease had devastated both the farming and rural economies.

However the third review, chaired by Northumberland hill farmer Don Curry, constitutes the outbreak's true legacy. It had wide terms of reference, looking generally into the future of food and farming in response to the challenges exposed by the disease. Nine people drawn from all parts of the food and farming world were appointed to help Don, including Helen Browning, Graham Wynne of the RSPB, and me.

Unlike previous commissions this one really made a difference. Much of that was due to Don (now Lord) Curry. Far from being a conventional hill farmer wedded to the agricultural support systems of the past, Don surprised us all with his radical ambitions, prepared to bang heads together to achieve a meaningful and progressive outcome. So we argued – sometimes even fought – about the problems in farming and food, their origins, the reasons for the lack of public engagement, and the solutions we needed. Don urged us to be bold and we were, uniting under his chairmanship to make our recommendations.

At their heart was the compelling case for making our food and farming systems more transparent and sustainable, for the integration of the farming and food chain, for reorientating farming subsidies to meet public interests and, above all, for reconnecting people with farming and food. The Curry Commission endorsed the integrationists and argued that *all* farmers should be encouraged to farm in an environmentally responsible manner, not just those in areas identified as especially important for nature and landscape.

We proposed an 'entry-level' scheme available to all farmers, with a higher-level scheme offering more generous payments and making more demanding requirements for more important sites. Above all we showed how more sustainable and transparent methods of food production, better education of and understanding by the public, and a more joined-up food chain to get food from 'field to fork' would make the farming and food system more sustainable and resilient to future shocks.

Food was at the heart of our recommendations, especially the need for transparency and visibility of all stages of the food chain. These were the days before much food was labelled or could be sourced online, and there were very few farm-gate sales; most food passed anonymously through many hands and processors before reaching consumers. The National Trust was in a strong position to lead by example, and we encouraged our tenants whose businesses had been devastated by foot and mouth to market their meat direct to customers: the Watsons in Coniston and the Relphs in Borrowdale led the way with their Herdwick lamb. Since then there has been nothing less than a revolution in interest in fresh, local food, with the Trust and many others leading the way.

This new enthusiasm for local food and the Curry Commission's recommendations marked a turning point for beauty too. As soon as the (delayed) General Election was over, MAFF was abolished and its responsibilities were passed to the Department for Food and Rural Affairs (DEFRA; no 'farming' in its title). To implement our recommendations the government took Don Curry into its machine, making him a semi-official extra 'Minister' within DEFRA and later ennobling him for his work. His championship ensured a continuing focus on reform. And as the new schemes were implemented, particularly the entry-level scheme allowing all farmers to be paid for their stewardship, it seemed that at last the beauty of the ordinary as well as the protected countryside had been recognised.

All these schemes had to be negotiated through the Common Agricultural Policy, which authorises all farm payments in EU member states. As a result, the CAP became progressively more responsive and balanced. Revealingly, when in 2005 the seven 1971 *New Agricultural Landscapes* sites were revisited, their quality had improved, due to tree planting, new hedgerows, better landscape and wildlife management, and stronger controls over farm buildings.

Once again though, the pressures of the new millennium have forced a retreat. Now, in times of financial restraint, a much bigger European Union is demanding new priorities for the CAP. The new (eastern) members are demanding investment, and concerns about population growth and food security have revived the emphasis on food production. After several decades in which farm support has been shifting in a direction that values beauty, nature and cultural landscapes, the wheel has turned away again. Some safeguards still exist through 'cross compliance': the conditions farmers must fulfil in return for financial support. But these are likely only to bind farmers to annual commitments, so benefits achieved from three decades of focused support for environmentally friendly farming may be lost. And the 2015 Conservative Party manifesto promise of a twenty-five year plan to 'grow more, buy more and sell more British Food' seems to signal an apparent return to the production focus of the past. After progress towards integration we are slipping back towards separatism again, though the arguments raging are couched in a new language: land 'sharing' (integration) versus 'sparing' (separation of interests).

Now there are even deeper reasons to worry. The very sustainability of farming in Britain may be reaching a crunch point. The UK government's National Ecosystem Assessment (2011) concluded that 'the condition of many soils in the UK is considered degraded . . . and there is continuing loss of soil carbon in arable systems.' In June 2015 the government's Climate Change Committee warned that, having lost eighty-four per cent of our fertile topsoil since 1850, we are still seeing erosion at the rate of 1–3 cm a year, placing our soils at serious risk. Lord Krebs, a member of the Committee, said 'soil is a very important resource that we have been very carefree with. At the moment we are treating our agricultural soils as though they are a mined resource – that we can deplete – rather than a stewarded resource that we have to maintain for the long term future.'

Yet measures that are good for beauty – especially payments to look after semi-natural habitats and landscapes – are also good for sustainability, because they hold carbon in the soil and stabilise the land. We may lose more from their cessation than we realise. So the risks posed by climate change need also to be factored into policy and practice. Above all, we need to safeguard carbon in land, and peat is where we should start, because peat locks in carbon more efficiently than any other soil.

Peat is a rare habitat internationally, occupying only three per cent of the world's land surface, but it stores a third (around 500 gigatonnes (gt)) of global carbon, more than twice the carbon in all the world's forests. The UK has about fifteen per cent of the world's peatlands, storing over 3 gt, the equivalent of over twenty years of UK carbon dioxide emissions. And peat is also a rich ecological resource and the foundation for beautiful landscapes: almost all the remaining upland peat in the UK is designated for either landscape or wildlife reasons or both. But around ninety per cent of peat bog habitat was lost in Britain during the twentieth century. There are now only about half a million hectares left, mostly in Scotland and the Pennines.

Moreover, not all peat is in good heart. The National Trust's High Peak estate including the Kinder plateau in the Peak District National Park is in desperately poor condition and far from holding carbon now actually emits carbon dioxide. This is because in the past it was damaged by industrial pollution, burning heather and overgrazing by sheep (whose numbers, encouraged by subsidies, increased by three hundred per cent after 1950). Like the peat in the fens it dried out, making it vulnerable to erosion by the fierce rain and wind that lashes these inhospitable uplands and, in hot weather, oxidisation which results in carbon dioxide emissions. Today a walk on the Kinder plateau can feel like a visit to the moon. Deep gullies have been carved out of the peat, and every new storm washes more material away, much ending up as peat deposits in water supply systems which then have to be filtered and cleaned before the water reaches people's taps.

Restoring the peat is therefore an urgent task, not just for the well-being of this National Trust estate but for the country and the planet. Radical changes are being implemented: gullies have been blocked to hold water on the plateau, sheep numbers reduced, access restricted (temporarily) and native woodland is being encouraged to creep up the stream-sides. Progress is being made.

National Trust rangers blocking gullies on Kinder Scout to hold water back and re-wet the peat to maintain its carbon content and restore the vegetation. (Courtesy of the National Trust/Leo Mason)

Then there is the future of lowland peat, especially in East Anglia. After the fens were drained these were the most productive soils in the country but the effect of two centuries of intensive cultivation has been devastating. They are drying out and blowing away: two-thirds of the peat soils in East Anglia that existed in 1985 will be lost by 2050. Two inspiring projects have set out to reverse the decline: the National Trust's plans to expand by one-thousand-fold the tiny Wicken Fen nature reserve near Cambridge, and the Great Fen Project's vision for a three thousand-hectare fenland habitat near Peterborough. These solutions will benefit landscape, nature, carbon and the local economy and are a far better use for the land today than an exhausted arable factory floor.

Though peat is our most valuable carbon store we need to apply the same principles to all soil. Soil stores five times as much carbon as forests, but loses carbon when it is farmed intensively and especially when it dries out. Carbon losses from soil have accounted for about ten per cent of UK carbon dioxide emissions since 1850, but unlike fossil fuels (which have been responsible for two-thirds) the soil carbon store can be built up by good management. But it takes around five hundred years to build an inch of topsoil, whereas we are losing it at a rate of 2.2 million metric tonnes a year.

We can, though, influence the carbon content of soil by the way we farm and manage it. Grasslands hold more carbon than arable land, and the biggest carbon losses happen when we convert grassland to arable, especially when the crop grown is maize. Between 1990 and 2000 grass-arable conversion was the largest contributor to soil-carbon loss in the UK. So we need to protect our permanent pasture, and reap the wider benefits it can bring, including the production of high quality grass-fed meat, because grazed soils also store carbon and water, protect wildlife and create beautiful landscapes. And there are wider opportunities here, too: the extreme flooding experienced in many parts of the country over the last decade, including in the winter of 2015, point to the need to use farmland proactively to help manage water. Floodplains need once again to perform their primary purpose – holding water back to prevent flooding downstream – and we need to slow the flow of water by planting trees and ensuring the land can absorb as much excess water as possible.

Mixed farming is better for carbon than monocultures, because it combines arable and grass cover. So is the application of animal manure, which enriches the soil, better than liquid slurry. Organic fertilisers are better than inorganic ones because they add carbon to the soil, protect soil from erosion and recycle organic matter on farms. On arable soils subtle but important differences in management can make a big difference: for example the angle and alignment of ploughing can either protect against or exacerbate soil or wind erosion. So there is increasing interest in low- or no-plough production to stabilise soils. Organic farming has been demonstrated to hold more carbon in soil than non-organic methods. We need to produce food, but we cannot risk undermining the integrity of our soils.

So there is, potentially, a powerful convergence of interests in farming for carbon and farming for beauty, with many practices shown to be good for carbon, good for nature and good for beauty while still being good (if not aggressive) for food production. In our small, crowded island, we do not have the luxury of using land for one purpose alone. We need – to go back to those post-war words – to harmonise our ambitions for food production, wildlife, access, landscape and cultural objectives, and to these we now need to add the even more challenging aspirations of long-term resource management for energy, water and carbon.

Farming created so much of the beauty of our countryside and many of its rich wildlife habitats. Farmers, therefore, are not the enemy of conservation but its stewards, given the right incentives and support. But farm support structures do not yet provide the right framework for the twenty-first century. They remain caught between pressures for highly mechanised food production which can compete in global markets, and demands for sustainable food production, wildlife and beauty. Moreover the pressures for greater food security have encouraged the land 'sparers' to revive their call for an industrial farming policy separate from safeguarding wildlife. The land 'sharers', of which I am one, must stand by our vision for methods of farming that respect and look after the soil; that honour the traditions and distinctive landscapes of farming in different parts of the country while not being a slave to them; and move forward without throwing away the legacy of the past.

The debate launched by Hoskins sixty years ago will continue. But the fight is now urgent as our soils, the foundation for life, beauty and nature, are now so vulnerable. There is no time to waste.

6

The curious case of trees

The Forest of Dean is a remote, mysterious place. It is a working, gritty, rural landscape; densely wooded in places and with open glades in others, scattered with communities and the visible elements of its coal-mining history. In the early spring of 2011 it was a hive of furious activity. Banners hung from buildings and trees, and people marched, singing 'This land is your land'. 'Hands off our Forest' was the refrain, and keeping the government's hands off the Forest of Dean was their objective.

For, astonishingly, one of the early decisions of the coalition government elected in 2010 was to propose that England's public forests, owned and run by the Forestry Commission, should be sold. I'd first seen the consultation paper by downloading it onto my Blackberry on a train leaving Paddington. I'd got a text from the office saying it had been released – 'read it, fast!' I did so, with a sense of mounting horror.

The paper proposed a radical change for the public forest estate in England: some 650,000 acres, similar in size to the National Trust's own vast landholdings, an area the size of Derbyshire. The whole estate: commercial woodlands, multi-purpose woodlands and ancient forests, was proposed for sale or lease. The campaign that followed culminated in far-reaching recommendations for the reform of forestry and woodland policy by the Forestry Panel, of which I was a member. It also represented one of the most profound and heartfelt arguments about beauty that I have ever witnessed.

But the row about trees in 2011 was not the first; far from it. Because although trees inspire our love and admiration, contributing immensely to the beauty of Britain, they have also – when the wrong trees have been planted in the wrong place – been the source of great conflict. The curious truth is that trees both create beauty and can destroy it. And they have been a regular cause of fights about beauty.

The UK has a woodland cover of only about twelve per cent (England's is less, at just over eight per cent), making us one of the least wooded countries in Europe; the average for other EU member states is thirty-seven per cent. But trees play a disproportionately important role in our landscape and they are the inspiration for much of our music, literature and poetry, and sense of who we are, for:

> Who hath not felt the influence that so calms
> The weary mind in summer's sultry hours
> When wandering thickest woods beneath the arms
> Of ancient oaks . . . ?
>
> (John Clare, 'Wood Rides')

In 1976, in *Trees and Woodland in the British Landscape*, Oliver Rackham wrote what is regarded as their definitive history. He explained why we both love trees and fight about them. His study was effectively an archaeological investigation 'because of their longevity and continuity and the many ways in which they interact with human affairs' and he drew heavily on what had motivated W. G. Hoskins twenty years before. He wanted us to understand the significance of human influence on the landscape so that it could be applied for good rather than bad purposes. Like Hoskins', Rackham's message was urgent: 'Time is running out. The historical flow of change in the countryside – an erratic trickle with spates now and then – has turned since 1950 into a devouring flood from which little, at least in the eastern half of England, is safe.' He wanted people to have a better understanding of trees and woodlands in the landscape so that we would protect and nurture them.

Our deeply rooted affection for trees and woodlands is sometimes described as a peculiarly British trait, but it is an emotion we share with many other cultures. Perhaps it stems from the fact that humans were all, once, more dependent on trees and woodland than we now are. But England was never a densely wooded country: the 'wildwood' that Rackham describes – the botanical recolonisation of the country after the last Ice Age ended about 11,500 years ago – was a varied woodland habitat, dominated by different species (lime, oak/hazel, hazel/elm, pine and birch) in different parts of the country according to soil type, climate and elevation. The climax 'wildwood' of about 4500 BC was multi-aged and characterised by open glades (grass pollen has been found as well as woodland species) where large mammals grazed, and is the land cover that would still naturally arise if there were no competition or intervention.

Though no true wildwood remains, our woodlands still demonstrate enormous diversity, reflecting the variability of our geology and soils. The ancient, twisted, low oak trees that clothe the lower slopes of Snowdonia are a world away from the massive standard oaks and beeches, the sentinels of lowland Britain. The alder and willow that line the banks of rivers are far removed from the birch and rowan that populate our hills. The luscious dankness of Wistman's Wood on Dartmoor – one of the oldest continuously wooded sites in England – could not provide a sharper contrast to the dry, sandy soils on which Scots pines stretch skywards in Thetford Forest.

The post-glacial woodland described by Rackham has, however, been subjected to more dramatic influences than that of climate and soils: the hand of humans and the competition for land. Thus the history of our inherited wooded landscape is fundamentally one of intervention and loss. For many centuries it has been impossible to find any woodland in Britain untouched by humans. So it is not just woodland's presence or absence that defines our landscape, but its management. Some touches have been lighter than others but human activity has, for millennia, been central to the woodland story.

Wood was the ultimate sustainable resource on which early society utterly depended. Woods and trees are versatile and indispensable: they provide food, fuel, building materials and shelter, and they are endlessly renewable. Prehistoric British settlers were skilled in working wood and making the tools, utensils, houses, furniture, carts and boats which made settled, domestic life feasible. The sophistication of their design and workmanship would impress us.

These relationships established a woodland culture, reflecting people's dependence on trees and wood for every part of their lives and livelihoods. Perhaps this is what survives somehow in our cultural memory, rooting the exceptional love of trees and woodlands we feel today. In some parts of the country an actual woodland culture still – just – exists. The Forestry Panel saw and felt it in the New Forest, the Forest of Dean and the Wyre Forest in the West Midlands.

Important though woods were, they competed with the need for land for crops and many grazing animals, so were cleared to make way for them. This happened early, so that even by the time of the Domesday Book the broad shape of the present British landscape would be recognisable to us, since the proportions of land used for farming, whether for crops or grazing animals, moorland and woodland were not very different from those we see today. The vast majority of Britain's woodland had already either been cleared or taken into management, the pace and process of change varying according to the ease with which the land could be cleared and what was needed from the woodland. Pre-Roman communities were particularly active clearers and (helped by the fact that the climate was warmer) extended plough-ing to some land that has not been cultivated since. Woodland that was cleared then, and ploughed but not kept in arable cultiva-tion reverted to moorland and was used for grazing, establishing large areas of heath and moor.

The lighter soils on the long, lowland ridges running across England were early candidates for settled farming, while the harsher climate and more rugged landscapes of the North and West remained more densely wooded for longer, with tiny fields carved out of the woodland, bounded by dense hedges and stone banks. If you walk along the Ridgeway or the Icknield Way in southern England today you can feel in touch with primaeval England, since these routes provided the easiest way to travel long distances above the wet, wooded valleys.

The Domesday survey of 1086 gives us the clearest picture of woodland cover in pre-mediaeval England. While much wood-land is recorded (often as 'wood for so many swine') it had already shrunk considerably. Rackham estimates that woodland covered just fifteen per cent of the Domesday-recorded area of twenty-seven million acres. Already, by Domesday, the true wildwood had gone (with the possible exception, says Rackham, of parts of the Forest of Dean) and all woodland was in active use. This included wood-pasture for pigs and other grazing animals; coppicing and the use of the smaller 'underwood' for firewood, charcoal burning, building (since wattle and daub construction required wooden rods); faggots and stakes for fencing; and rotational felling of larger trees for construction timber. The woodland's structure and appearance reflected these needs, with a mix of large trees and coppices, glades and charcoal-burning platforms.

Woodlands were also enjoyed by the upper classes, especially for hunting. In fact hunting was the underpinning rationale for the Royal Forests which were established after the Norman Conquest, based on William the Conqueror's introduction of the un-English doctrine that the King, uniquely, had the right to keep and hunt deer on other people's land. So the hunting forests, more a legal than a physical entity, were also more places of deer than trees. In fact the historic term 'forest' refers to a place set aside for hunting. These forests were not, therefore, densely wooded but contained open, tree-scattered glades, where deer, pigs and other wild as well as domesticated animals grazed, and they also included heaths, open countryside, villages and even towns, not all of it royal property.

Others had rights in the forests too: the landowner (when not the Crown) and commoners, whose rights included

Ancient Royal Hunting Forests such as Hatfield Forest once extended across whole counties and their elaborate management structures recognised the multiple interests in forests. (Courtesy of the National Trust/Paul Wakefield)

grazing, collecting fallen timber and burning charcoal. All these uses had to be regulated and so a complex machinery of governance grew up for the Royal Forests, to keep order over these rights, and to appoint specific roles, from the forest justiciar to the wardens, foresters and verderers to uphold forest laws in the courts.

Many Royal Forests are truly ancient: the New Forest, Forest of Dean and Wychwood are recorded in the Anglo-Saxon Chronicle; and Epping and Sherwood Forests are mentioned from the twelfth century. Each has its own character, with the moorland forests of Exmoor and Dartmoor contrasting with the fenland forest of Hatfield Chase. The biggest group was in a triangle between Oxford, London and Dorset offering the King the choice of fifteen palaces from which to chase deer. And the forests were large: by the end of the reign of Henry II, father of King John, it was estimated that a third of the country was subject to forest law, including the entire county of Essex.

With all these demands on them, forests were contested places. And the first fights about them were not about beauty but about hunting. The King drew revenues from the forests as well as hunting in them, and they were an important indication of power. So one of the main motivations of the Magna Carta, sealed in 1215, was to curtail King John's appetite for controlling forests. Clause 47 stated: 'All forests that have been afforested in our time shall at once be disafforested.' This did not mean cutting down trees, but the reversal of their annexation by King John, who had appropriated large areas of land for the Crown by declaring them Royal Hunting Forests. Magna Carta therefore aimed to free landowners from the application of forest law and enable them to hold property under common law.

But the 1215 version of Magna Carta did not last long. The Council of 25 Barons created to enforce Magna Carta – an unprecedented constraint on the rights of a king – proved ineffective. Within weeks John, with the support of the Pope, who described it as 'not only shameful and demeaning but also illegal and unjust' had renounced it, plunging the country into civil war which ended with John's death in October 1216. But when later versions of Magna Carta were reissued in 1216 and 1217 under his son Henry III, who came to the throne at the age of nine, many of its principles were upheld and strengthened. Indeed so important were the clauses relating to the forests that they were expanded and set into their own charter – which came to be known as the Charta di Foresta or Charter of the Forest.

It was the existence of this less well-known charter that gave Magna Carta its name. It was labelled the 'Great Charter' to differentiate it from the Forest Charter, which was shorter and focused on the still urgent need to remove large areas of countryside from the King's control. Clause 1 of the Forest Charter required the disafforestation of all forests created 'improperly' by Henry II (John's father); and clause 3 added similar forests created by Richard I (his brother) and John himself. It also required common rights of pasturage within legitimate Royal Forests to be returned 'to those who were formerly accustomed to have them'. It reinstated the rights of freemen: clause 9 declared that 'Every freeman shall agist [graze livestock] his own wood in the forest as he wishes and have his pannage [the right to forage pigs]. We grant also that every freeman may drive his swine through our demesne woodland freely and without impediment to agist them in his own woods or anywhere else as he wishes.'

The Charter concluded with the assurance that 'these liberties concerning the forest we have granted to all men . . . all these aforesaid customs and liberties which we have granted to be observed in our kingdom for as much as it belongs to us; all our whole kingdom shall observe, clergy as well as laity, for as much as belongs to them.' This was an early recognition of the universal interest in trees and forests.

The Forest Charter guaranteed to all freemen rights of access to forest resources and the freedom to manage land, and forced collaboration and respect for neighbours and holders of common rights. Unlike Magna Carta, which applied to literate freemen, the Charter of the Forest asserted the freedoms and liberties of *all* freemen, especially those living within royal or former royal forest lands. The subsequent management and governance of the Royal Forests, especially the rights of commoners and the court systems which have survived in the New Forest and Forest of Dean, have their roots in the Charter of the Forest which was not fully superseded in law until 1971.

The Charter also affirmed the common rights of people living in and near forests to graze cattle and pigs and to gather fuel and wood, and in doing so established principles that underpinned woodland management practices for many hundreds of years. They also shaped the common rights which, as we have seen, were so central to the arguments about beauty in the nineteenth century. We owe a great deal to the Charter of the Forest.

By contrast with the tensions over royal claims, the benefits of well-managed woodland to the local community were great, for a mediaeval woodland generated many products. First there were standard trees, which were not planted but left to grow to maturity to provide construction timber. These trees were interspersed with coppice, which was cut as frequently as needed, providing flexible poles for fencing, wattle-and-daub construction of dwellings and many other practical uses. Grazing animals were excluded from young coppice, but could happily co-exist with pollarding (coppicing from the boll of a tree, a couple of metres off the ground), a practice that was widely used in hunting forests.

Because they let in light, coppiced woodlands are characterised by drifts of spring-flowering plants, a rich insect life and ample nesting sites for birds. It is a managed system which produces an ideal mix of benefits which conservation managers strive to achieve today. But for many hundreds of years the vast bulk of woodland in Britain met all these needs as a result of their functional uses. Every aspect of a wood was valuable: trees might be grown for timber or to provide shade, or their products used for building, fencing, crafts or firewood. Charcoal was an efficient and portable fuel for domestic and early industrial use. Woodlands were busy, thriving places, far removed from the stillness we often associate with them today.

According to Rackham the specific planting of woodlands, to replace those which had been lost, or to grow trees for a specific use, was not common until the seventeenth and eighteenth centuries. One of these purposes was for beauty, and trees were planted to create deer parks and for ornamental purposes. Deer parks are frequently referred to in the Domesday Book and were common in mediaeval England. By Tudor times the idea of establishing trees to adorn the landscape, create a view or provide a setting for a country house had become fashionable. Johannes Kip's engravings of the late seventeenth and early eighteenth centuries show elaborate planting regimes surrounding country houses, with long avenues creating vistas into the countryside beyond.

And as we have seen, the eighteenth-century designed landscapes created by William Kent, 'Capability' Brown and Humphry Repton are now regarded as one of the supreme art forms of England, the central ingredient being artfully placed individual and clumps of trees, often reflected in shimmering lakes.

Woodland management was a culture and skill that once belonged to the majority of the population, but forestry – the art of cultivating trees for commercial or ornamental purposes – was different, and its founding champion in Britain was John Evelyn. A contemporary of Pepys, Evelyn was also a diarist and social commentator, and he was fascinated by arboriculture and timber production. His *Sylva: A Discourse of Forest Trees and the Propagation of Timber*, was the first formal publication by the Royal Society in 1664, and put the case for an enlightened transformation of the countryside, bringing abandoned and neglected wastelands (among them, controversially, parts of the Royal Forests) into productive use. Evelyn was also a garden designer and pioneer of horticulture, and the failure to save his home and garden, Sayes Court, later played a role in the foundation of the National Trust, but he will be remembered most for his advocacy of timber production, and his detailed practical advice on how to plant and nurture trees.

The urgent need was to meet the voracious demands of Britain's shipping fleet, central to the country's military and commercial success, for long, straight planks of oak. Though the Navy, as well as John Evelyn, had long warned that timber supplies for the royal dockyards were in jeopardy it was not until 1786 that a government Commission proposed that 100,000 acres of oak be planted to supply the Navy. In the interests of speed (a relative term) there was pressure to enclose land and establish oak plantations on Crown lands, especially in the Forest of Dean and the New Forest. This caused ructions as enclosures planted with monocultures of oak replaced the traditional glades and landscapes of the Forests, also displacing and upsetting the commoners. It was a sign of tensions to come.

These oaks were planted too late, of course, because demand for timber from the shipbuilding industry collapsed in the mid-nineteenth century as wooden ships were replaced by iron ones, well before the oaks reached maturity. However, the demand for timber

We love oak woodlands today but even these caused controversy when they were planted in the Royal Forests to grow timber for ship-building in the eighteenth century. (Courtesy of Latitude Stock/Alamy)

was by then growing exponentially to meet the demands of a growing population and the industrial revolution. Wood had fuelled Britain's early industrialisation, providing (as it had since the fifteenth century) pit props for the mining industry and charcoal to fuel lime kilns and other industrial processes, particularly iron smelting. As the nineteenth century progressed wood was still in demand and home-grown supplies were inadequate, so imports expanded. By 1914 the UK was importing 400 million metric tonnes of timber.

But the most dramatic event of the nineteenth century was a silent one: the collapse of woodland management. As cheaper foreign imports replaced home-grown timber, and coal, which could be transported cheaply by the canals and railways, replaced coppice wood as a fuel, the demand for the products of intensively managed woodlands fell. Local markets for wood products such as rakes, hoops and hurdles collapsed in the run-up to the First World War and finally perished in the agricultural depression of the 1930s. Coppice-with-standards was replaced by plantations of single-aged trees on the continental model. The skills of continuous management for multiple products involving the entire local community were replaced by experts focused on a single, long-term product: high-quality timber. So woodland management as a community process all but disappeared, and with it the woodland culture that had shaped so many generations. Thomas Hardy captures this transformation in *The Woodlanders* (1887), whose small community is disrupted by the arrival of an ambitious newcomer, one of the woodlanders noting phlegmatically 'She's the wrong sort of woman for Hintock – hardly knowing a beech from a woak [sic].' Planting and forestry became the preserve of the few, mainly large landowners.

By the early nineteenth century, too, new trees were appearing. Around 1790 Scots pine and larch were introduced into the Keswick area by the Governors of Greenwich Hospital and to Windermere by the Bishop of Llandaff. Step in Wordsworth, whose beloved Lake District was already beginning to suffer from the indignities of industrialisation. To his horror, and to add to railways, suburban villas and ore extraction, a new species of tree was invading the uplands:

> if ten thousand of this spiky tree, the larch, are stuck in at once upon the side of the hill, they can grow up into nothing but deformity; that while they are suffered to stand, we shall look in vain for those appearances which are the chief sources of beauty in a natural wood.
>
> (William Wordsworth, *Guide to the Lakes*, 1810)

This vision contrasted horribly with the landscape as he knew and loved it:

> Feathered with woods but not obscured – craggy and wild but not bleak or bare – bank and jutting stone moss-covered and fern adorned but not softened into effeminacy, or their natural beauty crippled by false art – dark, cool, lonely, and lovely, their wild grace at once rich and free.

Thus the stage was set for the first big clash between beauty and trees.

In the run up to the First World War the country's timber reserves were in a poor state. By 1914 ninety per cent of the country's timber was imported, and existing woodlands, including the Crown woodlands, were in a parlous state of management. Little was known about British reserves of timber, and there was no organisation capable of moving quickly to mobilise it should it be needed. In 1916 the government set up the Timber Supplies Department, which established sawmills and supply systems as quickly as it could. These consisted of haulage horses and horse-powered tramlines to extract timber and drag it to the already-congested railway lines for distribution. This was remarkably effective in difficult circumstances, but the coalition wartime Prime Minister David Lloyd George admitted that it had been 'a close run thing' and Britain had been closer to losing the First World War through a lack of timber than a lack of food.

At the same time as it set up the Timber Supplies Department the government commissioned the Forestry Committee of the Ministry of Reconstruction to 'report on the best means of conserving and developing the woodland and forestry resources of the United Kingdom'. Appointed in 1916 under the chairmanship of the Rt Hon Sir Francis Dyke Acland, it reported in 1917 and proposed the establishment of a Forest Authority, to be called the Forestry Commission. It would reduce Britain's dependence on imported timber, expand fast-growing softwood production in the UK and use 'wasteland' (meaning the hills) in the UK to grow timber and provide jobs. The Committee proposed that over 1.7 million acres should be planted by the end of the twentieth century and the first 200,000 acres within a decade, the majority by the state.

The plan was agreed, and by 1919 the Forestry Act was passed and the new body set up. It was given a budget and a group of energetic Commissioners with powers to acquire land (compulsorily if needed), plant trees and generate a woodland industry in Britain to compete with other countries. Moreover there would be grants and fiscal incentives to encourage landowners to play their part. Some of the products of this new forestry initiative, of course, were expected to be native hardwoods but there was a gathering interest in softwoods, especially larch and the fast-growing American Sitka spruce for which there was an expanding market, appealing to those who wanted a faster return. This was a very different vision for woodlands, requiring different skills from those that had evolved over many hundreds of years based on local management and their multiple, renewable products.

This, then, was the cause of forestry's first public fight over beauty. The infant Forestry Commission, keen to get started, sought quick wins that would establish a new dawn for forestry. It looked for land that was affordable and available, and for places where it could establish large blocks of planting. The uplands of England, Scotland and Wales were the obvious solution: the English Lake District among them. This was also the place where a first-class row was guaranteed.

As we have seen, Manchester Corporation had already provoked the outrage of the early amenity campaigners when it flooded Thirlmere. Insult was added to injury when it planted the catchment of its controversial reservoir with conifers, apparently believing that native broadleaves would pollute the water supply. But it was not just the presence of conifers that upset the Lake District's defenders: it was the uniform regularity of the planting, bringing awkward straight lines and rigidity into a landscape of rocky outcrops, charming curves and visual surprises.

Nothing could have provided a sharper contrast to the beauty of the Lakes than serried ranks of conifers marching across open country, paying no heed to the landforms below. Wordsworth's love for 'native beauty', 'the union of the child's imagination, through love and wonder, with the world of nature and the works of man' expressed in his *Guide to the Lakes* was shattered by this new form of landscape commercialisation.

But the Forestry Commission was undaunted. By the early 1930s it had planted nearly one-and-a-quarter million larches and over five million spruce on a thousand acres of Ennerdale and the Thornthwaite Estate near Keswick.

While these actions upset the newly established Friends of the Lake District, it was when the Commission acquired a colossal seven thousand acres of land in upper Eskdale that the Friends leapt into action. At first they tried to persuade the Commission to plant more broadleaf trees (only a tiny eighteen acres of Ennerdale had been planted with native trees) and to safeguard public access. But they became emboldened to try to stop conifer planting altogether after the novelist Hugh Walpole wrote to *The Times* decrying the planting proposals in Eskdale as bound to 'ruin it once and for ever'. Under protest, the Forestry Commission agreed to establish a Joint Committee with the Council for the Preservation of Rural England, the Friends of the Lake District's parent body. The CPRE members of the committee inspected the site and pronounced it unacceptable: none of the land should be planted. In reply, the Commission reduced but did not abandon its proposals.

A petition was circulated and by 1935 it had attracted thirteen thousand names, including many of the great and good in British society: Lords Lieutenant, Bishops, former Cabinet Ministers and eminent politicians (Beveridge and Maynard Keynes among them), University Vice-Chancellors, and heads of Oxford and Cambridge colleges and the major public schools. The petition was presented to the Commissioners, calling not only for Eskdale to be reprieved but for a moratorium on planting in the entire Central Lakes. In a debate in the House of Lords, Lord Elton compared the proposals to 'planting a petrol station in front of an ancient cathedral': abstinence, not mitigation, was called for.

John Dower, the architect of National Parks in England and Wales, drew up maps to define the area of the Central Lakes that should not be planted with conifers, and the campaign was fronted by the Rev. H. H. Symonds, a clergyman teacher who had retired to the Lake District at the age of fifty to devote himself to advocating for a National Park, the case for which he argued in his books *Walking in the Lake District* and *Afforestation in the Lake District*. A series of cantankerous meetings took place between the campaigners and the Commission until, in 1936, a historic agreement was drawn up in which an area of three hundred square miles of the central Lake District was declared exempt from conifer plantations.

This was an uneasy truce and the Forestry Commission's pride was hurt. But it was a lesson it had to learn time and time again, for the tensions between forestry and beauty were far from over.

In 1923 the Forestry Commission was given responsibility for the Crown Lands, including the ancient hunting forests, and its early relationship with these sensitive areas and their complex,

Stowe Landscape Gardens, where 'Capability' Brown learned his art. (© National Trust/John Millar)

One of Frank Newbould's posters, commissioned by the War Office to maintain morale. (© Imperial War Museum)

Some of what remains of the glorious Exmoor heather plateau, seen here from Trentishoe Down, looking towards East Cleave. (© National Trust/Paul Wakefield)

Left: Wicken Fen, the National Trust's 'nature reserve in a plastic bag', which helped us all think big for nature. It is now at the heart of a major fenland restoration programme. (© National Trust/Joe Cornish)

Right: The Large Blue Butterfly, photographed here at Collard Hill in Somerset, was successfully reintroduced after it became extinct in Britain. (© National Trust/Brian Cleckner)

Halvergate Marshes in the Norfolk Broads were the subject of a spectacular row in the early 1980s and a trigger for changing farm policy to protect beautiful landscapes. (© Broads Authority)

Remains of the open field, ridge and furrow system of mediaeval farming across much of central England can still be seen when the light is low. (© Tom Falcon Harding)

Intensive arable farming in much of lowland England has resulted in the loss of many landscape features.
(© National Trust/David Noton)

There is a powerful convergence of interests between farming and beauty when we strive for it: this is Corton Denham in Somerset.
(© David Crosbie)

The charity Common Ground's Apple Day has led to a revival of interest in local varieties of apple and locally sourced food. (© National Trust/John Millar)

A woodland scene. Coppicing, widely practiced for hundreds of years until the nineteenth century, delivers multiple benefits including useful wood products, glorious nature and enjoyment for people. (© Photoshot License Ltd/Alamy)

Lundy's rich maritime habitats had been severely damaged before it was finally declared the UK's first Marine Nature Reserve in 1986. (© Landmark Trust)

The mediaeval harbour wall at Mullion in Cornwall has been repaired many times, but it may eventually have to be sacrificed to the sea. (© National Trust/David Sellman)

Climate change is bringing more exceptional storm surges and severe weather, including coastal damage and floods to Britain. (© Helen Dixon/Alamy)

Coloured aquatint, 1805, after a drawing by Philip James de Loutherbourg. The French baroque painter's feeling for stage effects helped to clear the way for the vision of the romantics.

Coalbrookdale: 'too beautiful to be much in unison with that variety of horrors art has spread at the bottom' according to Arthur Young in 1776. (© The Institution of Mechanical Engineers/Mary Evans)

Though South East England is heavily populated, the land use planning system has protected its beauty by designating green belts, containing urban areas and protecting the countryside in between. (© John Miller/Corbis)

50 O BETHAU I'W GWNEUD CYN EICH BOD CHI'N
THINGS TO DO BEFORE YOU'RE 11¾

Nothing matters more than giving our children access to beauty. (© National Trust/Paul Harris, John Miller, John Millar, Arnhel de Serra)

interlocking objectives was not happy. In the New Forest the Commission blundered into controversy with plans to enclose and plant large areas over which common rights were held. This showed a lack of respect for the ancient traditions and complex relationships between the rights-holders and residents of the Forest, a replay of the oak-planting conflicts of more than a hundred years before. In 1949 the MP for Bournemouth, the aptly named Brendan Bracken, said of the Forestry Commission that it was 'a body of acknowledged incompetents which has done more to destroy our landscape than anything else in history, including erosion of the soil and the malice of Hitler'.

But as time passed the Forestry Commission became more responsive to public opinion, at least in some places. In the 1940s its largest forests were designated as Forest Parks and began to cater for visitors: these included Snowdonia's great forest, Coed y Brenin, Cumberland's Grizedale Forest and Dalby Forest in the North York Moors. Walking and cycling routes were laid out and car parks and campsites introduced so the public could enjoy them. Kielder Water and Forest Park, Britain's largest man-made forest, now aims to meet recreational needs as much as those of commercial forestry, and it attracts over 370,000 visitors a year to enjoy walking, cycling and sailing.

Wounded by criticisms of the aesthetics of its planting, in the 1960s the Commission employed Dame Sylvia Crowe as its first landscape architect. She was asked to remodel some of the early plantations and to design new ones that would fit better into the landscape. These aimed to soften plantation edges, introduce hardwoods in some parts of the plantations, and protect views and viewpoints, skylines and streams.

But the conflicts did not go away. One reason was that the 'bare wasteland' so attractive to forestry interests, public and private, coincided with many of the areas designated as National

Parks. One person's bare wasteland land is another's walking, landscape and wildlife ideal, and so the clashes continued. In 1961 the Standing Committee on National Parks published a pamphlet, *The Case for Control of Afforestation of Open Land in National Parks*, pressing for forestry to be brought under planning control. Its campaign was triggered by an article in *The Times* in March 1960 reporting that a newly formed private forestry syndicate planned to acquire 100,000 acres of 'bare land' within Devon, Cornwall and Somerset, and to make a further 250,000 acres of existing woodland 'fully productive'. The moorlands of Dartmoor, Exmoor and Bodmin Moor were the prime candidates for planting, and the precious ancient woodlands of Exmoor among those that would be 'improved'. Generous government grants and tax subsidies for forestry lay behind the syndicate's plans.

Though a row followed, forestry was still not brought under planning control, but the Forestry Commission agreed to improve consultation and to notify relevant authorities in designated areas in advance of its planting plans. A ministerial statement in July 1963 confirmed that while planting targets remained ambitious (the Forestry Commission aimed to plant 450,000 acres, mostly in Scotland and Wales, in the decade up to 1973), more regard was to be paid to landscape and public access. This slowed but did not stop bare-land afforestation: indeed one of my first tasks as the newly installed Secretary to the Council for National Parks in 1980 was to object to a peculiarly ill-judged free-standing diamond-shaped plantation on the Cnewr Estate, on the lower slopes of Pen y Fan in the Brecon Beacons National Park. We did not succeed in stopping it.

Though bare-land planting provoked outspoken responses, a quieter but just as significant assault was taking place in already established woodlands. A secondary purpose of the Forestry

Commission was to bring existing woodlands into more productive use, and to do so it provided generous grants to woodland owners to reinstate management, underplant woodlands with commercial timber crops and fell marketable trees. This had a dramatic effect on the landscape and wildlife value of Britain's woodlands.

These woodland were not, as we have seen, in good shape. Much had been effectively abandoned in the nineteenth century, leaving awkward, overgrown remnants of former coppicing and other management regimes. But many of these woodlands were not only exceptionally beautiful but also highly significant for nature conservation. Under the new regime the losses of ancient woodland – woodlands that have existed continuously since at least 1600 – were particularly severe, with new planting and commercial management having a devastating impact on their ecology. Many veteran trees, often of exceptional historic, cultural and ecological importance, were also lost due to felling or lack of care.

Looking back over this period the RSPB's 2013 *State of Nature* report calculated that in the previous fifty years sixty per cent of woodland species had declined and thirty-four per cent declined strongly: this includes woodland butterflies and birds (which had declined by seventeen per cent since 1970), invertebrate species and flowering plants. Eleven per cent of the 262 woodland flowering plants it assessed were on the red (endangered) list. The main reasons for the decline were the dropping of management techniques, like coppicing, that produce a mixed-age woodland; the lack of light and nesting sites in dense, uniform plantations; the removal of dead wood and leaf litter; and disturbance.

The biggest fight about trees and nature, however, had still to happen. This time it was about conifer planting in the Flow Country of northern Scotland, a bleak, remote, windswept plateau. This is the largest single habitat in Britain, immensely important in nature conservation terms. It has been described as the tropical rain-forest of the north, composed of 400,000 hectares of blanket bog. It is one of the world's richest peat bogs and a habitat for rare birds including the golden eagle, golden plover, greenshank and hen harrier. But in the 1980s all the foresters could see was a potential conifer plantation of immense proportions.

By 1987 sixty thousand hectares had been planted, just over half by the Forestry Commission and the rest by private investors, supported by grants and generous tax breaks. Owners could claim tax relief, exceptionally, at two points in the forestry cycle: when the trees were planted and when the timber was harvested. This made forestry attractive even when conventional returns were low, and had driven forestry onto more remote and 'unproductive' land where it was not in competition with intensive farming. This was, however, almost by definition land that was important for wildlife and landscape.

The RSPB called for planting to be stopped in 1987 and the NCC sought a moratorium so that a conservation solution could be worked out: it proposed to declare 172,000 hectares an SSSI. But there was no interest in a negotiated agreement and hostilities escalated. In the same year the conservation organisations published a string of lobbying reports, including one by us at CPRE (where by now I was), *Budgeting for British Forestry*, which sought the removal of the tax incentives that were driving damaging forestry, and one by the RSPB charting the negative impact of conifer plantations on rare birds.

In the spring of 1988 the NCC weighed in with its report *Birds, Bogs and Forestry*. It was launched in London (rather than Scotland) and used more direct and critical language than was usual for an official body:

An aerial photograph of the Sutherland Flow Country being planted
with conifers in the 1980s, encouraged by generous tax breaks.

Coniferous afforestation is destroying these peat-lands . . . Whilst two decades ago threats to these peat-lands on this scale would have seemed inconceivable, land use change unprecedented in its speed and scope is now in progress . . . Afforestation is inimical to the survival of moorland breeding birds . . . The area lost to forestry – most of it since the passing of the Wildlife and Countryside Act 1981 – represents perhaps the most massive single loss of important wildlife habitat in Britain since the Second World War. Decisions to promote appropriate conservation measures are needed promptly if the losses already sustained are not to increase.

This was a big story and the media loved it, delighted to link a conservation scandal with high-profile celebrity investors not previously known for their interest in forestry who were reaping the rewards of lucrative tax breaks.

Then, in his March 1988 Budget, Chancellor Nigel Lawson unexpectedly and decisively pulled the tax benefits for forestry. At CPRE we were delighted, because this was exactly what we had advocated, and at a stroke he removed the economic incentives not only for planting in the Flow Country but in many other upland areas. In his speech the Chancellor called for 'a better balance' between broadleaved trees and conifers, triggering further reform of forestry policy and incentives. The RSPB acted quickly in response, announcing its plan to purchase over 20,000 hectares of the Flow Country to create what would become its Forsinard Flows nature reserve. The result was a breakthrough for beauty and nature.

To its credit, after this terrible clash the Forestry Commission embarked on a programme to make peace with the people and

Today, large parts of the Flow Country are protected by the RSPB's
Forsinard Flows nature reserve. (Courtesy of Norman Russell/RSPB)

interests it had upset. Pressed by a series of Acts of Parliament (one
originating as a Private Members' Bill promoted by Dr David Clark
MP, later an enlightened Chairman of the Forestry Commission),
its statutory purposes were amended to include environmental
responsibilities and public access. Practice on the ground changed
too, with more responsibility delegated to local staff to build the
relationships, partnerships and management regimes that were
suited to different parts of the country. This is particularly important in the Crown Forests where the Commission's Deputy
Surveyor is an important figure in the landscape, and needs the
freedom to make decisions which respect local and historical traditions as well as contemporary needs. The new duties also shaped
grant schemes for private owners, encouraging them to adopt
higher standards of landscaping, nature conservation and public
access. As a result new planting became less provocative and there

was more focus on the multi-purpose management of existing woodlands.

By the late twentieth century the Public Forest Estate – as the Forestry Commission-owned and managed woodlands were known – had become an important presence and won much greater public support. The Commission, both as landowner and grant giver, had increased the planted area of Britain from its all-time low of five per cent before the First World War to around ten per cent, of which more than eighty per cent is in private (including charitable) hands. The Forestry Commission was repeatedly reorganised, and the threat of partial privatisation regularly floated. In the 1990s production and management of woodlands (Forest Enterprise) was separated from regulation (the Forest Authority), and since 2013 the Forestry Commission in Wales has been part of Natural Resources Wales, the successor body to the Countryside Council for Wales.

Perhaps surprisingly, after the fights of the past, we became allies. We did not want the Commission to be privatised, and we needed to work together to respond to new threats, including the influx of tree diseases and infections. Forty years after Dutch Elm disease had robbed much of lowland England of its elms, Acute Oak Decline, *Phythophthora ramorum*, ash dieback, Chalara, and many others required us to collaborate on mitigation, protection and lobbying for support from the government.

We also became better allies because, fundamentally, we all cared about trees and woodlands; and we were increasingly aligned in trying to ensure that the right trees were planted in the right place. We had more in common than the fights that had divided us. People find woodlands and trees, especially but not only our native broadleaves, enormously inspiring. Public recreation in woodlands has burgeoned since the millennium, with an estimated 300 million people visiting woodlands and forests every year, benefiting the visitors but also bringing the 'walking pound' – tourism income – to many rural areas. We know the sight of trees helps hospital patients recover faster, and their general restorative power, helping people with mental health problems, is becoming widely recognised. People support charities that protect woodlands and plant trees: the Woodland Trust now has nearly a quarter of a million members and owns 47,000 acres of woodland for nature, landscape and public access; just one of many organisations holding Britain's woodlands in conservation ownership.

And the potential for woodlands to do even more for our quality of life and help us create a more sustainable future is enormous. The woodland habitat of this country is, today, one of our most important reservoirs for wildlife. In 2011 the National Ecosystem Assessment, developed by DEFRA, highlighted the benefits it brings to the country's natural resources, by providing space and corridors for wildlife and helping keep our water and air clean. Moreover the UK's woodlands lock up carbon, storing an estimated 790 metric tonnes (Mt) of Carbon (640 Mt in woodland soils and 150 Mt in standing trees) and removing a further 15 Mt of carbon dioxide from the atmosphere each year, figures that would increase if we planted more woodland and trees. As our mediaeval predecessors knew so well, managed woodlands can provide an endlessly regenerating supply of sustainable wood for fuel, particularly if it is used locally. In recent years the National Trust has achieved significant carbon reductions by installing wood-fuelled boilers in properties where it can also re-introduce coppicing on its own woodland, for example at Castle Drogo in Devon, Scotney Castle in Kent and Sudbury Hall in Derbyshire.

And wood will be even more useful in a low carbon future. Wood-frame buildings have the lowest carbon cost of any construction method, and for every cubic metre of wood used instead of other building materials, 0.8 Mt of carbon dioxide is saved from the atmosphere. The twenty-tonne carbon footprint of a conventional house could be reduced to just 2.4 Mt by using timber for the frame, cladding, windows, doors and floors. Strength for strength, steel uses six times more energy to produce than timber, and timber-framed buildings also offer better thermal insulation than any other mainstream construction material: their energy use is six times lower than brick and four hundred times lower than steel.

We have also, surely, gone past the time when new planting risks conflicts with natural and landscape beauty. In fact we know how to do it well. In 1987 the Countryside Commission launched an inspiring vision to create a two hundred square mile forest landscape in the English Midlands. Drawing on a long tradition of woodland management in the area, and designed to rehabilitate the compromised, industrialised landscapes of the Midland coalfields, the National Forest has followed mediaeval rather than twentieth-century practices by absorbing new planting into the wider landscape, creating a patchwork of woodland and open glades, improving degraded landscapes and providing people with places to visit and enjoy a wooded landscape. Its vision was to re-create the multiple dimensions of woodland and forestry, and to encourage community involvement in all its activities. Just eight years later over eight million trees had been planted, with woodland cover across the National Forest area increasing from six per cent to over twenty per cent, bringing millions of people closer to woodlands for their enjoyment and inspiration. The local economy, community well-being and wildlife have all been given a boost: it is a model for the future.

Other successful new woodlands have been created around urban areas, in the Community Forests, and under the Forestry

Commission's community woodland scheme. The Woodland Trust has planted many new woods, most recently in honour of HM The Queen's Diamond Jubilee. And Boris Johnson, as Mayor of London, planted over twenty thousand individual street trees in London during his two terms of office, focusing on the areas with fewest trees and aiming to increase London's tree cover by five per cent by 2025.

Woodland wins on every front: it is good for people, good for nature and good for the economy. It is profoundly good for beauty. It offers a major contribution to our need to live more sustainably in future, and to do so in ways that are entirely compatible with beauty.

Against this background the decision in 2010 to sell off the Public Forest Estate in England was extraordinary. We knew some sales were coming: DEFRA, the government department responsible for forests and woodland in England, was under pressure financially, and the Forestry Commission had already begun a small programme of woodland disposals. But we had not expected such radical proposals. We had anticipated that some of the 'commercial forests', the conifer-dominated forests that were run as businesses and generated a profit, might be offered for sale, but none of us thought the non-commercial woodlands, especially the highly significant ancient royal hunting forests, would be included. We could not see how it made financial or policy sense to sell these woodlands, and nor could the public, who adored them. Yet that, it seemed, was what the government proposed to do.

As soon as the consultation paper was published we had to decide how the National Trust should respond. And as we talked, we considered whether we should offer the Trust as a backstop owner, a safeguard of last resort, if the government went ahead with this damaging proposal.

Overnight we studied maps showing all the Trust's land, including woodland, alongside that of the Forestry Commission in England. There were many places where we owned land near to each other, and sometimes it was even adjacent. We had a history of leasing land both from and to the Forestry Commission, some a long time ago on very long leases. So we were already tied together, and indeed were already negotiating with the Commission to buy some of its land as a result of earlier, more modest rationalisation proposals.

Our plan, after consultation with trustees, was soon decided. We would oppose the sale, but if the government persisted with it, we would say that as a last resort we would consider becoming owners of the forests ourselves. Along with everyone else, we announced our position and the debate began.

The public mood was deeply hostile: it was as if the government proposed to sell the Crown Jewels. Worse, it was as if the government was selling *our* jewels, for the forests were felt to belong to the people, as places for enjoyment and spiritual release. Because while the forests were owned by the government, it owned them for and on behalf of the people. That sense of a principle breached, that something of massive but non-material value might be snatched away, lay at the heart of the anger, drawing in new voices and encouraging innovative methods of campaigning, such as the online petition created by the organisation 38 Degrees.

There was unanimous opposition to the government's proposals, but to some even the smallest hint that the Trust might consider taking them on attracted wrath. John Vidal's headline in the *Guardian* on 29 January – 'National Trust ready to "step in" and save forests' – did not make us popular: objectors feared that by even hinting at being an owner of last resort, the Trust might offer the government a way out. We reaffirmed that our primary purpose was to stop the sell-off, and the next few weeks were frenetic. Along with many other organisations we met and talked to officials, Ministers and like-minded bodies, analysing the detail of the proposals. And the government's plan was soon exposed for its weakness. While there was clearly some conventional financial value in the so-called 'commercial forests', headed by Kielder in the North East and large plantations like Grizedale in the Lake District and Dalby in the North York Moors, the thousands of smaller 'multi-purpose' forests – so named because alongside timber production they were important for wildlife and public access – would barely break even. And the ancient hunting forests – the Forest of Dean, the New Forest, Cannock Chase, Rockingham Forest and Sherwood Forest – were loss-makers which needed investment. Hungry for money and with complex management requirements these were liabilities, not assets. Even the suggestion – proffered in response to objections – of the possibility of government-funded leases rather than sales went down badly; many of these forests had been in public or quasi-public hands for more than a thousand years and everyone agreed they should stay there. And the Public Forest Estate worked as an entity, with the 'commercial' forests providing a cross subsidy to the rest of the estate. The public forests weren't broken, and didn't need fixing.

Then, suddenly, the Prime Minister distanced himself from the proposals. On 16 February 2011, in response to a question from the Leader of the Opposition, Ed Miliband, asking whether he was happy with his policy to sell off the forests, he dropped it like a hot potato. 'The short answer to that is, no.' And it was over. The consultation paper was withdrawn. 'Forests sell-off abandoned as Cameron orders U-turn' was the headline the following day.

The government's next step was to set up the Independent Panel on the Future of Forestry in England, chaired by the popular Bishop of Liverpool, the Rt Rev. James Jones. Wise and experienced in matters of public controversy (he had recently been appointed to chair the review of the Hillsborough football disaster, still excruciatingly painful after twenty years), he had spoken against the forest sale in the House of Lords and was a well-known environmentalist. The eleven panel members, including me, were drawn from across the spectrum of interests concerned with forestry, and we had an important job to do. It was a job about the future that forests should have in public ownership: there was no more talk about selling off one of the country's most precious assets.

While the campaign had demonstrated how distant politicians and civil servants had become from what motivates people, the Forestry Panel had the chance, phoenix-like, to make an opportunity out of disaster and above all to reconnect with people. We looked at all the history, public conflict and passion and decided to engage not only with the future of the Public Forest Estate but also with the future of *all* the forests, trees and woodlands in England. In pursuit of answers we travelled the country, meeting people passionate about and expert in trees, woods and forests, and heard evidence from a wide spectrum of organisations and views. And then we argued: with each other, and with experts and lobbyists, before – under the Bishop's guidance – we drew together our final views.

Our report, which we published in July 2012, is far-reaching and significant, and achieved the rare accolade of receiving an unqualified welcome from all sides. At its heart was a determination to revive the woodland culture of England, and to reconnect people with trees and trees with people. It described how woodland and trees are critically important to us economically, socially and physically, and showed how more, better-managed trees, and a revival of the woodland culture would be good for people, good for nature and good for the green economy.

It sought action and a changed approach to woodlands and trees. It argued that we need to put wood and wood products once again at the heart of our lives, driven this time not by technology change but the needs and benefits of sustainability. We need to expand the woodland area of England in ways that deliver multiple benefits to people and places (we recommended increasing it from ten per cent to fifteen per cent, which among other benefits is equivalent to reducing carbon dioxide emissions by ten per cent). We need to bring our neglected, un- and undermanaged woodlands back to life, and make them more accessible to people. We need to plant many more street trees and bring trees and woodlands into our towns and cities, bringing their multiple benefits much closer to people. There are many opportunities to achieve these goals, particularly if we recognise woodland as part of our natural capital, expand the use of wood as a sustainable, renewable fuel and building material, and make tree and woodland planting a requirement in all new developments.

The Panel's report also required us, collectively, to think hard about our priorities, because it identified different long-term goals and a fresh perspective on woodlands, which had become so marginalised in public policy and thinking. It required the government to stop controlling the Forestry Commission (which we suggested, like the BBC, should have a Charter and be answerable to Parliament, not government) and to free it from the tyranny of short-term electoral cycles. And it required everyone to re-engage with trees, woodland and wood products to underpin the revival of one of our most enduring and – if we manage it well – endlessly renewable resources.

Three years on, though the government responded positively to the report, many of its recommendations had not been implemented. And yet as time passes we see even more clearly how vital woods are to our future, and the contribution a sensitive woodland policy and plan could make to our national well-being. We need to match the outcry in response to the proposed sale of the public woods with a similar sense of passion and determination to put woods back at the centre of our lives. The benefits to beauty – in its widest form – would be incalculable.

7

The coast – a
success story

A googled, bird's-eye view of the Mediterranean reveals the devastating impact of tourist development on its once-beautiful coastline. 'A string of fishing ports . . . the clarity of the mornings, the stillness of the sun-struck monochrome noons, the magic of the scented nights . . . the sky and sea were clear,' wrote Sybille Bedford in her autobiographical novel *Jigsaw* in the 1920s, of the stretch of coast between Marseille and Toulon. Today its charm has been sacrificed to dense development and busy roads. Large parts of Turkey, Croatia and Greece are heading in the same direction. Hotels and apartments fight for space with a sea view, beaches are lined with concrete and multi-lane roads carve their way through once remote and picturesque scenery. Yet spin your cursor north and Britain's coastline is – with exceptions – miraculously free of such incursions. Fields run to the edge of the coast, beaches are lined with blue and green not the grey of buildings, and cliff edges remain gloriously open and accessible. The evidence that the beauty of the British coast has been saved is inspiring and real. Yet it was just in time.

Indeed 'not a moment too soon' was the reaction of the local community as we signed the deal on the National Trust's acquisition of Wembury Point near Plymouth in 2006. A glorious peninsula within sight and sound of the city, Wembury had been occupied by the military since the war, and before that had hosted a holiday camp in the 1930s. Now its derelict buildings, abandoned lookouts and scruffy cliff-edges were surplus to the MOD's requirements and up for sale. The risk, of course, was that its history made it ripe for re-development, and Plymouth's housing developers were already eying the potential of this beautiful stretch of coastline. Yet it had other forms of potential too: to be a green lung for the people of Plymouth and to nurture nature. The RSPB was already managing part of the site for the rare cirl bunting, its only breeding ground in South West England, and other parts, though scrubby and overgrown, held huge possibilities for lowland-heath species of plants, birds and reptiles. Offshore, the famous Mewstone (also for sale) was a former prison and smugglers' hideout. Between the Mewstone and the shore porpoises, basking sharks and seals were frequent visitors. Amid the dilapidated former military buildings, Wembury's rock pools glittered in the sunlight, and we knew that once opened the whole area would be a delight for walking and wildlife-watching.

We launched an appeal to buy the site in 2005 and it was an immediate success. By 2006 we were in residence, removing the old military buildings or making them safe, improving the habitat and putting in footpaths and a small café.

This was a project for which the National Trust was well prepared. Coastline acquisitions, of beaches, headlands and cliff edges, had been one of our priorities since the 1960s. During my twelve years as Director-General we acquired over 120 miles: just before I left we completed our ownership of the White Cliffs of Dover, iconic symbols of England.

If the British people are known to have a special relationship with landscape and nature, then it is not a big step to explain our fascination with the coast. Somehow the coast has a special place in our sense of identity, perhaps because it encloses the extraordinary diversity and character of our landscape. The coast, too, has played a central role in our history, as both the first line of our defence and our door to the world. Certainly, the coast arouses emotions and passion. It is arguably more written about and celebrated than almost any other feature of our landscape.

There is, of course, no such thing as 'the' coast. Like every other part of Britain, our coastline is varied and characterful. The wide sandy beaches of the South and East with their crowded esplanades and kiss-me-quick traditions are a long way, literally as well as metaphorically, from the secretive Fleswick Bay, with its sparkling semi-precious stones, near St Bees' Head on the Cumbrian coast, or the isolated Po'rth Or on the Llyn Peninsula in north west Wales, where the sands 'whistle' as you step on them. Between the sandy coves of Cornwall and Pembrokeshire waves crash against ancient cliffs, sparkling in the sunshine or drenched with rain and looming out of the sea mist. The once black beaches of Durham, the detritus of coal-mining almost gone, now echo the miles of glorious pale sand on the stunning Northumberland coast. Then there are Norfolk's endless expanses of beach and salt-marsh; the eerie, echoing muddy creeks of south Essex and north Kent, the Thames estuary coasts where Dickens' vagrants hid; the bumptiousness of Skegness at the end of a long, long road in Lincolnshire; and the industrialised coasts of South Wales or around the ports of Bristol, Liverpool, Harwich and Hull.

No one in Britain lives more than about one hundred miles from the sea, and most of us have vivid memories of seaside holidays and visits. The coast therefore means something to all of us, yet there's a paradox at the heart of our relationship with it today. Though the coastline of Britain – deeply varied and indented – has played a large role in our island's story, we no longer think of ourselves as a maritime nation. The relationship most people in Britain have with the coast is occasional and recreational. It is almost as if we have turned our backs on the sea.

Once-dominant activities have declined: the number of fishermen in the UK fell by three-quarters between 1938 and 2011, from 48,000 to a little over 12,000. Ship-building and boat-building, once among Britain's biggest industries, are confined to a handful of locations. The number of people working in businesses dependent on the sea is now tiny compared with those who earn their living from coastal tourism and leisure.

Yet for millennia the coast was key to the character of Britain, our culture and our development. The sea was, for thousands of years, easier and faster to navigate than land, and the succession of communities who colonised our islands all came by sea. The earliest settlers, after the last Ice Age, came over land bridges that joined us to the continent, mainly in the Palaeolithic and Mesolithic periods, attracted by our green and verdant land. Around 6000 BC Britain became separated from continental Europe as sea levels rose, followed by the Neolithic revolution, which marked the beginning of settled agriculture, and further in-migration during the Bronze and Iron Ages.

So the coast was, for many, the point of arrival and dispersal. But it remained important: the Romans, Vikings and Anglo-Saxons were skilled sailors and fishermen whose livelihoods depended on the sea and its products; and their political success derived from their ability to occupy new lands. For the first few centuries AD the cultural and trade links for eastern England were closer to Germany, Denmark and Scandinavia than to the rest of England and Wales; a fact recalled in the remarkable site of Sutton Hoo, near Woodbridge on the Suffolk coast, where an early seventh-century Anglo-Saxon nobleman, thought to be King

Raedwald, lies buried in his ship along with his weapons and elaborately decorated fighting helmets, accompanied by shield-clad warriors.

For large numbers of people, including those inland, the products of the sea – fish and cetaceans, kelp and other seaweeds, birds' eggs and some mammals, including seals – were indispensable sources of food and oil. Boat-building was an important industry by late mediaeval times, with ships forming both the frontline of Britain's defence and the route to discovery, exploration and exploitation of other lands. Farming colonised the coast as it did the interior, but its footprint was lighter: only occasionally did intensive cultivation reach the coastal edge.

For the coast is the place where the underlying geology that shapes our landscape is most clearly visible. Unless it is built over, the coast exposes its bones to view: the ancient granite rocks that form the craggy north and west coasts; the folded sandstones and grits of much of the South West; the Jurassic limestone and chalk cliffs of the South; and the cliffs of glacial waste that are found on the east coast. The coast is an ever-changing place, reflecting the fact that Britain itself is still on the move, our islands gently tipping downwards in a south easterly direction as the tectonic plates on which we stand continue to shift. In fact the coast is the most dynamic element of our landscape. It has grown and shrunk under the influence of natural and (more recently) human forces, and it continues to change today.

Many legends speak of lands lost beneath an encroaching sea: Dogger Bank, off the east coast, hints at the former land bridge with continental Europe and parts of the Isles of Scilly were drowned some 1,500 years ago, giving rise to fables of the lost land of Lyonnesse. From mediaeval times there was talk of a lost 'Welsh hundred', Cantref y Gwaelod, thought to have existed in what is now Cardigan Bay, and it is still possible to walk along the exposed

Sarns (causeways of boulders contained within boulder clay) into the bay when the tide is right.

The historic loss of land on the east coast of England, particularly in the East Riding of Yorkshire, East Anglia and Kent is well documented. More than thirty settlements on the Holderness Coast that were listed in the Domesday Book have been engulfed by the sea. The Suffolk village of Dunwich is but a shadow of the port that rivalled London before it was lost to erosion in the thirteenth century. The last church to be lost, St Peter's, in 1912, was recorded in a watercolour by Turner before it succumbed: the bells of Dunwich are still said to toll mournfully in a storm.

If land has been lost by natural processes it has also been gained. There is constant movement along the coast, sometimes very locally and sometimes on a grander scale. Sand, gravel and smaller stones are in continual flux. Beaches rise and fall; sand-dunes accumulate then blow; shingle beds build then scatter; spits build up and then fracture. Land slips into the sea; wave-cut platforms extend the land. Sometimes these natural processes produce extraordinary results: the eighteen-mile long shingle bund of Chesil Beach, its rounded pebbles perfectly graded, getting larger towards Portland; the satisfying roundness of the almost perfect chalk circle that constitutes Lulworth Cove; and the exquisite beauty of the natural arch of the Green Bridge of Wales in Pembrokeshire.

But in recent centuries human intervention has resulted in profound changes to the coast. From mediaeval times onwards this was most often the reclamation of salt marshes for grazing, achieved by enclosures within estuaries, including from the much-diminished Wash and Morecambe Bay. As salt water was excluded by bunds, the land gradually built up enough fertile soil to sustain pasture and sometimes even ploughing. Many of our best-known lowland grazing marshes, including Romney Marsh and the Somerset Levels, were created by this process.

The church was at the forefront of coastal reclamation from the thirteenth century onwards, just as it was in creating the great sheepwalks of northern England: it had a long tradition of using the skills of Dutch engineers even before the famous Vermuyden drained the fens. And if the shoreline moved so could settlements: the port of Harlech in Wales became separated from the sea, while New Winchelsea was rebuilt inland after a terrific storm destroyed its predecessor.

There were many small-scale modifications of the coast, including the formalisation of natural harbours as they were gradually protected and enlarged. At Mullion and Boscastle in Cornwall sea walls were built to protect the harbour against surges and high tides, and natural barriers were reinforced with boulders. All around the coast these improvements ensured safe harbours, landing places and transport links for the fishing industry to land and get its products to market. Safety at sea was important too: during the seventeenth century local arrangements for warning of dangers at sea were taken over by Trinity House, whose distinctive lighthouses – no longer manned – stand with a striking beauty around our coasts today.

The great ports were at the forefront of Britain's population growth and industrialisation by the eighteenth century, establishing vast enclosed harbours, wet and dry docks, fish landing and processing apparatus, transport hubs and all the paraphernalia and activity associated with the mass movement of people and goods. These coastal towns were noisy, dirty and smelly but full of life and excitement; the whole world came to the streets around their harbours and docks.

The Georgian seaside resorts grew rapidly in popularity as the fashion for sea-bathing and fresh-air cures caught on in the eighteenth century, led by Royalty. The resorts, especially as they expanded in Victorian times, were sea-colonisers too, because as well as hotels, boarding houses, promenades and theatres they constructed piers and esplanades whose fingers extended into the ocean, giving people the experience of raw weather, sights and smells that the land alone could not provide.

By the nineteenth century ambitions for coastal reclamation were resurgent again, and construction works claimed land for building and farming in the Ribble, Tees and Dee Estuaries, and on low-lying land around Cardiff and Bristol. These supported the development of major cities, providing land for generating power, canals, railways and industrial sites. For along with its intrinsic qualities the coast provided convenient transport corridors, access to water for cooling power stations and locations for infrastructure for ports.

But it was when industrial energies faded and the coast became a magnet for retirement living, holidays and tourism that the voice for the defence of its beauty was stirred. As a nation we both discovered the coast anew and began to destroy it.

The very first gift of land to the National Trust, in 1895, was the few acres of land looking out to sea above Barmouth in North Wales. And it was given by Fanny Talbot specifically to curtail Barmouth's expansion and 'avoid the abomination of asphalt paths and the cast-iron seats of serpent design'. Dinas Oleu, the Fortress of Light, represented all that Octavia Hill had dreamed of for the new Trust: 'It is delightful to think that one beautiful sea-cliff has already been given – a bit of British coast held in trust for the nation. Will there be more such gifts to record this time next year?' she wrote in her *Letters to Fellow Workers* in 1894.

There were, because the need for coastal protection was already apparent. The early countryside campaigners were appalled by the dismal quality of much development on the coast. And the shanty town of Peacehaven epitomised the worst of it. It began as a speculative purchase of land above chalk cliffs in the parish of Piddinghoe

The National Trust's first acquisition was the coastal plot
of Dinas Oleu above Barmouth, given by Fanny Talbot.
(Courtesy of the National Trust/Joe Cornish)

near Lewes on the south coast by a showman, Charles Neville, in
1916. His company advertised plots for sale in the *Daily Express*,
and invited the public to enter a competition to name the new
town. The winner (the name Peacehaven was suggested by Ethel
Radford from Leicestershire) won her plot, but his trick was to
offer 'free' plots of land to the runners-up, conditional on payment
of a stiff conveyancing fee. Eighty thousand people entered the
competition and he declared over 2,500 of them runners-up, landing himself a small fortune. The *Daily Express* sued him, challenging his proposition as a scam and it eventually won the legal case,

but the publicity brought thousands of willing colonisers. By 1924 around three thousand people had constructed ramshackle dwellings, made from whatever material they could find: old railway carriages, army huts and lean-tos, like the 'plotlands' movement of the same period which saw people throughout Britain occupying and building cheap homes on unused land.

Peacehaven's development story was unusual but the desire to live on the coast was not. The health-giving benefits of the sea air, combined with relatively cheap land, meant that developers were quick to spot an opportunity. Neville himself went on to build the settlements of Saltdean and parts of Rottingdean, and many others followed, leaving Cyril Joad in *The Untutored Townsman's Invasion of the Country* (1945) to note despairingly, 'The south coast along the greater part of its length is already done for.'

CPRE led the campaign for better coastal protection by commissioning a report on the coast and the damage that was being caused by unplanned development from Wesley Dougill, a planner from

Peacehaven on England's south coast was the first example of coastal sprawl and triggered the fight for coastal protection.

Liverpool University, which it published in 1936. He wrote 'we are witnessing today what can be termed without exaggeration a national movement seawards. As a result of it the seaboard is being quickly built up.' By 1942 the Commons Preservation Society had set up a Coastal Preservation Committee and was lobbying hard, giving evidence along with CPRE to the Scott Committee, urging greater controls. The Scott Committee noted the establishment of 'permanent and semi-permanent camps for urban populations on holiday' of which 'several hundred had been set up before 1939'. Its general view was that the coasts should be used for recreation, viewing 'with favour ... the further provision of ... commercial holiday camps and holiday villages', but it recognised that this policy needed to be applied with care, because of the risk to beautiful coastlines. Therefore the wartime government commissioned J. Alfred Steers, a lecturer in geography at Cambridge University, to survey the coast and identify the areas of greatest scenic quality. His report, drawing on his personal survey of most of the coastline of England and Wales, was published in 1946 and was the first strategic review of the coast.

In addition to controlling coastal sprawl the campaigners wanted to reduce the military occupation of large sections of the coast, since the Ministry of Defence's landholdings had doubled from 225,000 acres in 1939 to over 550,000 acres by 1960, involving the construction of ugly buildings and numerous fortifications, as well as barbed wire fences that excluded the public. As late as 1967 the MOD still occupied 134 miles of coastline, including long lengths in Kent, Cornwall, Dorset, Carmarthenshire, Pembrokeshire, Lincolnshire, Suffolk and Essex.

Following the 1949 Act the beauty of the coast had an official champion in the National Parks Commission, and for its scientific value the Nature Conservancy. The National Parks Commission was acutely conscious of the threats, and it was no accident that its first tranche of ten National Parks in the 1950s included some important coastlines: Pembrokeshire was designated almost entirely because of its coast, and significant parts of Exmoor and the North York Moors, and smaller parts of Snowdonia and the Lake District are coastal. Gower, a stunning coastal landscape and habitat in South Wales, was the first Area of Outstanding Natural Beauty to be designated in 1956, and others with striking coastlines followed, especially the Northumberland Coast (in 1958), much of Cornwall (in 1959; to some people's disappointment, because it had been an early candidate for a National Park) and the North Devon Coast (in 1959).

But these designations left large areas of coastline unprotected and vulnerable to unplanned sprawl. And although the National Trust had begun to acquire coastline, especially in Cornwall (its earliest property there was Tintagel's Barras Nose in 1897, and many other small stretches followed in the 1930s and 1940s), it was only expected to make a tiny contribution. Something needed to be done. By the early 1960s a deputation from CPRE's Coastal Committee had convinced the Minister of Housing and Local Government that there was a serious problem. As a first step the Ministry issued a Circular, in 1963, asking local authorities to initiate studies of the coast, to safeguard natural beauty and mitigate or remove eyesores. By 1966 the National Parks Commission had persuaded the Ministry to launch the largest-ever study of the coast and the planning issues affecting it. The Commission convened nine regional conferences bringing together all the affected bodies, land-based and maritime, and drew up maps and data covering the entire coast of England and Wales. Its purpose was unambiguous: to protect the beauty of the coast, as John Cripps, the Chairman of the (by then) Countryside Commission wrote when presenting the report to Ministers: 'the money and changes [we recommend] are needed to ensure both that we provide better for present requirements and that we shall be able to pass on to those who come after us this vital part of our national heritage conserved and enhanced, not further despoiled.'

Though the exercise concluded that 'only' a quarter of the coast of England and Wales was already developed or earmarked for development, it marked a determination to protect what was left, for it was undoubtedly under threat. The report pinpointed the main problem: the new car-based mobility and dispersal of holi-day-makers and their increasingly diverse demands for all kinds of recreation – sailing, canoeing, water skiing, motor-boating, diving and swimming. Whereas once people had taken a train to a large resort for a conventional beach holiday, now they could travel wherever a road could take them. Caravans were the source of much attention: from being so unusual in 1951 that their numbers were not even recorded in the British Travel Association's annual survey, by 1955 they were used by two million holiday-makers and by 1967 4.5 million. The number of day trippers was expanding even more rapidly than those taking holidays. But dispersal was the main worry, for with it came pressure for holiday camps and chalets, car parks, golf courses and other recreational facilities and new roads.

The Commission also looked at other problems facing the coast. The resorts were beginning their long decline because they no longer met the needs of the increasingly mobile and more demand-ing tourists. The Commission also described the scourge of coastal eyesores, even in National Parks: ugly caravan sites, derelict land, dumped industrial spoil and abandoned military buildings. Some coastal areas were scarred by established industrial development, such as refineries, chemical processing plants, aluminium smelters and steel mills, and new threats were appearing in the form of exploration for oil and gas, new power stations and plans for port expansion.

From the 1950s onwards the popularity of caravans brought
new questions about how the coast could be protected.
(Courtesy of the National Trust/John Miller)

The Commission came up with commendably clear solutions.
New planning policies should be devised specifically for the coast,
both to determine the scope and quality of development where it
was needed, and to ensure that beautiful and still-undeveloped
stretches of coastline were protected from inappropriate changes.
Industrial coasts were to be defined and contained, and where
there were competing pressures local authorities should be given
the means to reconcile the claims for recreation, commercial development, nature conservation and quiet enjoyment.

The Commission proposed extending the then innovative
proposals for 'management agreements' between private landowners and public bodies, so that the most beautiful lengths of
unspoiled coast would continue in the uses (mostly low-density
grazing) that made them so valued. To protect these, they

recommended a new designation, Heritage Coasts, where planning policies would be strictly applied and low-key public access and sympathetic land management would be encouraged.

Many local authorities were ready to adopt these recommendations as part of their own planning processes, but the Heritage Coasts plan needed the government's endorsement. It gave it, but not as a statutory planning designation. It was left to the Countryside Commission to persuade local authorities to adopt the idea, which the Commission encouraged with funding for Heritage Coast Officers and the preparation of management plans. To kick-start the process the Commission ran pilots in Suffolk, Purbeck and Glamorgan between 1974 and 1977. They were such a success that by 1980 nineteen English Heritage Coasts were in place, with a further five in the 1980s, seven in the 1990s and one in 2001, some of course overlapping with existing National Parks and AONBs. In the same period fourteen were designated in Wales. In total a third of the coastline of England and Wales has been designated as Heritage Coast. And the National Trust now owns about forty per cent of it.

By the 1960s the National Trust was thinking seriously about its own contribution from coastal protection. It was by then a very different organisation from the one its founders had set up, and was heavily loaded with the weight of taking on as many as a dozen country houses a year. It might have been forgiven for thinking it had enough on its plate. But the threat of a rapidly suburbanising coastline resonated within the National Trust and its resulting campaign, Enterprise Neptune, launched in 1965, was arguably the Trust's most proactive and influential ever.

Dinas Oleu had, as Octavia Hill hoped, been followed by other coastal properties and by 1960 the Trust owned about 175 miles of coastline, including the Farne Islands (acquired in 1925), Tennyson Down on the Isle of Wight (1927) and, from the 1940s, White

Park Bay and the Giant's Causeway in Northern Ireland. But the Neptune campaign represented an altogether more strategic approach to the challenge of coastal protection.

The idea for Neptune is attributed to Christopher Gibbs, who in 1962 was the new Chief Agent. He had already saved a number of precious stretches of coastline in Pembrokeshire, witnessing there desperate pressures for commercialisation of the coast: holiday parks and bungalows, caravans and chalets, industrial development and military equipment, much of it within the newly created Pembrokeshire Coast National Park. But he was backed by an even more powerful advocate, Lord Antrim, who was the Trust's Northern Ireland Chairman and a passionate defender of the Antrim coast. He had launched and led the Ulster Coastline Appeal, and on the strength of its success was instrumental in the preparations for a Trust-wide role. By 1965 he was Chairman of the whole National Trust, and it was no surprise that the Trust's Executive Committee was persuaded to launch a national appeal to buy up coastline around the whole perimeter of England, Wales and Northern Ireland.

The idea came none too soon. The Trust estimated that about five miles of coastline were being built on each year, particularly near popular holiday destinations. Gibbs asked Trust agents around the country for a rough assessment of how much of the coast was worth protecting. In reply they guessed about a third, and with that ball-park figure in mind the decision to launch the campaign was made.

The Trust's Council, however, wanted to know more precisely where and what the Trust should seek to acquire. Conveniently one of the greatest authorities on the British coastline, the now Professor Alfred Steers, was a member of its Estates Committee. Steers recommended a new survey and the Trust commissioned Dr John Whittow, a young geography lecturer at Reading University, to carry it out: he estimated that they would need to cover over three thousand miles to complete their work around the coasts of England, Wales and Northern Ireland. Gathering together a group of thirty-four graduate students and three lecturers from his department, Whittow and his colleagues spent the summer of 1965 mapping the coast. They worked quickly on this mammoth task, on a shoestring budget, and to a simple formula.

First they categorised land use into one of fourteen categories, which were hand-drawn onto maps. When Whittow brought the maps together, he consolidated the information into just three categories: land beyond redemption (usually because it had been built on); land which was managed and in active use (including by the Ministry of Defence) but could possibly be restored in future; and land which was free from development and therefore a target for protection. On the basis of these maps around nine hundred miles were identified as pristine, in need of protection and therefore ideally to be acquired, and the Trust adopted this as its target. It was remarkably close to the agents' original guess.

These nine hundred miles were astonishingly beautiful. They included most of England's South West peninsula, much of the coastline of Wales, North West England and Northern Ireland, especially Antrim. Northumberland's beautiful beaches were also on the list, along with much of what remained undeveloped along the south coast. The least promising areas, recalled John Whittow many years later, were 'the East Anglian coast, a low-lying coastline with an enormous number of caravan parks and holiday villages . . . the entire coastal area south of Brean Down in the south west coast was also overwhelmed.' But in his recommendations to the Trust only that which was irretrievably lost, or utterly safe, was excluded. And from the moment the target was adopted, Neptune became central to the Trust's ambitions. It was an extremely popular campaign, externally and internally. Some regional agents, with Cornwall's Michael Trinick in the vanguard, never missed a chance to acquire a stretch of coastline that could be looked after by the Trust. Stories abound: on one occasion the agent for South Wales, Hugh Griffiths, confessed, after showing a series of beautiful slides to an admittedly sympathetic Estates Committee, that he had in fact already sealed the deal. Another story suggests that the slides that were used to dazzle the committee were, always, the same ones.

The audacity of the Neptune campaign was astounding. It was deeply ambitious for a modest-sized charity to set out to acquire nine hundred miles of coastline, yet the Trust was undaunted. Partly this was because it was so buoyed up by popular support: its willingness to take risks, plan ambitiously and for the long term, make commitments and acquire beautiful, vulnerable coastline generated a massive and positive public response. The risks paid off and Neptune's popularity made a significant contribution to the growth in the National Trust's membership from 158,000 in 1965 to 540,000 only a decade later. Unprecedented support came too from official bodies: the government agreed to match the Trust's initial Neptune fundraising appeal pound for pound, and many local authorities donated land and money to the Trust.

Neptune had a bigger impact too. In fact it played an important role in the re-democratisation of the Trust because this was a new style of acquisition. Almost all the land acquired was made immediately available for public access, benefiting millions of people including non-members. This was both philanthropic and, to some, demonstrably closer to the founders' vision than the acquisition of the country houses of the rich. Paid for by readily offered legacies and gifts (and needing much smaller endowments than built properties) the coastal estate built up rapidly. Within four years of Neptune's launch one hundred miles had been added to the Trust's coastal estate; by 1980 Neptune had funded a further

220 miles. In 2015 it stood at 775 miles, within touching distance of the original nine hundred mile target.

A frightful row about Neptune, one of the biggest in the Trust's history, brought further pressure for democracy. The catalyst was the Trust's first professional fundraiser, Commander Conrad Rawnsley (grandson of the founder Canon Hardwicke Rawnsley), who was brought in to lead the Neptune appeal. However his proactive, combative style ran counter to the more cautious approach of the Trust's leaders, and he wanted both to spend more money on the campaign and to make progress faster. With relationships already tense, they fell out spectacularly following Rawnsley's public criticisms of the Trust at a press conference he called at Saltram near Plymouth, where because of its failure to back his fundraising methods he called the Trust 'inert and amorphous', condemning the 'old boy net' by which it was run and, most damaging of all, describing it as 'incompetent'. It was, he said, 'Bankrupt in ideas, bankrupt in leadership, bankrupt in the common touch, bankrupt in its sense of what the people need and in the alacrity with which it set about providing it'. The Extraordinary General Meeting that followed his sacking in 1967 led to a review of relationships with members and, eventually, to a more open and responsive National Trust. But though the row was painful and embarrassing it did nothing to diminish the enthusiasm of the public and the Trust's members for the Neptune campaign.

This was because the Trust did what it said it would: it bought land, stopped ugly development and cared for hundreds of miles of beautiful coastline and the historic structures associated with it. For a coastal visitor today the sight of a National Trust sign welcoming visitors is an indication of quality, certainty and good management. And sometimes it is even more than a force for protection. The so-called Black Beaches of the Durham coast were acquired in 1988 and symbolically named as the campaign's five-hundredth mile under the leadership of Oliver Maurice, then Director for the North East. It was the first stretch of degraded coastline to be purchased for the purpose of improvement, not protection – those beaches had not been on John Whittow's maps.

The mines of the Durham coalfields had for decades tipped their spoil on the cliffs, covering the beaches with a foul shroud of black waste. But by the 1980s the coalfields were closing, and Maurice saw the potential for the beaches to recover their lost beauty. Working in partnership with the local authorities and, in an inspired move, appointing ex-miner Denis Rooney as the Trust's first head warden there, time and tide are gradually but systematically washing the beaches clean. It is a renaissance which has been recognised nationally and beyond, with the Durham Coast being given Heritage Coast status in 2001; in 2010 the project was declared the Winner of the UK Landscape Award and the UK nomination for the European Landscape Award.

But the beauty of the coastline is not just about its aesthetic and cultural appeal. The coastline is just as important for its wildlife. The National Parks Commission's 1966 study calculated that nearly 540 miles of the coastline of England and Wales were designated under the 1949 Act either as a National Nature Reserve, SSSI (450 miles, the vast bulk) or local nature reserve. And nature conservation is just as important out to sea as on land, but here progress lagged well behind. As late as 1977 the Nature Conservancy Council's seminal *Nature Conservation Review* looked no further to sea than the intertidal zone of estuaries; and it was not until 1979 that specific measures for marine conservation were recommended when it jointly published a report with the Natural Environment Research Council (NERC): *Nature Conservation in the Marine Environment*.

Scientists had been alerted to the need to protect the marine environment by the oil-polluting wreck of the *Torrey Canyon* in

1967 and as the fashion for scuba-diving revealed the wealth of Britain's underwater wildlife. From the 1960s local naturalists had pressed the case for protection of 'underwater reserves' for Skomer Island in West Wales, Kimmeridge Bay in Dorset, Wembury near Plymouth, the Farne Islands in Northumberland and St Anthony's Head near Falmouth. Lundy was proposed as a voluntary marine reserve in 1971 but the first and only local nature reserve established specifically to protect marine biology was in 1973 by Torbay Borough Council, at Saltern Cove in south Devon.

Disappointed by the failure to follow this with protection of other marine sites, the voluntary bodies lobbied for and succeeded in getting the ability to declare marine nature reserves in the 1981 Wildlife and Countryside Act. But by 1983 none had been created and the NCC reported to the World Conservation Strategy that 'marine ecosystems are the Cinderella of nature conservation in Britain'. Lundy was a particular problem: though it has the finest diversity of any marine site in the UK, with a multitude of sea squirts, starfish, colourful jellyfish, sponges, pink sea fans, Devonshire cup corals as well as basking sharks, dolphins and grey seals, by the 1980s it was badly over-fished, its coral reefs were damaged and its native fish populations had plummeted.

Though evidence was amassing country-wide that sea life was declining catastrophically, it was happening offshore and almost invisibly, and there were strong counter-voices, especially from the fisheries industry, to any attempts to constrain commercial activities.

The Nature Conservancy's 1984 *Nature Conservation in Great Britain* finally brought some progress when the seas around Lundy were designated as a marine nature reserve in 1986, followed by Skomer in 1990 and, much later, Strangford Lough in Northern Ireland (1995). It is also proposed to designate the Menai Strait in

North Wales. But even with the agreement in 1992 of both OSPAR (Oslo and Paris Conventions for the Protection of the Marine Environment for the North East Atlantic) and the European Union's Habitats Directive (containing provisions for marine protection) it was not until the late 1990s that the government drew up plans for Special Areas of Conservation for marine habitats, and not until 2002 that it accepted the case for a more strategic approach to marine conservation in *Safeguarding our Seas: A Strategy for the Conservation and Sustainable Development of our Marine Environment*. It took until 2004 for the long-advocated 'no take' zone around Lundy to be implemented.

Though the role of official bodies was important, the campaign to expose the crisis facing marine wildlife was led by the voluntary bodies, including The Wildlife Trusts, RSPB, WWF and Marine Conservation Society, working through Wildlife Link to add weight to their efforts. Campaign after campaign was launched, including The Wildlife Trusts' *Our Dying Seas* which documented the extent of marine losses, and raised high profile objections to fishing by-catches, especially dolphins trapped in fishing nets. Basking sharks were tagged to highlight their distribution and vulnerability; campaigns were launched with chefs and supermarkets to encourage consumers to buy and eat fish only from sustainable sources; and profile-raising efforts including 'fish-scale' petitions calling for a Marine Bill were used to sustain the lobbying effort.

The slow progress was doubly frustrating because it had been known for many years that over-fishing was a serious problem. Emerging from the local, sustainable industry that had occupied many coastal communities for hundreds of years, the commercial fishing fleets that developed in the nineteenth and twentieth centuries took fishing to new levels and by the 1970s there were clear signs of over-fishing. In British shores, mackerel was the first species whose decline was noted, but by 2000 cod, haddock and plaice had been so aggressively fished that their numbers crashed, especially in the North Sea. Tensions between nations over fishing grounds grew, and once again the European Commission was the broker for action. The Common Fisheries Policy (CFP) is as old as the Common Agricultural Policy and had similar objectives to support productive fisheries, although it always had a theoretical responsibility to preserve fish stocks. Overfishing and dramatic declines in catches eventually forced a reconsideration of the CFP, with controls being introduced for the first time in 2007 and more ambitiously in 2010. Fish stocks are now beginning to recover, helped by consumer pressure encouraged by bodies like the Marine Conservation Society, which tells consumers whether the fish they are buying are from sustainable sources.

A similar battle was fought, and gradually won, over marine pollution. Again, the disastrous oil spill from the *Torrey Canyon* in 1967 brought the issue to public attention, leading to international agreements such as the London Dumping Convention of 1972. More widespread was the problem of localised pollution, including the discharge of raw sewage into the sea which continued until the 1970s. The European Commission's 1976 Bathing Water Directive was an early attempt to clean up the sea, focusing especially on beaches where people bathed and paddled. The Blue Flag campaign originated in France in 1985 to reward municipalities for complying with sewage treatment and bathing water quality standards. It spread throughout Europe, and the sight of a blue flag flying at a beach remains a valuable form of public reassurance today. In Britain the Blue Flag campaign was supplemented in 1990 by a new organisation, Surfers Against Sewage. Its members took radical action, publicising filthy beaches and polluted water by wearing gas masks and dumping in Parliament inflatable models of the unmentionable sewage-related objects that ruined the enjoyment of their sport. Our beaches are in better condition thanks to their action, and more recently they have joined the campaign for coastal protection, recognising the joys of surfing in a beautiful as well as a clean environment. Inspired by their work, in 2000 the National Trust employed a former surf champion, Robyn Davies, to run surf classes on the Cornwall coast, helping visitors to see the connection between looking after the coast and being able to enjoy it.

While our beaches have become less polluted, we still face the more pervasive and insidious threat of litter and plastic waste, and this fight has not yet been won. Surfers Against Sewage reported in 2012 that the volume of litter washing up on British beaches had almost doubled in fifteen years. The Marine Conservation Society's annual survey in the same year reported that over forty per cent was public waste: discarded plastic bottles, broken glass and empty cans, and general rubbish. Fourteen per cent was fishing related and nearly five per cent sewage-related. More than thirty per cent was from unidentified sources, assumed to have been dumped by sea vessels either accidentally or deliberately. The consequences are serious: apart from the health risks and the damage to people's enjoyment, plastics may never fully break down and will remain in microscopic form for thousands of years, causing injury to fish, birds and mammals.

Though the challenges were daunting and remain so, the story of coastal protection has been one of steadily growing success. But it reveals more clearly than any other element of the fight for beauty that success is not about holding things static, but is a constant process of managing change. The National Trust discovered this with a vengeance in the early 1990s.

In the early 1980s it had bought some land, a hotel and three of half a dozen 1840s cottages perched on the edge of a cliff, in the hamlet of Birling Gap on the Sussex coast, near the iconic Seven Sisters cliffs. These chalk cliffs had long been slowly, though unpredictably, crumbling into the sea at a rate of about a metre a year. Knowing this, the Trust had initially planned to demolish the buildings and let nature take its course, but it ran up against local opposition. Eventually the Trust agreed to keep the hotel going as long as it was viable, but it could not guarantee to protect the cottages; indeed the one nearest the edge of the cliff had to be demolished in 1996. A fierce local campaign ensued, with locals pressing the Trust to install coastal defences to protect the remaining cottages and the hotel. As (then) a member of the Trust's Council, I supported the Trust's decision to resist pressures to try to hold the site static. Not only was this physically impossible, it ran counter to any sensible view of the future, since further losses of the cliff would be inevitable.

Birling Gap, seen here with temporary access arrangements, where erosion threatens the viability of living and working near the cliff edge. (Courtesy of the National Trust/David Sellman)

217

In 2000, just before I joined the staff, an emotional public inquiry had taken place, with local people arguing for coastal defences to be constructed to protect the cliff, accusing the Trust of being blind to their views. The Trust stuck to its position, though it was painfully aware of the strength of local feeling. In the end the Trust 'won' the public inquiry because the Inspector agreed that one day, regardless of any defence scheme, the cottages would fall into the sea. It was a distressing lesson in public and community relations, from which we learned much.

It was soon clear that we could face similar situations all around the coast. At Studland, in east Dorset, the Trust had to move the beach huts back twice in ten years as the beach retreated by two or three metres a year. Further west, the footpath at Golden Cap had to be moved back twenty-five metres from the cliff edge to accommodate erosion. A severe storm at Formby on the Lancashire coast took twelve to fifteen metres of sand off the beach, dumping it miles along the coast. At Mullion Cove, in Cornwall, the cost of repairs to the mediaeval harbour, increasingly battered by storms, was becoming unsustainable: by 2005 the Trust had spent £1 million on repairs since 1990.

Other rows were brewing too. A few miles west of Birling Gap, the Cuckmere River reaches the sea at Cuckmere Haven. Here is another group of coastguard's cottages, sitting picturesquely against the backdrop of the undulating white Seven Sisters cliffs: it is one of the most photographed views in England. Nobody would build cottages there today: they perch on the edge of the rapidly eroding cliff and have been uninsurable for years. They are vulnerable, yet unsurprisingly their owners love them and believe they should be defended. Expensive, concrete-pouring solutions have long been advocated in attempts to stabilise the coast. But even if such solutions could protect the cottages (and that is doubtful, for long), it would not be the end of the matter. 'Hard' coastal defences would deflect the force of the waves elsewhere, possibly causing greater damage.

Instead the Trust wanted to do something much more modest and, we hoped, more in tune with nature. For despite appearances the Cuckmere estuary is far from a natural place. The meandering river is a contained force, bounded by green fields which were reclaimed from the sea after the Second World War. Where the river meets the sea there is a large bund which is vulnerable to being breached in a storm surge. Though it provides some security for the grazing land and the cottages now one day it will fail, the estuary will flood, and the cottages will almost certainly be lost.

The Trust's idea was to create a small breach in the bund, allowing the sea to invade the land intermittently and in a managed way. This would, in time, re-create the salt marsh that pre-dates the grazing land, helping to contain and manage future seawater inundations. The landscape would be returned to a more natural state, accommodating all but the most severe storm surges, and there would be no need for major construction works. But though this solution would provide modest protection for the cottages the Trust could not guarantee their long-term survival.

Though it seemed the right thing to do, there were objections. The cottage owners were unhappy, and some local people were concerned that the restored salt marshes would be a less attractive and accessible landscape than the improved grassland. We had a similar experience at Cotehele, in Cornwall, where we proposed the re-creation of salt marsh to provide a natural buffer against tidal surges on the river Tamar. Local objectors preferred the improved grassland to salt marsh, and the project stalled. And at Cuckmere we failed to convince the Environment Agency so, for now, the status quo remains.

Faced with an accelerating number of challenges around the coast, and increasingly concerned that climate change might be exacerbating the speed of change, we commissioned a risk assessment of our entire coastal estate. Published in 2005, *Shifting Shores* demanded action by us and others. For it showed, beyond question, the extent to which our coasts were changing; and that in certain places, especially in Dorset, Sussex, much of East Anglia and Yorkshire, we should expect even more dramatic changes over the next twenty years. Ten years later, a revisiting of the same sites has confirmed the predictions.

In response to these findings we agreed that it made no sense to fight the rising sea or treat it as an enemy against which we had to defend ourselves: instead we should take a strategic, long-term view, working with nature rather than against it. This meant accepting the inevitability of change. Many of the nation's most distinctive coastal landmarks, some of which the Trust owns, such as the Needles on the Isle of Wight or Old Harry Rocks near Studland, were created by coastal erosion and one day would be lost to coastal erosion. We had to accept that we could not hold the coastline still. This meant challenging the assumption that the Trust's job was to keep things as they are, or were when we acquired them.

The effects of climate change were clear: we found evidence both of sea level rise and an increasing risk of extreme events. Our coastal risk study drew together all the available information from the Environment Agency's Indicative Flood Risk Maps, DEFRA's FutureCoast initiative and the UK Climate Impact Programme's predictions of sea level rise. It concluded that over the coming century 169 sites along some 608 km (sixty per cent) of National Trust-owned coastline could lose land through coastal erosion; and that some losses might be significant, involving as much as between one and two hundred metres of erosion. A further 126 sites covering over four thousand hectares were found to be already at risk from tidal flooding, and thirty-three more low-lying sites would be at risk over the coming century. Those affected include

Blakeney on the north Norfolk coast, Orford Ness on the Suffolk coast, Northey Island in the Blackwater estuary, East Head near Chichester Harbour, West Wight on the Isle of Wight, Golden Cap in Dorset, Porlock on the north Somerset coast, Westbury Court Garden, a seventeenth-century Dutch-style garden in the River Severn floodplain, Llanrhidian Marsh near Swansea and Formby Sands north of Liverpool.

A further factor influencing our decisions was that hard sea defences are not only expensive but can have unpredictable side effects. The Trust owns the spit, East Head, on the west Sussex coast at the entrance to Chichester Harbour. This has long been starved of a steady supply of sand and shingle by the hard defences built to protect housing on the Manhood peninsula (East and West Wittering and Selsey) and is now regularly breached. So rather than invest in hard defences ourselves, we promoted a strategy of sensitive adaptation, adjusting to natural forces as they occurred. So at Formby Sands we moved the car park to the back of the dunes, where it would not disturb the natural processes of shifting dunes, and we re-routed the Sefton coastal path. At Porlock in Somerset we created a new salt marsh, which now attracts waders, ducks and plants that had previously been only rare visitors; otters have moved in and people enjoy the wildlife.

But if the dynamism of coastal protection poses a significant challenge, so too does the reconciliation of aesthetic concerns with the generation of renewable energy. Modern wind turbines were rare in Britain until the turn of the twenty-first century, though windmills have been part of the rural scene for hundreds of years. A new generation of wind turbines has been steadily appearing, and under the EU's Renewable Energy Directive, agreed in 2009, the UK must meet fifteen per cent of its energy needs from renewable sources by 2020. This led to a boost in subsidies for renewable energy, though some of these were controversially dropped in 2015.

Since the coast is windier than many inland locations, it is in many ways an obvious place to start. The Crown Estate, which manages Britain's seabed from the coast out to the twelve-mile nautical limit and is responsible for licences, has played a big role in stimulating coastal renewable energy. And after a slow start development is now rapid: under licence from the Crown Estate there are currently over one thousand wind turbines with a capacity of over 4,250 MW, and capacity for another 27,000 MW has been consented or is under construction, including on Dogger Bank and in the North Sea. The Crown Estate reports that four per cent of Britain's energy is now met by wind generation, and that on a particularly windy day in early 2015 wind farms met twenty per cent of the UK's energy need. Large offshore wind farms have already been built off the north coast of Wales, near the Dee estuary, and off the Essex, north Norfolk, Lincolnshire and Cumbria

Wind turbines on land and at sea are vital sources of clean energy. They can harm beauty but not if we locate and design them well. (Courtesy of the National Trust/Joe Cornish)

coasts. Many on-shore wind turbines have also been installed: many have been disputed but it has also proved possible to position turbines carefully to avoid damage to landscapes.

Renewable energy is clearly a vital part of our response to climate change, but the location of wind turbines can be problematic for the landscape and nature protection movement, because of their visual impact and the risk of bird strikes, particularly on migration routes. The National Trust has struggled to reconcile its deeply embedded concern for protecting beautiful landscapes with its equally profound commitment to the 'permanent preservation' of our environment, which requires a responsible approach to resource management. Sometimes there are straightforward clashes: I was glad when the proposed South West array in the Bristol Channel, very close to Lundy, a place I love, was dropped for financial reasons. But if we are to take climate change seriously, as we must, renewable energy generation must play a significant role, and we must seek designs and locations that are compatible with beauty. This is not impossible: the National Trust has shown how many smaller-scale renewable projects, from wood fuelled boilers to mini hydro-generation, small wind turbines and the installation of solar panels on roofs can be happily reconciled with aesthetic concerns and cumulatively can make a significant contribution to energy generation. A single, beautifully designed hydro-electric scheme in Snowdonia supplies enough electricity to light the entire National Trust estate in Wales; and renewable energy generated on Trust properties in Northern Ireland produces twenty-two per cent of the Trust's total energy demands there.

It is the vast wind farms that dominate the skyline in all directions that trouble those who love beauty, but there are places where wind turbines can be located without harm to treasured landscapes. And the solution, surely, is not to ignore questions of beauty or dismiss them, but to debate the issues, openly exploring designs and seeking places where installations for renewable energy can respect our long-held commitments to landscape and nature protection. We need to find places where wind turbines can sit comfortably in the landscape, and develop technologies such as wave power, solar generation and the extraction of thermal power from the sea, all of which have great potential. Encouragingly there is a growing number of studies commissioned by National Parks, AONBs and Heritage Coasts to identify where and how (and where not) renewable technologies can be accommodated without damaging the spirit and quality of these special places.

Our coastline, therefore, continues to be a place of which new demands are made and where new challenges are posed. But we have learned that above all else we need to plan for its future in a more joined-up way. We can accommodate appropriate change if we know what we are trying to achieve. And a long-term vision for the coast is becoming clear. It should be a place for creative conservation, not exploitation. Many local authorities and conservation bodies are now promoting Integrated Coastal Zone Management, an approach that looks at the coast in the round and tries to plan for all its needs in a harmonised way. The New Economics Foundation has proposed a 'Blue New Deal' to support economic activities on the coast that create jobs and support conservation aims. And nationally the government accepted the challenge and passed the Marine and Coastal Access Act in 2009, with the aim of 'ensuring the clean, healthy, safe, productive and biologically diverse oceans and seas by putting in place a new system for improved management and protection of the marine and coastal environment'. Proper, effective marine protection is being extended – Marine Conservations Zones now protect twenty per cent of English waters – so finally the slow, grudging historical pace of marine conservation is being put right.

With these, and the earlier advances made in protection of the beauty of our coast, we have surely come a long way from the fears of the 1960s that our coast would be ruined beyond redemption. Or have we? Vigilance remains essential. Passing a law does not mean that it is always implemented or upheld. The Devon and Dorset Wildlife Trusts fought a ten-year campaign to protect Lyme Bay from scallop dredging, which literally scrapes the ocean floor, removing not only live scallops but every other living thing, leaving a murky desert behind. A sixty-square-mile exclusion zone was finally agreed there in 2008, and there are now signs that the sea bed is recolonising. The National Trust has had to fight off damaging developments at Runkerry, next to the Giant's Causeway, Ireland's only World Heritage Site. In spite of the rigorous protection supposedly in place, consent was granted in 2012 for a resort and spa, including an eighteen-hole championship golf course, a 120-bedroom hotel and seventy-five houses. Fortunately the money did not materialise and it has not been built; many of us hope the application will not be revived because of the damage it would cause to this world-class site.

Sometimes, however, the simplest ideas work best and offer the clearest vision for the future. The most inspiring commitment in the Marine and Coastal Access Act is for a path to be created around the entire coast of England, following the precedent of the recently installed all-Wales Coastal Path. These ideas have their roots in the fight for beauty, inspired by Tom Stephenson's *Long Green Trail*, the Pennine Way, which opened in 1965. There are already five coastal trails. The first three opened in the 1970s: the dramatic 186-mile Pembrokeshire Coast Long Distance Footpath, the Cleveland Way, more than half of whose 110 miles hugs the north Yorkshire coast, and the 630-mile South West Coast Path. The North Norfolk Coast Path and Peddar's Way, which includes a fifty-mile coastal stretch, opened in 1986, and the all-Wales Coastal Path opened in 2012.

Creating these paths is not straightforward. The historic rights-of-way network was not designed for recreation, so access to and along the coast was very patchy, with many natural and human obstacles such as field boundaries, cliffs and rivers. Access is even more difficult if the land is intensively farmed and impossible where housing, urban or industrial developments block access to the sea. Routes have to be surveyed, landowners persuaded and signs and waymarking, stiles, bridges, gates and fencing put in place.

For a long time the farming and landowning bodies' official view of coastal paths was negative. Coastal land was, for them, simply part of their business and they saw few advantages in letting people walk over it. Dogs, bikes and horses were even less popular. But as the coastal paths became better established and popular the mood changed. For the people walking them that is no surprise: the Pembrokeshire and South West paths are, in fact, the only way truly to appreciate these splendid coasts. And before long even sceptical farmers woke up to the opportunities to provide facilities for walkers: bed-and-breakfast accommodation, bunk-house barns, cafés and guided walks. And for every hardy soul walking the entire length of a path, there are hundreds using short lengths for local walks, attracted by good signposting, access to the sea and wonderful views. So local pubs, cafés and countless small businesses flourish because of the patronage of path users.

The benefits of the all-Wales Coastal Path have been measured. The 870-mile-long path was begun in 2007 and completed in 2012 at a cost of £14.6 million. Using it, and the 182-mile-long Offa's Dyke National Trail, it is now possible to walk the entire perimeter of Wales, the first country in the world that can make such a claim. In 2013 Natural Resources Wales calculated that the coast path had attracted 2.82 million visitors in the previous twelve months, bringing £32 million into the economy. In a single year, it had paid

The all-Wales Coastal Path, seen here near Stackpole in Pembrokeshire. (Courtesy of the National Trust/John Millar)

for its start-up costs twice over. Moreover the study found 5,400 tourism-related businesses within 2 km of the route and estimated that the new path had led to the creation of the equivalent of 112 new jobs. The 'walking economy', including a revival in local food products, is now an established part of the future of rural areas. Just as important, extraordinary experiences are now available to everyone: the sight of thousands of seabirds on Skomer and Skokholm, ospreys on the cliffs near Tremadoc, the chance to eat freshly caught crab and lobster, to enjoy the vast, glorious beaches of Gower, Cardigan Bay and the Llyn, and to glimpse seals and basking sharks in shallow waters. The entire diverse and beautiful coastline of Wales is accessible, creating and sealing a bond of affection that will not easily be broken.

The English Coastal Path, approved by Ministers in 2015, will bring similar benefits: physical and spiritual refreshment for people and a sustainable underpinning of the economy of remote and beautiful places. If its business case was all that mattered, it is unanswerable. But it is not all that matters, so we should be bolder. We should make more than a coast path, by designating a deep coastal zone where conservation, access and sustainable jobs are priorities, and where adaptation to change is positively encouraged. Within that zone, the coastline can evolve in the knowledge that it is providing a natural resource 'bank' for the nation.

Our coastline offers so much: outstanding wildlife and beautiful landscapes; inspiring experiences for people, benefiting their health and well-being; and places that can sustain thousands of small rural businesses, including in farming, fishing and tourism. We have saved our coastline, provided (or are developing) appropriate public access to it, and are making good progress on marine conservation: now let us harness its potential as a positive tool to help us manage the inevitable changes that climate change will bring. Our success in caring for the beauty of the coast shows how we can add immeasurably to the quality of our lives, ensure economic health and well-being, and bequeath places of great beauty to future generations.

8

Cultural heritage –
how caring for the past
creates a better future

It is impossible to separate the fight for protecting our built and cultural heritage from that for the beauty of landscapes and nature, for as Hoskins showed us ours is a cultural landscape, shaped and reshaped by human hands over centuries. The fight to preserve what remains of our past has been as powerful a driving force for beauty as any. This chapter charts that fight.

Yet there is an irony here, because although each generation loves and wants to protect its past, we are at best ambivalent about much of the present and often positively uneasy about the future. We do not admire today's municipal buildings as we do the great town halls of the past, and modern housing estates are often far less appealing than a thatched cottage or restored Georgian or Victorian terrace. We object to new high speed trains, yet railway preservation societies lovingly restore the very steam engines and iron bridges that so appalled Ruskin. So what do we love from the past and why? What are the elements that constitute beauty in our cultural heritage? And can we use the experience of protecting our past to ensure that we leave a legacy worth protecting to future generations?

Ruskin abhorred steam railways, yet today enthusiasts
work hard to keep them running, as here in north Norfolk.
(Courtesy of the National Trust/Rod Edwards)

A prior question, though, is what we even mean by 'heritage'. One of my early experiences at the National Trust was a straightforward challenge to what we stood for. 'Blair Babe's £1m slum'. I winced as I read the headline in the *Daily Mail* in 2002, as we launched our appeal to acquire the last remaining courtyard back-to-back houses in Birmingham. I was cross about the 'Blair Babe' slur (I'd been a civil servant in the Cabinet Office for two years before coming to the National Trust, hardly a sign of political allegiance) but crosser still about the word 'slum', which told me that we still had a long way to go to show that heritage was about celebrating *all* of our histories, not just those of the rich and famous, and how broadening its appeal would make the beauty and inspiration of our cultural history more accessible to everyone.

The Birmingham back-to-back houses, before and after restoration by the National Trust.

(Courtesy of the National Trust/Robert Morris)

The back-to-backs, or blind-backs as they are sometimes called, are small three-storey houses backing onto each other around a central courtyard: some facing inwards, the others facing the streets. They were once typical of Birmingham's housing stock but had nearly all been demolished in clearances since the 1960s. They were certainly at the opposite end of the spectrum from the stereo-typical view of the National Trust's stately offer. Yet their tiny rooms, lovingly decorated and dignified, spoke to the upbringing of millions of Birmingham residents and had been built as both homes and workplaces, the engine rooms of the City of a Thousand Trades, where their home-based workers made window catch-ments, glass eyes or watch hands. And once we had restored and opened the back-to-backs to the public, they received the highest praise from visitors, recalling as they did the stories of urban living and confirming a new and growing enthusiasm for 'everyone's' heritage.

This story is just one example among many showing how the heritage movement has evolved. But its messages have been repeated time and time again throughout the movement's history. Because although the first advocates for heritage were antiquarian scholars, from the eighteenth century their expert preoccupations were complemented by a growing popular fascination for history and the built heritage. And this popular support, endlessly generat-ing new ideas, challenges and interests, is what has driven heritage protection forward.

Before any formal preservation measures were in place people were flocking to ruins and historic sites, inspired by Walter Scott's novels, popular poetry, articles in weekly magazines and a prolifer-ating number of tourist guides to the mediaeval castles, ducal homes and royal palaces of Britain. They were also, as we saw in chapter one, following Gilpin to the New Forest, the Lake District and the Wye Valley and the Romantic poets to beauty spots throughout the land. Elizabeth Bennet was far from alone (except, perhaps, in her fascination for Pemberley) in touring a number of 'remarkable places through which their route thither lay; Oxford, Blenheim, Warwick, Kenelworth [sic], Birmingham etc.' when in *Pride and Prejudice* (published in 1813) she embarked on a distracting tour with her aunt Mrs Gardiner.

This counterpoint between expert preoccupation and popular appeal has shaped the heritage movement's evolution. Initially, though, the experts were in charge of what was saved. The Society of Antiquaries of London was established in its 'modern' form (it had Elizabethan roots) in 1707, and its primary interests were standing monuments, ancient buildings such as those of the Universities of Oxford and Cambridge, and the royal palaces. Its first secretary, William Stukeley, visited the most important monuments and recorded threats to them with a growing sense of alarm. Stonehenge and Avebury were being ploughed, with housing speculators breaking up the stones for building materials; visitors were sneaking souvenirs from historic sites; and Hadrian's Wall was being pillaged to construct the adjacent military road. He was appalled that turnpike roads, railways and houses were being built, and farmers were ploughing fields, without regard for the hundreds of thousands of ancient monuments – burial chambers, megaliths and stone circles – that were scattered throughout the landscape, and for which there was no form of protection at all.

To champion these sites the British Archaeological Association was founded in 1843 and the Archaeological Institute the following year. Their members led the defence of ancient sites, with Sir John Lubbock (later Lord Avebury), a banker turned MP, pressing for ancient monuments to be left *in situ* rather than being collected for museums. This was key to the movement's later development, because it recognised the importance of place and context, which

Ancient monuments including Stonehenge attracted
visitors before any protection for heritage sites was in place.
(Courtesy of the National Trust/Rachel Topham)

are lost when a site is broken up and its artefacts dispersed. Leading by example, he purchased the land containing the critical sites of Avebury, Silbury Hill, West Kennet Long Barrow and Hackpen Hill. He also promoted a Private Members' Bill just as (in 1868) the Society of Antiquaries was seeking to establish a commission to protect historic monuments, publishing a list of 531 monuments that should be safeguarded. The proposal for a commission languished, and Lubbock's Bill (with its own painstakingly prepared schedules of sites) failed, but it shamed the government into producing a Bill of its own.

That Bill was the brainchild of the First Commissioner of Works, George Shaw Lefevre, and it became the Ancient Monuments Act 1882, offering the first protection for ancient sites. Shaw Lefevre was no uninterested official because he had been one of the founders of the Commons Preservation Society in 1865 and he wanted to achieve the same success for ancient monuments. He had sought a right of compulsory purchase of ancient monuments by the Office of Works, but all he got through the Bill was a list of sixty-eight monuments that the Office could, by agreement, accept as a gift or purchase; and a fine of five pounds for anyone convicted of damaging a monument. It was weak, but it was a start.

And it was a start that the first Inspector for the Office of Works, General Pitt-Rivers, used to great advantage, deploying all his persuasive skills to bring fourteen ancient monuments from the schedule into guardianship within a couple of years, and begin the process, supported by the Ordnance Survey, of mapping ancient monuments across the country.

The Office of Works was fully alive to the public's enthusiasm for the built heritage, and by the early twentieth century its interests had expanded to embrace royal palaces including the Tower of London, and castles and military structures such as Tynemouth and Dover Castles. One of its early successes was to negotiate with the Ministry of Defence to take over their day-to-day management. Since this came with a budget, repairs could be undertaken that sustained rather than damaged the historic interest of the buildings. And the Ancient Monuments Act 1900 picked up the mood of the times by enabling mediaeval as well as prehistoric sites to be taken into guardianship, just as the infant National Trust was rescuing important examples of mediaeval vernacular architecture including Long Crendon Courthouse in Buckinghamshire and the Tintagel Old Post Office in Cornwall.

When Charles Reed Peers was appointed as Chief Inspector in 1910, the Office of Works established him in a separate Ancient Monuments Department within the Office with its own board, staff and expertise. His energy led to the acquisition by the government of the first Roman site, Richborough Castle; the first mediaeval site, The Fish House in Mere, Somerset; and the first privately owned castle, Kirby Muxloe in Leicestershire. He oversaw dramas, too, such as the near-loss of the fifteenth-century Tattershall Castle with its splendid Tudor fireplaces. It had been sold to a speculator in 1910 but as its valuable fireplaces were removed for sale a storm of protest erupted. It was rescued by the derring-do of Lord Curzon, the former Viceroy of India who had a passion for historic buildings. He sped to Lincolnshire to buy out the owner within a twenty-four-hour deadline, before tracking down and purchasing the fireplaces, and presenting the castle to the National Trust.

Each crisis led to an expansion of what could be protected. In 1913 the Ancient Monuments Act widened the definition of a historic monument to any that justified public interest on historic, architectural, traditional, artistic or archaeological grounds,

Tattershall Castle was rescued thanks to the derring-do of Lord Curzon who tracked down its stolen fireplaces and returned them to the castle, which he then handed to the National Trust. (Courtesy of the National Trust/John Hammond (left) and Carlton & Sons)

though it still excluded ecclesiastical buildings and inhabited houses. It provided three new mechanisms: a (rarely used) Preservation Order; the ability to schedule significant monuments; and provisions for properties to be held in guardianship by local authorities.

This Act was significant because it also set up an advisory Ancient Monuments Board, stacked with proactive experts. Chaired by Lionel Earle, the Board decided to define and protect a 'national collection' of the monuments and buildings that would constitute a representative sample and tell the story of Britain. It considered, in turn, the most important ancient monuments from each period of history, then monastic buildings, city and town walls, and castles. It was well on the way with prehistoric forts and Roman remains when the First World War broke out, but it had achieved its goal: the foundation of the National Heritage Collection.

The war years curtailed the Board's work, just as they did for nature and landscape. Lack of money was a constant problem in the depressed inter-war period; and the same tensions we saw earlier erupted over agricultural and forestry improvements. Ploughing of ancient sites was a perennial problem, and there was a crisis at Grime's Graves in Norfolk when in the 1920s the newly established Forestry Commission planted the recently scheduled monument with young trees, causing Charles Reed Peers to write despairingly: 'the state must set an example, or it is hopeless to expect private owners to abstain from profiting by the destruction of any monuments they may own.' The Treasury offered no help to the Board in its attempts to buy sites to safeguard them, saying in 1924 that it should not 'waste its resources on schemes which, however desirable from the aesthetic point of view, do not enrich the country or add to its commercial equipment'. So much for beauty.

Yet during the lean 1930s heritage was not forgotten, thanks not least to the energetic First Commissioner of Works, George Lansbury. He used the unemployment crisis to employ out-of-work miners at ancient monuments. His workforce of 1,300 men reinstated moats at castles including Helmsley, Portchester, Pickering and Beaumaris, sometimes rather too enthusiastically. He swept aside criticisms of the amount of money he spent, throwing himself at every new challenge. Under his leadership Hadrian's Wall was saved, after plans to quarry stone right up against the wall led to new safeguards for setting and context, through the Ancient Monuments Act 1931 which allowed the protection of areas 'comprising or adjacent to an ancient monument'. He was also a benefactor of the National Trust, raising the money to acquire Sutton House in Hackney, which had been the home of Ralph Sadleir, Privy Councillor to Henry VIII, and was one of the last remaining Tudor buildings in East London. More acquisitions for the public estate followed: the purchase of Bowes Castle in the Pennines, the Augustinian Abbey of Haughmond in Shropshire and Mulcheneny Abbey in Somerset; the generous gift of Middleham Castle in Yorkshire; and in 1937 a part-purchase, part-gift deal to secure the splendid Kenilworth Castle, already a popular visitor attraction.

By the mid-1930s the 'national collection' had grown impressively to over 270 monuments and was still expanding. It included the 'star' sites of Stonehenge and Maiden Castle, Rievaulx Abbey and Carisbrooke Castle, but also forty-six mediaeval castles, thirty monasteries and twenty-one Roman sites, though nothing dating from later than the late mediaeval period. They were very popular: by 1935 the 122 sites open to the public were attracting about 2.5 million visitors.

But now a new crisis appeared for which no one was prepared. A combination of the Depression, the Great War and unprecedentedly high taxation meant that many of the great families of

Britain had lost their heir, their fortune or both. Moreover the practicalities of running large country houses had become near-impossible with staff not returning after the war or no longer content to work in service. And while the families' London houses sat on valuable, realisable real estate, the future for country houses, packed with extraordinary and often idiosyncratic collections, expensive to staff and run, was bleak. Meanwhile occupied houses and their collections were excluded from the protective legislation developed so painstakingly over previous decades. Not only were they outside the scope of the Ministry of Works, there were those who felt it was not for the government to rescue the country houses of the rich.

Yet everywhere country houses and their collections were disappearing. Some were abandoned; others sold or leased as schools, hospitals and nursing homes; some burned to the ground (not always accidentally) and others were deliberately demolished. Between 1914 and 1918 alone more than four hundred houses were lost. Between 1920 and 1950 an average of thirteen houses a year disappeared, easily another four hundred, their collections sold or dispersed.

Stimulated by Christopher Hussey, the energetic editor of *Country Life*, the National Trust found itself at the heart of a passionate debate to save the country house, though its Christian Socialist founders might have turned in their graves. Their focus had been on mediaeval architecture and open spaces and they had only ever acquired one country house, Barrington Court in Somerset, bought in 1907 against Octavia Hill's advice. Barrington was a beautiful Jacobean house but it was in a terrible state of repair, with chickens scratching in the state rooms when it was first visited by National Trust officials, and it had no indigenous contents. It cost the Trust a fortune, nearly bankrupting it in the process. The words 'remember Barrington!' still echo within the Trust, and it was because of memories of Barrington that in 1968 the Finance Committee Chairman (and later Chairman) Roger Chorley invented the Chorley Formula to calculate endowments. Since 1976 no property has been taken on without one.

But by the late 1920s the founders were dead and the Trust was being run by well-connected people within or with the ear of government. In 1934 the Trust's first professional head, Donald Matheson, invited his friend Lord Lothian, who owned Blickling Hall in Norfolk, to speak at the Trust's AGM. He called on the National Trust and the government to save the country house. He encouraged the Trust to set up a Country Houses Committee, which it did in 1936, and persuaded the government to pass the National Trust Act 1937, enabling owners to transfer country houses to the Trust with a tax-free endowment and, if the Trust agreed, to remain in residence. A visionary step had been taken.

The Act offered a lifeline for families in dire straits, but giving up their country houses was a profound and irrevocable step. Few volunteered until James Lees-Milne, the first Secretary to the Country Houses Committee, took to the road in the Trust's little Austin, and set off around the country to talk to country house owners, recording his travels in his droll, witty diaries. Visiting Wallington in Northumberland, he wrote in September 1942: '[I] found the Trevelyan family overpowering in spite of the kind welcome they gave me', and when, after dinner, he could not avoid a game of general knowledge questions he recorded that:

> Every single member of the family gets 100 out of 100. The son in law [John Dower, described as 'working on post-war National Park schemes . . . very left wing . . . and important'] gets 80, Matheson [the Secretary of the National Trust] gets 30. I get 0. But then I am a half-wit.

Deeply humiliated I receive condolences from the Trevelyans and assurances that I shall no doubt do better next time. I make an inward vow that there will never be a next time.

Most prospective donors took much persuading, though some, including the Trevelyans, did not. Nor did the Manders, a Midlands manufacturing and political family who were desperate for their fifty-year-old Arts and Crafts house, Wightwick Manor in Wolverhampton, to be thought of as meritorious. It was the first to be accepted under the scheme, despite not being on Christopher Hussey's list of endangered houses, helped no doubt by Sir Geoffrey Mander's generous endowment.

James Lees-Milne who, as secretary to the National Trust's Country Houses Committee, was responsible for persuading many country house owners to join its rescue scheme. (Courtesy of the National Trust)

Beyond the core arrangement, whereby the Trust took on ownership and a permanent obligation for building repairs, each deal was different. Often only the immediate surroundings of land were included, for the families (wisely for them, it turned out) were advised to hang on to the bulk of their landed estates. Nor were the contents always passed to the Trust, even though the presence of an indigenous collection is the distinguishing feature of the country house in Britain. But the additional burden of owning and safeguarding contents was often a step too far for a National Trust trying desperately to make ends meet. The house was the priority.

Privately Lees-Milne agreed. 'In fact my loyalties are first to the houses, second to the donors and third to the National Trust. I put the Trust last because it is neither a work of art nor a human being but an abstract thing, a convenience,' he wrote in March 1943. And if anyone in later years criticised some of the deals he negotiated (and they did) the answer is quite simply that without him many more houses would have been lost. In any case, too many were: John Cornforth calculated that while the Trust took around one hundred houses, more than seven hundred were lost between the years 1900 and 1970. By 1974 the fate of the country house was still so uncertain that Roy Strong commissioned the exhibition *The Destruction of the Country House* at the Victoria and Albert Museum. It recorded the National Trust's contribution but charted in poignant detail the hundreds of houses that had gone and others that were still at risk. Its black-and-white photographs showed crumbling piles, burning chimneys and partially demolished walls, waiting for the next swing of the stone ball.

So Lees-Milne's first and primary job was safeguarding houses, and he was realistic enough to know that the state in which the impecunious National Trust could hold them was not the last word. He wrote:

All we can and must do is continue preserving, as carefully as we can, the fabric and contents of a representative number of country houses. The fact that we are now keeping them mummified does not matter. On the contrary it is all to the good. Future generations may discover alternative uses which will bring them to life again without impairing their mystery and their magic. They will be grateful to us.

The National Trust was of course heavily dependent on public policy and finance to achieve its rescue of the country house. Apart from the tax advantages, an invaluable source of help was Hugh Dalton's National Land Fund, set up in 1946 when he was Chancellor of the Exchequer, with an endowment of £50 million to secure culturally significant property as a memorial to those who had died in the Second World War. Its primary focus was countryside but money was also given to enable the National Trust to acquire the exquisite mediaeval house and estate, Cotehele, in Cornwall. In 1948 Dalton's successor as Chancellor, Stafford Cripps, asked the Ministry of Works for a list of the most important houses at risk that were not already protected by the Trust. A list of fifty-two was swiftly produced, and a further forty-one were added when the list was broadened to cover a representative selection of British architecture and historical periods. The country house, built as a conscious adornment of the landscape, had won a formal place in Britain's valued heritage estate.

The question then was whether these buildings could be saved without either the government or the National Trust having to acquire them; and so the Historic Buildings and Ancient Monuments Act 1953 authorised a grants programme for the Ministry of Works. The grants were (for their time) significant, starting at a total of £250,000 a year and climbing to £700,000 a year by 1970. To dispense the funds, the Ministry was advised by a new Historic Buildings Council, on which sat significant and knowledgeable figures like Christopher Hussey and Hugh Euston, later the Duke of Grafton. But many houses they considered were in crisis and needed more than a grant to save them, so when Dyrham Park near Bath was put on the market in 1956 and its contents offered to Sotheby's, the Historic Buildings Council urged the Ministry of Works to buy it and its most important contents. In sums that seem astonishingly small today the house and twelve acres of land were bought for £5,000 and a large part of the contents for £42,000. Dyrham was given to the National Trust and by 1961 was open to the public.

There were, however, many important historic buildings and sites in private ownership throughout the country that deserved protection and would never be candidates for public ownership. So the Town and Country Planning Act 1944 introduced the ability to 'list' inhabited buildings of recognised importance. By 1959 over 73,000 had been listed (the figure is around 500,000 today), and owners were required to seek consent before demolishing them or making significant changes.

But there was no coherent view of heritage: listed buildings were the responsibility of the Department of Town Planning and its officials were completely separate from those in the Ministry of Works who were responsible for scheduling and guardianship. Moreover the limitations of trying to protect isolated sites and buildings were becoming clear, especially as the fashion for wholesale urban redevelopment began to gather momentum. What remained of war-ravaged town centres in, for example, Coventry and Plymouth were demolished in a manner more cruel than the Blitz, and reconstructed with little sensitivity to what had previously existed. Horrified by what was happening Duncan Sandys, a Conservative MP and former Housing Minister with a passion for history and architecture, founded the Civic Trust in 1956, and by 1960 more than three hundred local societies, often long pre-dating the Civic Trust, had affiliated to it. Each society was dedicated to protecting the character, history and beauty of their historic towns and cities and several had begun life as local branches of Miranda Hill's Kyrle Society, founded in the 1870s to bring beauty into people's lives.

The Civic Trust's advocacy for historic town centres chimed with Richard Crossman's views as Minister of Housing and Local Government from 1964. He was privately appalled by some of the urban redevelopment proposals he was asked to approve, and asked the Council for British Archaeology for a list of the most vulnerable and important historic towns. This was quickly supplied; it cited fifty-one towns including Durham and Alnwick, and when Duncan Sandys promoted a Civic Amenities Bill as a Private Member, Crossman backed it and it passed in 1967.

The result of Sandys' Act was that local authorities could designate Conservation Areas: whole streets and squares marking the historic core of a city, town or (later) village. Within the designated area, property owners had to apply for consent to change the external appearance of a building or architectural feature. It was not fool-proof but it protected many places which would otherwise have been demolished or dismantled piecemeal. It also encouraged the conservation of modest, domestic-scale buildings in an urban setting rather than focusing only on prestige buildings. A terraced street, market place or a jumble of mediaeval shambles might not be deemed significant in its own right, but as a group it captured the ambience and spirit of a place that was otherwise too easily lost.

The idea that there were *areas* of historic significance was gathering momentum internationally too. Driven by the appalling destruction of heritage and cultural property caused by bombardment, looting and illegal export during two world wars, the United Nations Educational, Scientific and Cultural Organisation (UNESCO) was founded in 1948. Initially focused on research and information exchange, by the 1960s the idea of a World Heritage Trust was being mooted. This stemmed from the UN's decision to list the world's most important National Parks and equivalent reserves. From the outset this included cultural landscapes such as the Khmer archaeological fields in Cambodia and the mediaeval parliament site in Iceland. The World Heritage Trust idea was proposed to the IUCN General Assembly in 1966, by which time Stonehenge had joined the list, and by 1972 a World Heritage Convention had been agreed, with the aim of protecting a wide range of places across the world that encompassed monuments, buildings, cultural and natural sites. In 2015 there were twenty-nine World Heritage Sites in the UK, and one candidate, the cultural landscape of the Lake District. They are the most significant cultural heritage sites in our country and theoretically the best protected.

Though charismatic and determined individuals led the fight for heritage protection, they would not have achieved success without public support, and it was that support that sustained and extended the movement. The public's enthusiasm was largely expressed by the popularity of visiting sites. In fact the Ministry of Works was way ahead of the National Trust in the early days; in 1962 its sites attracted 5.5 million paying visitors a year in England compared with the National Trust's 1.2 million and private owners' 4 million. The Trust was not yet fully engaged in the visitor business, being almost overwhelmed by the challenge of accepting, surveying, restoring and opening as many as a dozen country houses a year under the Country Houses Scheme. In 1955 the Trust still had only 100 staff and 56,000 members, and the aesthetes (the curators represented by Lees-Milne) were in the ascendancy, lording it over the more plodding 'hob-nail boots' (land agents) who were responsible for looking after the Trust's land holdings. And the curators were acutely conscious of the pressures posed by large numbers of visitors: Robin Fedden, the National Trust's Historic Buildings Secretary, wrote in 1967 'there are buildings where "preservation" seems in danger of sacrifice to "access" and where numbers destroy any sense of a house as a home, and make almost impossible creative contact with the past, and with art, and the art of living, that a house enshrines.' The atmosphere for visitors was formal, reverential and hushed.

But the Trust could not, and did not, ignore people's enthusiasm for long. And indeed it was the acquisition of country houses and the enormous estates that came with some of them, often as part of the endowment, that turned the Trust into a mass membership, big property-owning charity, enabling it to do far more for beauty than had been envisaged by its founders.

Its exponential growth started in the 1960s, when workers began to get weekends off and families could afford a small car. The middle-class 'day out' was born and the National Trust was perfectly placed to take advantage of it. Visits to National Trust properties soared from one to two million between 1959 and 1969, and the tiny membership department, working in the Blewcoat School in Victoria, central London, was already feeling swamped when Ted Fawcett was appointed head of membership in 1969. His eagle eyes saw huge opportunities to expand the membership, and he began training property administrators to recruit people when they visited. He also introduced table-top shops selling tea towels and small souvenirs.

The effect was galvanising. Along with the visits, membership soared – from 150,000 in 1965 to 540,000 a decade later – and the Trust had to overhaul the management of its membership. It became a reluctant pioneer in computer use, anxious to replicate the personal touch of its old card-index system when it established a new-fangled 'call centre', the Ravensbourne Registration Service, in Beckenham. Soon the Trust had become a mass-membership organisation and, to widespread astonishment, reached one million members in 1981. There are still a few 'I'm one in a million' car stickers around.

Visitor numbers also rose because there was more to see and visit. The 1970s, 80s and 90s were incredibly productive and successful decades for the National Trust. The V&A's 1974 exhibition *The Destruction of the Country House* had revitalised interest in its protection, and highlighted the vulnerability of the country house. As if to illustrate the point, Mentmore, an extravagant Victorian country house in Buckinghamshire, was by 1977 under threat of sale, along with its extraordinary collection of fine art, furniture, and gold, silver and enamel objects. An impassioned and lengthy campaign was launched, but the government declined to save it and the contents were dispersed in one of the largest ever country house sales. The conservation movement was appalled, and when the National Land Fund was re-born as the National Heritage Memorial Fund (NHMF) in 1980, it was sympathetic to safeguarding other country houses and even more sympathetic to the National Trust as a suitable owner. Acquisitions helped by the NHMF included Belton House near Grantham, Calke Abbey and Kedleston Hall near Derby, Canons Ashby in Northamptonshire, the ruins and gardens of Fountains Abbey and Studley Royal in Yorkshire, and Stowe Landscape Gardens in Buckinghamshire. These are all places of the highest conservation significance, and with their estates and gardens added immeasurably to the Trust's appeal.

In fact gardens are one of the Trust's greatest successes. Though initially many were acquired as an adjunct to a house, they have proved enduringly popular and hugely significant as both historic landscapes and the source of horticultural inspiration. And since the Trust proactively acquired its first garden, Hidcote, in 1948, gardens have rightly occupied a central place in its thinking and offer to members and visitors. Often even more popular than the houses, gardens have taught the Trust how to manage people as well as the historic properties it owns.

National Trust visitors, especially to country houses, felt more than a frisson of privilege, especially in the early days. They were the first generation to be admitted in any numbers to these hallowed, once private, houses. But as Robin Fedden was all too aware, their visits created new challenges: the weight of feet on floors and carpets, dust and dirt, and risks from handling and accidents to precious objects. Country houses that had been visited by their families and their retinues only a few times a year were getting more wear and tear than they had ever had in private hands. By the 1970s it was clear that an ad hoc process of cleaning and repair was no longer good enough and the Trust's professional staff decided to do something about it. Its first Housekeeper, Sheila Stainton, set up a textile conservation workshop to oversee the sensitive cleaning and repair of curtains, carpets and furnishings, and then, working with Hermione Sandwith, produced *The National Trust Manual of Housekeeping*. This was first published in 1984 and revolutionised the care and maintenance of the Trust's collection, explaining exactly how each material and item in a country house should be cared for, and with which techniques and instruments. From the careful, pony-hair brushing of porcelain to the gentle hoovering of floors and the delicate use of beeswax on wood, each edition (two were published during my time as Director-General alone) thicker and heavier than the last, instructed on the proper method of care.

Buttressed by these safeguards, and nurtured to a high level of presentation, the properties flourished and the Trust's popularity grew. Building on Ted Fawcett's ideas, visitors were welcomed and guided around properties in an increasingly professional manner, volunteer numbers soared and the Trust widened its appeal to families. Under Angus Stirling's leadership educational activities flourished and the Young National Trust Theatre was launched. The Trust's popularity seemed unstoppable.

Yet by the time I arrived at the Trust in late 2000 it was clear that country house management and presentation needed, again, to move on. People were changing and expectations were changing. Though brilliantly effective for conservation, there was a risk that the Trust's protective approach would put people off. Before being interviewed for the job of Director-General I'd taken my middle daughter, Rose, around a country house in Cornwall. Even she, a butter-wouldn't-melt child, was shushed and frowned on as she chattered during our visit. These buildings were not saved just by continuing to exist: they needed to speak to people, to embrace them and to mean something to them.

And so that's what I set out to do, stealing the phrase 'arms open conservation' from a visit to the US National Parks Service to explain what I meant. I wanted people to feel involved, enthralled and engaged in the spirit of place, and not be simply passive observers of it; I believed the Trust could only make that possible by enabling people to feel more at home, more welcome, and less inhibited by rules and regulations. The 'arms closed' approach, where the Trust took charge, telling people what they could and couldn't do, and the prevalent 'do not touch', 'do not sit here' and 'do not walk on the grass' signs had, I believed, gone beyond what was necessary for high conservation standards, and risked alienating people in a world where the appetite for being instructed was ebbing. It was time, I believed, to move on from Lees-Milne's 'mummification' and bring the houses to life. I wanted our supporters to see our conservation work in action and to feel part of the Trust's great and inspiring cause.

And so in 2002 I stood somewhat gingerly on the grand stair-case of a Victorian Gothic country house near Bristol, a fraying silk carpet beneath my feet and a damp, slightly mildewy smell in the air. The great entrance hall, its high, domed ceiling above us, was crowded with journalists and influential members of the heritage movement. I was there to announce the launch of an appeal to save Tyntesfield, one of the best surviving and most complete Victorian country house estates in the country, from sale and certain break-up. And in doing so I promised that the National Trust would manage Tyntesfield under new principles: with our arms open, with the public fully involved, observing all the processes of conservation and able to participate in them.

This was a decisive moment for the National Trust and it launched a new approach to heritage conservation. Our appeal was astonishingly successful, raising £8 million in three months from the public alone; though the sum raised would eventually reach

Tyntesfield, acquired by the National Trust, pioneered the 'arms open conservation' approach. (Courtesy of the National Trust/John Millar)

over £40 million when all sources were included, especially gener-ous grants from the National Heritage Memorial Fund and the Heritage Lottery Fund which were – happily – conditional on my 'arms open' approach being implemented. So Tyntesfield paved the way for a revolution in the way country houses, and increas-ingly their estates and the countryside, would be managed. Today a visit to any National Trust place demonstrates its legacy, and the housekeeping rules have been recast by conservation experts to enable visitor enjoyment. Liveliness, warmth, activity and a lived-in feel is everywhere: pianos are played, billiard games are in progress, ropes have nearly all gone and children are encouraged to walk on the grass, play and picnic. It is warm and welcoming, very different from the formality of the past.

The acquisition of the Birmingham back-to-backs marked a similar moment of change. Already under discussion when I arrived as Director-General, the Birmingham Conservation Trust (BCT) had spotted the significance of the small group of build-ings next to the Hippodrome Theatre that was to be demolished to make way for a new block of flats. Their unpromising exterior (bedraggled terraced frontages offering Oscar's Fast Food and the services of a taxi-hire company) belied an almost complete courtyard of back-to-back houses with their laundry and commu-nal wash house intact. The condition inside the houses was poor but retrievable. It did not take long for trustees to agree that, notwithstanding the £1 million fundraising challenge, we should accede to the BCT's request to take them on and open them to the public.

There were critical voices, of course, the *Mail*'s article sneering at our decision to take on 'slums' being one of them, and it reminded the Trust of the fuss when it had acquired Paul McCartney's house, 20 Forthlin Road, in 1996. Yet the Beatles' houses (we also acquired John Lennon's Aunt Mimi's house in 2002) are enduringly popular, not least because they tell the story of suburban living, evoking half-lost memories of formica kitchens, lino floors, flying ducks on walls and pink silk bedspreads.

By the time I left the National Trust towards the end of 2012 membership had reached an astonishing four million and it is growing steadily still. It now opens over 250 great houses and gardens to the public, as well as dozens of smaller houses, industrial sites and mills, cottages and follies. It is the most popular heritage organisation in the world, a sign of people's hunger for beauty, and of the depth of the relationship between people and place. A relationship that is inspired when the spirit of a place is liberated, born from bricks, mortar and contents and enhanced by atmosphere: the way a house has been occupied, the experience its visitors have and the way its stories are told. All these elements give a place its character and authenticity; all this is why people respond so warmly. And it is perhaps what James Lees-Milne meant by 'alternative uses which will bring them to life again without impairing their mystery and magic'.

What happened within the Trust in the early 2000s marched with a wider process of growing public fascination for heritage. English Heritage, the child of the Office of Works, was established as an arm's-length public body in 1983, and in 2015 was split into Historic England, the regulator and champion for all England's heritage, and the English Heritage Trust, the body holding and managing the much-enhanced National Heritage Collection, now composed of over eight hundred sites. English Heritage launched its own membership scheme in 1983 and now has around a million members. Historic England has extended further the definition of historic significance, and now lists twentieth-century buildings and examples of significant public-sector architecture such as prisons, hospitals and police stations. The Heritage Lottery Fund, successor to Hugh Dalton's Land Fund, has also pioneered a broader view of heritage, encouraging its grantees to engage with and embrace new audiences, showing that history is not only about the lives of the rich and powerful but for everyone, everywhere. Since 1994 the HLF has dispensed a staggering £6 billion on heritage projects and it continues to spend £375 million a year, bringing unprecedented investment and opportunity into the sector.

Heritage protection, then, has done well, consolidating its place as a central element in our care for the beauty of our country. But what it has done best is look after heritage sites and broaden their appeal. So despite all the achievements charted here the question, for beauty, remains: has it done enough to bring heritage values into the mainstream, beyond heritage sites? Or has our wider heritage, like nature and the landscape of the wider countryside, been stripped of its significance and beauty?

One of the most important developments in recent years is Heritage Open Days, founded in 1994 by the Civic Trust as part of European Heritage Days. Its aim was to enable people to see places in their own communities that were not normally open to the public. From the beginning the initiative was a great success and by 2014 (by now under the National Trust's umbrella) was attracting over three million visitors over a four-day period in England, 200,000 visits to Scotland's Doors Open Days and similar numbers to Wales' Open Doors events. The initiative has sparked interest in the historic places that exist, often unnoticed, in local communities and revived enthusiasm for everyday history as well as special sites. It does the bulk of its work through volunteers, reflecting the movement's skill in involving them; over 62,000 help the National Trust alone.

At the same time a burgeoning interest in industrial archaeology, whether steam trains or old mine-workings, factories or water-wheels, has drawn new audiences and activists into practical restoration efforts, encouraging people who enjoy rolling up their sleeves and making things work. The same cog-wheels and engines, crafted cast-iron and soaring brick-chimneys that so appalled Ruskin have inspired more recent generations. So we are capable of adapting to and absorbing change, not just in response to the passage of time but by the intrinsic qualities of the object in question: its design, construction and purpose.

But if we are serious about protecting the beauty of the past we need to satisfy more than nostalgia. Previous generations built and planned for the future, and we must do so too. For heritage is not just about how we look after the past, but how we consider the needs of future generations and the legacy we will leave them. And here our attitudes to history come into play. History helps us understand where we have come from as a society and as individuals: for many of us, it is our foundation. But history is not static. Our view of history is mediated by our understanding of current events as well as those of the past, and our understanding is shaped by our own experience. History gives us perspective and experience helps us address future uncertainties. History is, then, as much about the future as it is about the past.

And if we want to pass on a legacy of which we are proud, we need to embrace the future as well as the past. A snapshot of the dilemma this poses was presented in the early 2000s when the heritage movement was confronted with a government that appeared to have no interest in history at all. The incoming Labour government, indeed, seemed to believe that history had begun in May 1997, the date of its election. The Department of National Heritage did not last long: while the new government enthused about pop stars, fashion icons and media figures, and the media responded with its soubriquet 'cool Britannia', the department's name was changed to Culture, Media and Sport, making no reference to heritage. History was dropped from the compulsory education curriculum after the age of fourteen. The Millennium Dome, representing that moment of idealised celebration of the passing of the twentieth century, was a forward-looking, history-free zone. History was relegated to, well, history.

Yet the public refused to play along. Outside government circles there was an apparently insatiable appetite for the very thing that officialdom ignored. Acres of newsprint, novels, biography, analysis and endless films and TV programmes were devoted to history. The *Downton Abbey* phenomenon was in the making. And in the summer of 2003 people were joining the National Trust faster than the birth-rate: one new member every forty-two seconds.

But as a movement we felt we had no traction. So we decided to fight for a greater recognition of heritage and history. In 2000 the heritage movement came together, just as the wildlife bodies had done in the early 1980s, to form a new charity, Heritage Link. Jointly with English Heritage we published *Power of Place*, setting out the reasons why heritage was good for the country, good for people and good for the economy. It explained the richness an understanding of history brings to individuals and decision-makers, the large and growing dependence of tourism on heritage, and the joy it brings to people's lives. And, drawing on the experience of all the heritage bodies we showed how heritage is for everyone and is all around us. 'The historic environment is seen by most people as a totality. They value places, not just a series of individual sites and buildings. What people care about is the whole of their environment' wrote Neil Cossons, then Chair of English Heritage.

DCMS responded in late 2001 with *The Historic Environment – A Force for Our Future*. It nodded in the right direction but its only substantial commitment was to widen the remit of the Green Ministers to include heritage; otherwise its recommendations simply played back what other heritage bodies – local authorities, English Heritage and charities like the National Trust – could do.

We came back with more evidence. After the catastrophe of foot and mouth in 2001, when the countryside had effectively been closed, we had seen a surge of enthusiasm and the revitalisation of the rural economy as people flooded out into the countryside after weeks of being denied access. The Trust could see – and an independent study, looking at the reopening of Cragside and Wallington, by Newcastle University confirmed – the real stimulus our properties gave to their wider area. The research demonstrated that one of the main drivers of employment and economic activity in the countryside today is tourism or leisure-related, often associated with a historic asset; and moreover that where the National Trust has a presence it packs a significant, sustainable, economic punch. In fact the research showed that there is a multiplier of between five and seven jobs for every individual job the Trust creates in a local economy.

But again the government's response was lacklustre. All we had done was show that heritage is good for the economy: important, but no more convincing than many other sectors, equally keen to attract the government's attention.

So finally we decided to launch a campaign, to generate an understanding of the intrinsic value of heritage: we called it *History Matters – pass it on*. It was based on our fundamental belief that history is central to many people's lives, and the need to show how much it matters. But crucially it was also about the future, seeing history as a way of engaging people in what is yet to come.

Over the summer of 2006 all the main heritage bodies in the UK – the National Trust, English Heritage, the Heritage Lottery Fund, Heritage Link and the Historic Houses Association – held hundreds of events and activities. We gave out *History Matters* badges and asked people to fill in postcards saying why history mattered to them. On 17 October, *One Day in History*, we asked people to write about their lives, and collected all the scripts into a rich archive which the British Library agreed to keep for future social research. A young, aspiring MP – David Cameron – contributed one. Historians, media figures and TV personalities spoke up for history. Overall, more than 1.2 million people took part in less than five months.

The overwhelming message was that people *did* feel that history was central to their lives and, moreover, that without understanding history, they would struggle to make sense of today and make good decisions about tomorrow. People told us that history enriches their lives, and helps them feel connected. They didn't necessarily need or want to be experts: their fascination was derived from curiosity or the opportunity to connect history to their lives; hence the growth in interest in family and local history. Perhaps their ancestors had worked in a historic house's kitchen; or on an estate farm; or lived in a back-to-back. Perhaps they had walked these paths or looked at this view.

But people also told us that they did need some knowledge of history to make sense of it, and the strongest messages we received were about history teaching in schools. History was too often taught in snapshots: unless children studied history in depth (and fewer did, each year), they learned about the Romans, the Tudors and Hitler, but not what connects them or the long timeline of which they are a part. They had little sense of the order in which important events occurred, or the social and economic changes that have taken place in Britain over time, or what has shaped us as a nation. As a society we risked losing our sense of narrative and connectedness.

Partly as a result, people rely increasingly heavily on their own experience: family memories, visits to museums, historic sites or walks, and their enjoyment of looking at landscapes and buildings to inform themselves of history and to get a more vivid picture of the realities and the communities of the past. People told us they needed those experiences to enrich and inform their lives: so in turn the heritage groups have an enormous responsibility, since they may provide the only encounters with history that many people experience.

History Matters was not a policy-wonk campaign, asking for specific changes to the law, or policy. It was a heartfelt, unabashed plea for history to be recognised, valued and used to make better decisions today and tomorrow. It was, moreover, an impressive coming together of the heritage movement in the UK around a simple, clear message: *history matters – pass it on.* And since then we have seen steps forward in the teaching of history in schools, including an overhaul of the history curriculum to introduce a stronger narrative element. Whether it is enough remains to be seen, but what is clear is that people's personal experience of history through places, and the power of the spirit of place, is and will remain a critical way of being exposed to history.

History Matters also raised important questions and challenges for the movement. Are we too locked into our sites rather than looking out to the wider world? Do we just look backwards instead of forward? In tracing the evolution and patterns of past lives, can we awaken a sense of responsibility and choice to help us shape the future as well as enjoy the past? Can we use the historic environment to help us evoke concepts of stewardship and responsibility for all our surroundings?

In the last twenty years the heritage movement has undergone a revolution, rediscovering its roots which lie in popular appeal. Expanding the process of conservation and research, often focused on individual buildings, heritage has become concerned with everywhere and is the preserve of everyone. Though we unquestionably need experts and expertise to help us open our minds to the power and significance of buildings, history and landscapes, it is clear that heritage bodies should do more to enable people to discover the meaning and relevance of places for themselves, and to understand how places and their history can be meaningful to us all as citizens today. And increasingly, we realised, that is what we must do if we are to pass on a legacy worth leaving for future generations to enjoy.

We have done well in protecting our history, especially our designated historic sites. The challenge now is whether we are leaving anything worthwhile for future generations. As we go on to discuss the main engine of change in this country, urbanisation, can we draw from the experience of looking after our past to help us shape a better future?

9

Urbanisation and why good planning matters

The fight for Britain's beauty has not been only about stopping bad things, though that has certainly had its place. It has also been about how we do new things and the standards and expectations we have of our future. The most dramatic transformation of Britain in the last two centuries has been the process of urbanisation, and it has been neither easy nor comfortable for those who care about beauty; nor indeed from many other perspectives. But while urbanisation has posed arguably the biggest challenge for beauty it also, now, presents the biggest opportunity. If we can make our new and existing urban areas more beautiful, sustainable and functional we will benefit most people and build a better future.

On a chilly, bright spring day in 1989 I stood with Hugh Finn, the Chairman of CPRE's Kent branch, on the downs near Arpinge in Kent, looking down on the site where the Channel Tunnel terminal would be built. We'd just come from the green fields around Ashford which were destined for mass housing development. A high-speed railway was planned to take trains to the Channel Tunnel, a new international station at Ashford was to be the hub for tens of thousands of new houses and Kent's roads and motorways were being upgraded. Its Garden of England beauty felt more fragile than ever. Hugh Finn, a successful and worldly farmer, had a passion for the Kent countryside but was also pragmatic about its future. 'The thing is,' he said, 'we aren't going to object in principle but it all depends how this new development is done – it could be dreadful or it could work.' So the person he took me to meet was Sandy Bruce-Lockhart, recently elected to Kent County Council (he later became its Leader and later still Chair of English Heritage). His personal mission was to keep Kent beautiful while accommodating these changes. And his priority was to pursue the least-damaging route for the high-speed Channel Tunnel Rail Link. He insisted on parish meetings along every inch of the route, and forced modifications which helped it to pass less intrusively

In the 1980s and 1990s much of Kent's countryside looked and felt like a construction site: this is the M20 being built near Maidstone. (Courtesy of Derry Robinson/CPRE)

through the countryside. He achieved what Ruskin would not have believed possible, a new railway that has largely been accepted into the landscape, due not least to detailed consultation with local people and a willingness on the part of the rail company to listen, and make changes.

The pressures on Kent, though intense, were not unusual. And Finn's approach was consistent with CPRE's throughout the country. If development was agreed through the local or (in those days) county development plan we would not object, but we would fight exceptions to development plans or proposals on land within the green belt, where each breach threatened to undermine a hard-won principle. But in the late 1980s and early 1990s the pressures on the countryside seemed to be growing exponentially, and we soon worked out why.

A new phenomenon, the reverse of urbanisation, was occurring. For the first time, more people were leaving the cities than moving in to them, and the countryside was feeling the pressure. But this wasn't just bad news for the countryside, it was bad for towns and cities, because as they emptied the lifeblood drained from them. Unless we became urban campaigners too, argued CPRE's Head of Planning Tony Burton, we would never succeed in protecting the countryside.

His argument was compelling and typically well researched and rehearsed. I knew he was right. But it was a big leap of faith and credibility for a rural protection society to take on the vision of urban regeneration. Yet CPRE's *Urban Footprints* campaign, which we launched in 1992, became one of the most important we ever ran. It was also successful because our concerns resonated with those of many others. Just three years later there was a 'brownfield first' policy for new housing, and after five years an Urban Taskforce was commissioned by the government, chaired by the architect Lord Rogers, to 'establish a new vision for urban regeneration' that would 'bring people back into our cities, towns and urban neighbourhoods'.

More than eighty per cent of the British population now lives in cities, suburbs or towns. Some are thriving, creative and beautiful places but too many are not. Yet these are precisely the places that must offer us good places in which to live and work if we are to face the future with confidence. Our track record in managing urban change is not good. The process by which we became an urban nation was far from comfortable and we are still living with that legacy. It is time to put that right, and ideas about beauty, supported by good planning, can help us.

Less than three centuries ago the British population was overwhelmingly rural and based in tiny settlements. It took the world's earliest industrial revolution, combined with rapid population growth, to turn us into an overwhelmingly urban society. Between 1750 and 1900 the population of Britain multiplied five-fold and small towns like Glasgow, Newcastle, Manchester and Sheffield became vast cities. Within those 150 years the UK was transformed from a nation of farmers and rural labourers to one of urban workers.

This is the story of urbanisation: how it changed the face of Britain and how people fought for beauty as it unfolded. It is also the story of counter-urbanisation, which threatened to undermine our cities at the end of the last century. It is also the story of the values and principles we need to apply if we are to bequeath to future generations places that are good and beautiful to live in. This book has had much to say on rural beauty so far, but urban beauty is just as important, and both are vital for the future.

The very word 'urban' often strikes a dissonant chord today, perhaps because it has too often been associated with the sprawl and ugliness of many industrialising and chaotically growing cities. But the roots of the word and much of its experience, as Raymond Williams explored in *The Country and the City* (1973), are positive:

urbanity, civilisation, culture and beauty, with its origins in ancient Greece. And the earliest towns and cities in Britain were crowned by beauty: built around religious foundations they were centred on inspiring cathedrals as at York, Ely, Winchester, Canterbury, Gloucester and Worcester. During the Roman occupation of Britain, London and Cirencester were the largest of nearly thirty planned, elegant Roman towns.

The population of England fell after the Romans withdrew, some think from about four million to fewer than two million, but grew again in the twelfth and thirteenth centuries as towns developed as hubs for civic services and markets, and the base for craft guilds which were the main generators of trade and wealth. The main commodities were grain, fish, salt, wool, cloth and metals. Though today's buildings are from a much later period, we can get a glimpse of the importance of the mediaeval market-place from the beautiful seventeenth-century market halls that survive, for example, in Tetbury and Chipping Campden in the Cotswolds.

By the fourteenth century these market towns were growing rapidly. Always the largest, London reached a population of about fifty thousand by the 1340s, not long before Chaucer wrote his *Canterbury Tales*. But having reached a peak of between five and six million, England's population crashed again as around one in three people succumbed to the Black Death in the late 1340s. It took a long time for the population, and cities like York and Oxford, to recover, and England only regained its pre-Black Death population at the end of the sixteenth century. By then trade routes were opening up and people were moving to find work, especially in the fast-growing cloth industry. As we have seen, wool, the raw material for the cloth trade, had a huge impact on the landscape, but it was an influential urbanising force too, especially when, by the fifteenth century, English wool had captured the domestic market and become a vital export. Wool processing was concentrated in the

West Country, East Anglia and the West Riding, where there was both ample high-quality wool and plentiful water for wool-washing and powering the mills, with easy trade routes to ports. Wool-fuelled prosperity spread, with Long Melford in Suffolk, Stroud in Gloucestershire, and Halifax, Leeds and Wakefield in Yorkshire growing into towns adorned by great and glorious 'wool' churches and wool-merchants' manor houses. By 1520 Totnes in Devon was one of the twenty most prosperous provincial towns in England.

England's industrial revolution began early and it was based on the iron industry, which began in areas with a plentiful charcoal supply such as the Forest of Dean, the Sussex Weald and the Yorkshire Cleveland Hills. When the blast furnace was invented, cast iron for wheels, axles, guns and bullets could be manufactured, and by the late sixteenth century blast furnaces were spreading into South Wales, northern England, Derbyshire and Birmingham, laying the foundations for the industrial revolution. By then, too, coalfields had been established in the Tyne, Wear and Trent valleys and in Nottinghamshire and Yorkshire, overtaking the use of charcoal. Mineral (lead, tin and copper) and salt extraction was stepped up, and paper manufacturing began in England in the mid-sixteenth century.

In 1611 John Speed, whose town plans and county maps remain popular today, identified 605 market towns in England. Most had populations of fewer than a thousand, and though they were classed as market towns their leading tradesmen were still farmers or graziers and animals commonly roamed the streets: in Leicester 'pigs and cows went their way about the town . . . and as late as 1610 it was necessary to forbid winnowing [the separation of grain from chaff] in the streets'.

London massively outstripped other cities (the next largest was Norwich with fifteen thousand people) with a population of a quarter of a million by 1600, but despite its rapid growth it was tiny by contemporary standards. The view from the dome of Sir

Christopher Wren's 'new' St Paul's Cathedral on its completion in 1720 was still of the fields beyond.

During the seventeenth century advances took place in agriculture, technology and transport, with the first turnpike roads and their tollgates appearing around 1700. Trade and commerce were expanding at home and abroad; the East India Company, symptomatic of British colonial ambitions, was established in 1600 and grew to dominate trade with India and the Far East. But though the population was growing, even as late as 1800 the majority of people still lived in the countryside, since most processing of farm and woodland products, coal-mining and mineral extraction took place in rural areas.

The population explosion coincided with the moment when John Rickman, a Northumbrian-born government statistician, was given charge of the first official census. He had to calculate backwards to estimate that the population in 1700 had been six million, but his 1801 census recorded 8.9 million people and the number was later revised up to 9.2 million. It caught the moment of change, for from 1780 the population figures show a classic explosion, driven by both a growing birth rate and a declining death rate. People were moving, too, into the fast-growing cities of London, Liverpool, Manchester, Leeds, Sheffield, Birmingham, Coventry, Wolverhampton and Stoke-on-Trent, drawn by the new industries.

Arnold Toynbee places the beginning of the industrial revolution (a phrase he coined in the 1880s) in Britain at about 1760, and W. G. Hoffman, in his seminal study of industrialisation in the 1950s, calculated that 1780 was the first year in which the annual rate of industrial growth exceeded two per cent, where it stayed for over a century. But its early manifestations were relatively small scale and local, and some of the first images of the industrial revolution were not of ugliness but pride. Some early mill owners, such as the Greg family at Styal, whose cotton mill was constructed in

1784, built their houses proudly overlooking their factories and commissioned paintings to record them. This was also, of course, the time of significant commissions of new houses, gardens and parks.

But the first clashes with beauty were not long in coming. Arthur Young, in his *Annals of Agriculture* in 1776, captures the shocking impact of the new industries. Writing of Coalbrookdale, where Abraham Darby was pioneering the smelting of iron ore, he said:

> it is a romantic spot, it is a winding glen between two immense hills which break into various forms, and all thickly covered in wood, forming the most beautiful sheets of hanging wood. Indeed too beautiful to be much in unison with that variety of horrors art has spread at the bottom: the noise of the forges, mills and with all their vast machinery, the flames bursting from the furnaces with the burning of the coal and the smoak [sic] of the lime kilns.

And George Borrow, whose *Wild Wales* records his itineraries in the 1820s, describes looking over Neath and Merthyr Tydfil:

> I had surmounted a hill, and had nearly descended on that side of it which looked towards the east, having on my left, that is to the north, a wooded height, when an extraordinary scene presented itself to my eyes. Somewhat to the south rose immense stacks of chimneys surrounded by grimy diabolical buildings, in the neighbourhood of which were huge heaps of cinders and black rubbish. From the chimneys, notwithstanding it was Sunday, smoke was proceeding in volumes, choking the atmosphere all around.

Three industries led the industrial revolution, generating the productive power that leveraged the exploitation of the natural resources of this country: the textile industry, the iron industry and the coal industry. Between them, they changed the face of Britain.

Textile manufacture took off in the eighteenth century, leaving behind the hand-powered wool industry on which mediaeval England's prosperity had been based. John Kay's flying shuttle was patented in 1733, Lewis Paul's spinning jenny in 1738 and Arkwright's water frame in 1769. These enabled innovations such as machine-knitting and the development of specialist weaving and cloth production: wool in Leicester, cotton in Nottingham and silk in Derby. Soon even wool was being imported as home production could not keep up with the demand.

The iron industry was revolutionised when Henry Cort patented in 1783 the process for using coke to fire the furnaces for making high grade wrought iron, freeing the forge-masters from their dependence on wood. Coke furnaces multiplied across the West Midlands, South Yorkshire and North Durham. Abraham Darby's iron bridge, the first in the world, was built in Coalbrookdale in 1779. As well as iron, the introduction of brass (the alloy of copper and zinc) stimulated the metal trades industry of Birmingham, the City of a Thousand Trades, whose workers were home- rather than factory-based.

Coal, though, was the great enabler. From being a country dominated by ores and minerals (Cornwall having been the world's largest producer of tin and copper) coal production in Britain grew from a mere three million tons in 1700 to ten million tons a century later, then expanded massively with forty-eight million tons being mined by 1854 and 185 million tons by 1914. It was Britain's universal fuel: used to heat domestic houses, to produce lime for mortar and farming, for smelting and metal-working; and it took the place of wood in the manufacture of salt, sugar and soap, in the making of glass, bricks, tiles, and for dyeing and brewing. James Watt's steam engine, patented in 1769, not only revolutionised the production of coal, by enabling mines to be pumped free of water, but also fired the machinery and transport revolution it triggered. Coal was king; as Arthur Young wrote in 1791: 'all the activity and industry of this kingdom is fast concentrating where there are coal pits.'

Coal had to be transported, of course, and before the railways its main carrier was water: over three thousand miles of canals were built between 1660 and 1850, adding to nearly seven hundred miles of already navigable rivers.

But it was the movement of people that forced the fastest change and triggered the unmanaged growth of many cities, fuelled by both an exodus from rural areas and a rapidly growing population, especially in the industrialising Midlands and North. Josiah Wedgwood opened his works in Burslem in 1759 after which the Potteries towns' populations burgeoned. Liverpool, trading across the Atlantic, including with the West Indies, grew from 10,000 people in 1720 to 78,000 by 1800, and over 350,000 by 1850. Manchester grew eight-fold in the eighty years between 1720 and 1800 and another four-fold to over 400,000 people by 1850: its suburb of Medlock going from open country to 'forests of chimneys, clouds of smoke and volumes of vapour, like the seething of some stupendous cauldron' in the few years after 1836. In just five years between 1831 and 1836 a total of 156 new streets were built in Sheffield.

It was not all ugliness and poverty. The centres of these cities were the focus for extravagant construction and reconstruction, with civic buildings, town halls and art galleries commissioned to show off the wealth and sophistication of the city and its leading figures: Sheffield's Cutlers' Hall was built in 1832; Liverpool's St George's Hall in 1854 and Manchester's Gothic Town Hall in 1877. New urban parks were established and laid out with elaborate planting schemes and recreational facilities for the public; the first in Preston in the 1830s, followed by Birkenhead, Derby and Southampton. London's first public park was Victoria Park, in Hackney, in 1842, and many others followed, adding to its earlier commons, pleasure gardens and royal parks (often former deer parks). By 1900 most towns and cities in Britain had one or more public parks providing benefits to all the population, especially the opportunity for health-giving exercise in the cities' crowded centres.

Elegance was the dominant feature of the spa towns, where the restorative powers of mineral-rich spring water attracted people to bathe and take cures, in Bath, Harrogate, Buxton, Cheltenham and Tunbridge Wells. And attractive coastal resorts sprang up after the Prince of Wales (later George IV) visited Brighton in 1783, making fashionable sea-bathing and imbibing the bracing coastal air. John Nash's elaborate Brighton Pavilion was built between 1786 and 1822, and Scarborough, Margate and Worthing developed piers, guest-houses, theatres and assembly rooms.

London too had its prestige buildings, extensive parks and elegant boulevards, but it was also the place of deepest contrasts. In 1801 a million people, one in ten of the English, were Londoners. Its public squares and glamorous buildings, as well as its size and strategic influence, were the cause of envy, but still for every beautiful street there were acres of poverty-stricken chaos, and it was described in 1841 by a German visitor as an 'extraordinary admixture of the beautiful and the mean'. And for the majority of its residents it was mean. Dickens' *Oliver Twist*, written in 1837, describes the grim Jacob's Island, close to Tower Bridge:

> the inhabitants of the houses on either side lowering, from their back doors and windows, buckets, pails, domestic utensils of all kinds, in which to haul water

up . . . crazy wooden galleries come on to the back of half-a-dozen houses, with holes from which to look at the slime beneath; windows, broken and patched, with poles thrust out, on which to dry the linen that is never there; rooms so small, so filthy, so confined that the air would seem too tainted even for the dirt and squalor which they shelter.

And as Cobbett, travelling through England in the 1820s, described, the soul-destroying greed of London, 'the great Wen', sucked people and the wholesome produce of the countryside into its all-consuming, miserable clutches.

The social consequences of filthy, overcrowded courts and alleys, and poorly built houses with no sanitation or clean water raised serious moral questions. Octavia Hill's maternal grandfather, Thomas Southwood Smith, a doctor, was a leading figure for social and sanitary reform. His friend and colleague Edwin Chadwick, who had trained as a barrister but was fast becoming a social reformer, was employed by a Royal Commission appointed to look into the operation of the Poor Laws. Appalled by what he found, at his own expense he undertook and published in 1842 a *Report on the Sanitary Condition of the Labouring Population*. He concluded:

That the various forms of epidemic, endemic, and other disease caused, or aggravated, or propogated chiefly amongst the labouring classes by atmospheric impurities produced by decomposing animal and vegetable substances, by damp and filth, and close and overcrowded dwellings prevail amongst the population in every part of the kingdom, whether dwelling in separate houses, in rural villages, in small towns, in the larger towns – as they have been found to prevail in the lowest districts of the metropolis.

Anyone who could do so escaped from such horrors. Although we think of suburbs as a twentieth-century phenomenon the first were built a hundred years earlier to house those who could afford to live apart from their place of employment to avoid the noise, dirt, smoke and bustle. Thus the merchants, cutlers, better-off shop-keepers and emerging professional classes built spacious and elegant houses in Camberwell, Lewisham, Stepney, Hackney, Islington or Kensington, and their equivalents in northern cities. Though many of these houses fell into disrepair in the first half of the twentieth century they are now again among the most desirable (and expensive) places to live.

By the mid-nineteenth century the railway had begun to impose itself on urban and rural landscapes alike. George Stephenson's locomotive engine, developed in 1814, triggered investment in local railway lines. Though initially unco-ordinated, by the 1840s railway lines were radiating out from London and connecting all the major towns of England. The rail-way had the most extraordinary impact. Land hunger broke out as stations were constructed, driving up property values nearby, and the railway termini were the excuse for extravagant, monu-mental buildings, such as the Midland Grand Hotel at St Pancras, now restored. Many shared Ruskin's dislike of railways, 'the iron veins that traverse the frame of our country'. George Eliot's Dorothea Casaubon in *Middlemarch* feared its arrival, knowing it would bring profound change to the landscape she loved. Dickens described in precise detail the impact – he likened it to 'an earth-quake which rent the whole neighbourhood to its centre' – of the construction of the Camden Town cutting in *Dombey and Son*: 'carcasses of ragged tenements, and fragments of unfinished walls and arches, and piles of scaffolding, and wildernesses of bricks, and giant forms of cranes, and tripods straddling above nothing'. But the railways could scarcely be ignored as they transformed the cities, connected the towns, and enabled new markets by transporting goods so quickly. And today we value much Victorian infrastructure, especially the railways, not least because we appreciate the skill and quality of their design.

England was rapidly becoming an urban country: in 1851 half of England's population lived in towns but by 1911 it was four-fifths of a population that had nearly quadrupled in size since 1801, from nine million to 32.5 million. The economy was fired by coal, which served not only domestic industry but the world's, with nearly one third of the 185 million tons extracted in 1914 exported. The dependence on iron gave way to steel in the 1870s, stimulated by demand from the railways.

As early as 1911 the grip of the North was receding with the decline in prosperity of the old coalfields. Manufacturing was shifting away from the coalfields to Teesside, the East Midlands and Home Counties, and around the railway towns of Crewe, Swindon and Rugby. The railways were also responsible for a new breed of dormitory towns, which sprang up between ten and thirty miles from London. The railway companies were in the land-speculation business, offering knock-down fares to the new breed of commuters to whom they also sold a house on land they developed near their stations. It was a highly profitable enterprise and of the four million houses built in England and Wales between 1851 and 1911 most were in the South East. Radlett, Dorking, Sevenoaks and Amersham grew around London, and Altrincham and West Kirby (Wirral) around Manchester and Liverpool. The railways also brought the coastal resorts within easy reach, with Bournemouth, Blackpool and Southport reaching their heydays in the early twentieth century.

Different elements of urbanisation triggered different aspects of the fight for beauty, as we saw in chapters one and two. While Octavia Hill's mission was to bring physical beauty into the life of the most deprived urban residents, including her housing tenants, the early twentieth century challenge was to stop sprawl by containing urban areas and protecting the countryside. But running through both of these were harder questions which are still very much in play today, to decide *how* and *what* should be built to meet people's needs, especially housing and its design. This, and the place of beauty within it, is a debate that has preoccupied all those who have sought to address the many challenges thrown up by urbanisation.

As the nineteenth century drew to a close public authorities accepted that they had a responsibility for improving people's lives, and their primary concern was public health. So the top priority for the early municipal authorities was slum clearance and providing new housing, though what they constructed was very different – to Octavia Hill's dismay – from the small-scale, intimate developments, based around a personal relationship between landlord and tenant that she had fostered. Re-housing often meant relocation to large, new, purpose-built accommodation, and the population in the centres of Birmingham, Leeds, Liverpool and Manchester fell as the slums were cleared and people moved to new housing in outlying areas. The 'hollowing out' process that would reach its peak in the late twentieth century had begun.

But Octavia Hill was not alone in believing that there was more to life than fulfilling material needs. Some of the earliest providers of new housing were not public bodies but philanthropic industrialists, to whom the adverse effects of appalling housing and living conditions on their workers were evident. Motivated by religious as well as human concerns, they wanted to create places where good and healthy lives would reap good and healthy workers.

The first experiment had been at New Lanark, when a cotton mill built at the Falls of Clyde was accompanied by a manufacturing village designed on the principles articulated by Robert Owen in his *New View of Society* (1816): 'Any general character, from the best to the worst, from the most ignorant to the most enlightened, may be given to any community, even to the world at large, by the application of proper means.' New Lanark's owner, Mr Dale of Glasgow, applied those 'proper means' to build a new community with houses, a school and chapel to provide for the workers and their families educational, moral and social support structures.

Others followed his lead. In 1879 the Quaker Cadbury family decided to move their cocoa and chocolate business from its central (Broad Street) Birmingham site to an estate four miles south of the city, in a village called Bournbrook. They named their new site Bournville, and built sixteen houses for workers alongside the factory. They were so popular that by 1900 the estate consisted of 313 cottages, schools, a Ruskin Hall and Friends' meeting house, and it was surrounded by parks and gardens. Beauty and good design were central elements in the plans.

In 1888 the Liverpool-based Lever Brothers' soap-making firm moved from Warrington to a new factory complete with a model village, Port Sunlight, on the banks of the Mersey. Its 720 attractive houses, of Arts and Crafts design, with gardens and communal green spaces, church and Sunday schools, shops, hospital and museum, were a world away from its workers' former homes. As Mr William Hesketh Lever explained, his vision was to 'build houses in which our workpeople will be able to live and be comfortable . . . To know more about the science of living than in a back slum, and in which they will learn that there is more enjoyment in life than the mere going to and coming from work.'

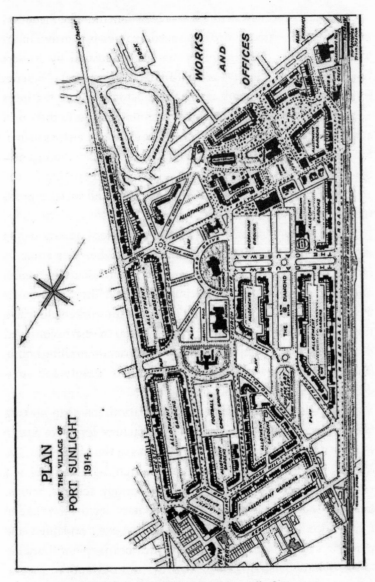

Port Sunlight – one of the philanthropically driven new settlements providing good housing, civic life and a pleasant environment for the employees of Lever Brothers.

On a smaller scale, Joseph Rowntree in York founded the village of Earswick in 1902 for 'the improvement of the condition of the working classes ... by the provision of improved dwellings with open spaces, and, where possible, gardens ... with such facilities for the enjoyment of full and healthy lives'. The parallels with Octavia Hill's housing schemes are clear. But these were still small-scale initiatives when seen against the magnitude of the problems facing the urban poor, to which a more ambitious response was needed.

In stepped the unlikely figure of Ebenezer Howard, a short-hand writer in the House of Commons. He had spent too long listening to the verbose speeches of MPs, whose expressions of dismay at appalling living conditions in cities were matched only by the paucity of their actions. Inspired by Ruskin and Morris and their search for utopia he published in 1898 *Tomorrow! A Peaceful Path to Real Reform*. In it he argued for nothing less than razing the discredited cities to the ground. In their place new communities free from the evils of urbanisation should be built. Those communities – he called them Garden Cities – would draw on the sanitary health and clean living of the countryside, and unite the advantages of an energetic and active town life with the beauty and delight of the country. His pamphlet opened with Blake's 'Jerusalem', and was littered with quotes from Ruskin, Tolstoy and Goethe. It was as much a moral proposition as a practical plan, but it set out what was needed: the purchase of land (six thousand acres), a central, circular form for the Garden City which on a thousand acres would house thirty thousand people in 5,500 separate lots. There would be a surrounding 'green belt' of five thousand acres of agricultural land, with occasional buildings (convalescent homes and the like) catering for a further two thousand people. The Garden City would have six magnificent boulevards converging on a central garden containing public and municipal buildings including a town hall, concert and lecture hall, theatre, library, museum, picture gallery and hospital.

Unlike previous 'out-of-town' developments this was not to be a suburb or dormitory; in fact it was their antithesis. It was to be a self-sustaining community with its own ethos, economy and autonomy. Howard imposed a strict limit of 32,000 people; and imagined his Garden Cities grouped around a central city connected by futuristic railway systems. The existing cities, especially London, would be purposefully depopulated, their slums pulled down and their empty spaces filled with parks and gardens. Howard's ideas were a profound rejection of the unplanned chaos of the eighteenth- and nineteenth-century cities and a commitment to co-ordinated town planning and social improvement.

Howard then had to get a Garden City built. By 1899 he had established a Garden City Association (on which George Cadbury, among others, sat) and by 1903 the company, First Garden City Ltd, was issuing shares and searching for a suitable location. The following year it lit on the tiny hamlet of Letchworth in Hertfordshire, and appointed as architects Raymond Unwin and Barry Parker, devotees of Ruskin and the Arts and Crafts movement. But their, and Howard's, ideals were heavily compromised in the construction of the City. The railway was driven through the middle rather than kept to the periphery. Unwin and Parker's designs were deemed too expensive so cheaper, and inevitably uglier housing was substituted, and the location of the railway and industrial plants meant that the city became divided between a working-class north and a middle-class south. Moreover the typical Letchworth resident was caricatured in the press as a bit of a crank. Nevertheless the population reached nine thousand by 1914 and with its parks, gardens and leafy lanes became attractive to those fleeing London. In the end, though, Letchworth and its successor Welwyn Garden City became what Howard did not want them to be: middle-class commuter towns.

Despite Howard's efforts, London was anything but abandoned and, as we have seen, Clough Williams-Ellis' 'octopus' of suburbanisation continued to expand its tentacles outwards, triggering the second big fight about beauty. London County Council decided to stem the sprawl. In the same year (1935) as the Ribbon Development Act was passed, it accepted Raymond Unwin's proposal for 'a narrow green girdle' around the city, made in the *Second Report of the Greater London Regional Plan Committee*. A Green Belt (London and Home Counties) Act followed in 1938, introducing one of the most important principles of twentieth-century planning, the green belt, whose purpose was to separate town from country and prevent sprawl. It was later reinforced by Duncan Sandys' 1955 Green Belt Circular which encouraged all local authorities to consider establishing one. Introducing it to Parliament, Sandys said, 'for the well-being of our people and for the preservation of the countryside, we have a duty to do all we can to prevent the further unrestricted sprawl of the great cities.' By 1969 there were fourteen green belts around major cities: Bournemouth and the south coast towns, Bristol/Bath, Birmingham/Coventry, Oxford, Cambridge, Sheffield, Nottingham/Derby, Chester, Cheltenham, York, Merseyside/Manchester, Leeds/Bradford, and Tyneside and Sunderland. One more was designated around Durham in 1995.

Urban containment was the watchword for the protection of beauty in both town and country. It was motivated by the need to stop sprawl into the countryside, but what happened within towns and cities was at least as important. And so the 1944 White Paper *The Control of Land Use*, emphasising the principle of the 'right use of land,' was swiftly followed by the commissioning of Sir Patrick Abercrombie to draw up a plan for the reconstruction of London after the war. It had problems both old and new: in addition to its legacy of slums, large areas had been destroyed by bombing, people had been moved out of the centre, and there was industrial upheaval due to the focus on wartime production. It needed rethinking and replanning. Abercrombie's *Greater London Plan* was published in 1944 to meet the government's objectives of 'providing the foundations for Greater London upon which homes, work and fresh food can be supplied not only quickly but permanently in full measure'.

To achieve this he proposed four concentric zones: an inner ring, the heart of London, where industry would be moved out and green space moved in; a second ring of well-planned suburbs; third the green belt, at ten miles wide far bigger than Unwin's 'green girdle'; and fourth an outer rural ring within which eight new satellite towns would be located, each with accompanying industry, housing and social facilities. Abercrombie was determined that the future would be different from the past: 'Would a repetition of London's sprawl be something we would want to show our allies as our contribution to the remaking of the world?' he asked, rhetorically. As important, to him, as the technicalities of planning for London's future was the quality of design: 'if we . . . produce something really worthy of humanity today, we may be sure that posterity will honour us for its inheritance.'

His words reflected frustration at the desperately poor quality of much of what had been built in the 1920s and 1930s. In the Garden Cities, architectural standards and good design had at least been an explicit objective, but as Abercrombie commented, 'London . . . can take no pride in the bulk of the 600,000 houses that were built on her ever-expanding outskirts between the wars.' Though architects were always engaged for public or municipal buildings, Abercrombie blamed both the builders and the Building Societies for their complete lack of interest in the design of housing. The rows of bungalows or sham Tudor houses, the failure to consider indigenous materials or building styles, or the poor workmanship of much of what was built combined to result in houses 'shelled out like peas' in which communities never formed.

Once again, though, it proved easier to build anew than to improve what was already there. The idea of New Towns, in Abercrombie's outer ring, was picked up with alacrity by the government and implemented by the New Towns Act of 1946. Although the process got off to a bumpy start, thanks largely to Lord Reith's intervention New Towns were built around London at Stevenage, Crawley, Hemel Hempstead, Harlow, Welwyn Garden City, Hatfield, Basildon and Brackley; at Ayliffe and Peterlee near Durham; Cwmbran in the Welsh Valleys and Corby in Northamptonshire. They were seen as an ideal solution to the country's housing needs, providing good places for people to live. But in practice there was little to differentiate them from the suburbs and many became lonely places to live, leading to the epithet 'new town blues'.

The government's next step was more profound, with its introduction of the Town and Country Planning Act 1947 which brought almost all kinds of development (except, of course, those relating to agriculture and forestry) under planning control. It was a central part of the post-war vision for a balanced, harmonious approach and its aim was to guide development to the most appropriate locations and resist it where it would cause damage; so protecting the countryside and helping towns and cities to grow in an orderly way. Its main instruments were Development Plans for each local authority, co-ordinated to ensure the nation's overall needs were met. By covering the whole country they were intended to provide certainty about where housing, factories and commercial buildings, schools, hospitals and roads should be built and where they should not. It also enshrined the principle that good agricultural land should not be wasted by building on it.

Stevenage New Town, planned and built in the 1950s to accommodate
overspill from London. (Courtesy of the JR James Archive)

The 1947 Act represents the essence of good planning within
the post-war vision: necessary development should be enabled,
but uncontrolled sprawl should be stopped and important public
interests, including the protection of the beauty of the countryside,
should be safeguarded. What it could not always dictate was how
development needs should be met, and although well intentioned,
the pressure to continue clearing slums and re-house people led to
decisions that today we think of as mistakes, especially high-rise
flats replacing terraced streets and large housing estates with too
few community facilities.

The government also needed to plan for new infrastructure: the
power stations and lines that from the 1950s were needed to supply
people with electricity. The National Grid had been established in
1926 to co-ordinate Britain's fragmented electricity supply, and by
1950 a 275 kV transmission system for the whole of the UK was in

place. Increasing demand for electricity led to pressure for new power-stations – often coal-fired stations on major rivers such as the Trent in Nottinghamshire, though the first generation of nuclear power was introduced in the 1950s (one, Trawsfynydd, controversially located in the Snowdonia National Park) – and a grid system updated to carry 400 kV electricity, which was completed by the 1960s.

There was at that time little debate about whether these were necessary and little consideration of their impact on the landscape. Only the National Parks Commission had a mandate to consider this, and its annual reports from the beginning record concerns about the visual intrusion of overhead lines, for example in Langdale and Martindale in the heart of the Lake District (1950), next to Hadrian's Wall in Northumberland and through Snowdonia's Vale of Ffestiniog (1952). In its Second Report (1951) it says, 'we . . . believe that in both the National Parks and elsewhere in the countryside there are areas of exceptional beauty where it will be essential for lines to be laid underground if serious disfigurement is to be avoided.' But for cost reasons this proved impossible, and it took until 2015 for the National Grid to agree to put underground some of the most intrusive power lines. Its decision will benefit Dorset near Winterbourne Abbas, the New Forest near Hale, the Peak District near Dunford Bridge and the same stretch of the Vale of Ffestiniog that so troubled the National Parks Commission in 1952. But high-voltage power lines were never the only problem: in the rapidly developing 1950s it was just as often local electricity and phone lines, their trailing wires disfiguring historic villages and towns, that triggered complaints.

The planning system did its best to cope with all the demands on it, but by the 1950s the cumulative impact of the clutter of streetlights and signposts, overhead wires and road improvements invading the countryside, the suburbanising effect and poor quality of design of most new buildings, and the insidious shift of housing and other developments out of once-vibrant town centres once again caused rebellion. The critics were again architects, and Ian Nairn was their voice, writing in a special edition of *The Architectural Review* of 1955 entitled *Outrage* that:

> everywhere where the borough engineer cracks the town wide open with road-widening . . . or obliterates the market-place with a useless flower-garden, and everywhere outside where one department or another dumps a camp, a housing estate, or a sewage disposal plant into the indifferent wild – everywhere we are levelling down two ideal extremes to a uniform mean: a mean which is a threat not simply to our felicity but to our continued development as more than an order of termites.

The sins were many. The wholesale redevelopment of town centres like Coventry destroyed the patina of an evolved mediaeval town, even one that had been bombed in the Blitz. The new tower-blocks, often (deliberately) architecturally brutal, had failed in their purpose: they were not only more wasteful of land because of the bleak, dead spaces in between them, but they also destroyed the community spirit of the older terraced streets. Suburban estates continued to creep across once rural areas. *Outrage* accused the planning profession of 'twisting the Brave New World' envisaged by post-war idealism to 'become the decanting of overspills evenly throughout the country – Subtopia'.

Yet the perennial problem of finding sites for large numbers of new houses did not go away and the planning system was the best mechanism to decide how and where to accommodate them. In the early 1960s a second generation of New Towns was built at Telford, Redditch, Skelmersdale, Runcorn, Warrington and

Urban renewal could get it wrong, obliterating all signs of the past and shattering communities – today we can do better. (Courtesy of Wikimedia Images)

Washington. Towards the end of the decade Milton Keynes was proposed on an altogether bigger scale, and large expansions were agreed for Peterborough and Northampton. By 1971 the twenty-eight New Towns in Britain (twenty-one in England, two in Wales and five in Scotland) accommodated 1.4 million people, and many more were housed in large extensions to existing settlements. The Lower Earley development near Reading of the late 1970s was typical of its time and design, with a variety of off-plan choices for house-buyers, though none bore much relation to the vernacular architecture or local materials of the area. CPRE's ambitions of the 1930s for the embracing of local building styles and materials in new developments seemed a forlorn hope.

The car, of course, was responsible for many of the problems. For an ever more prosperous population, car ownership represented freedom, and in the 1930s a young engineer, William Morris of Oxford, had provided the answer. His first invention, the Bullnose Morris, was made in 1912 but by the 1930s his affordable family car, the Morris Minor, was universally popular. In 1935 there were over a million private cars on the road, and between 1951, 1961 and 1971 the proportion of households owning a car leapt from just over ten per cent to twenty-nine per cent to forty-four per cent; it is now over seventy-five per cent. The pressures of traffic caused problems in town and country, with new roads bulldozed through town centres, and dual carriageways and (later) motorways built to move traffic faster between towns, while the suburbs became almost entirely car-oriented. From the 1960s onwards the car dominated planners' thinking, making housing developments even more land hungry, taking people off the streets and contributing to suburban isolation as well as unsustainability.

Recalling earlier generations of conservationists, Philip Larkin summed up the risk that the countryside would be subsumed by the car's greed:

> I thought it would last my time –
> The sense that, beyond the town,
> There would always be fields and farms,
> Where the village louts could climb
> Such trees as were not cut down;
> I knew there'd be false alarms . . .
>
> . . . And that will be England gone,
> The shadows, the meadows, the lanes,
> The guildhalls, the carved choirs.
> There'll be books; it will linger on
> In galleries; but all that remains
> For us will be concrete and tyres.
> (Philip Larkin, 'Going, Going', 1972)

Back in the 1920s the car had not at first been seen as a threat. Indeed 'motoring' was associated with the townsman's natural desire to explore the countryside. The Roads Beautifying Association was founded in 1928 by Wilfrid Fox as a positive measure to ensure that the new roads being built around London were attractive and well designed, and in 1954 the Department of Transport set up a Landscape Advisory Committee which scrutinised all proposals for new roads and improvements: it lasted until 1994. When Roads Minister John Hayes gave CPRE's annual lecture in 2015 he called for beauty to be taken more seriously in road design; his intervention, though welcome, was a reminder of the days when his department had tried to do just that.

Because roads and road improvements were soon, inevitably, in conflict with beauty. It was, after all, roads that had triggered the scourge of ribbon development, and were blamed for urban sprawl. During the 1920s the number of motor cars on the road was doubling each year and petrol stations with garish fascias began to proliferate, the first one opened by the AA at Aldermaston in Berkshire in 1920.

The first stretch of the M1 opened in 1959, triggering a mixture of pride, freedom and curiosity. But as the early motorways filled up an altogether more controversial relationship developed. By the 1970s the Department of Transport's road programme consisted of large numbers of bypasses, road improvements and new motorways or near-motorway-standard roads. While many were justified they required vast quantities of quarried aggregate and were often very poorly designed, cutting through beautiful countryside and historic parks without apparent regret. The National Trust became embroiled in damaging proposals affecting Saltram House near Plymouth, Petworth Park in Sussex, which would have been bisected by a bypass, and Ascott House in Buckinghamshire, threatened by a bypass for Wing. While the last two were stopped, the construction of the A38 through Saltram Park was a rare occasion when the concerns of the National Trust were overruled.

By the 1980s the fight about roads had become intense. The problem was traffic growth forecasts which the department appeared honour bound to meet. But new roads generate more traffic, so more roads needed to be built to accommodate it, in an ever-perpetuating circle. As a result, the ambition of the roads programme grew, and the environmental groups turned *en masse* from mitigators to objectors. The first 'motorway' to which CPRE objected in principle was the upgraded A14 from Felixstowe to the M6/M1 junction in the Midlands, which threatened a particularly tranquil part of rural Northamptonshire. The distribution sheds and undistinguished development which now line long stretches of this road show how justified our concerns were. As the roads programme grew, the fights became ever more bitter and high profile, and road protestors became celebrities who were admired and criticised in equal measure. But eventually the brutal destruction of St Catherine's Hill near Winchester to deliver the M3 extension, and the controversial A34 Newbury bypass (where 'Swampy' famously led the protesters, who tunnelled, climbed trees and lay in front of bulldozers) forced a retreat. And though these bruising encounters and the financial restraints of the 1990s and 2000s curtailed the ambitions of the roads programme, many road schemes are now reappearing, justified as a way of kick-starting the economy.

In towns and cities the fights about cars were just as intense. The 1950s and 1960s witnessed a series of brutal road schemes which demolished historic town centres and constructed concrete flyovers: the M4 within London, Spaghetti Junction outside Birmingham and the vast interchange at Hangar Lane in west London. Communities were chopped in half and air pollution levels rose. Colin Buchanan's *Traffic in Towns* report (1963) tried to turn the arguments on their head. Rather than focus on how to keep traffic moving, Buchanan argued, the first priority should be people and the quality of the urban environment: roads should be subjugated to other needs. His wise report was only feebly implemented and though many town centres have been pedestrianised we are still grappling with the problem of urban traffic and pollution. Yet the modern alternative to town centre redevelopment – the out-of-town shopping centre – was hardly better. Shopping malls attract huge numbers of cars and pull investment out of town centres, triggering a contemporary version of 1930s sprawl. Roadside clutter – signs, kerbs, road markings and street furniture – can dominate the view.

It is hard, therefore, to conclude other than that the city has been in decline ever since the entirely meritorious attempts to clear the slums began. In spite of concerns about the profligate use of land which underpinned the first planning laws, in practice planning policy has struggled to fulfil its aims of both sustaining the cities and protecting the countryside. The Garden City movement, New Towns and the expansion of suburbia were all signs, some explicitly stated, of a lack of confidence in the cities. In an increasingly market-led system of housing provision, homes were built where the market wanted them, and that was neither in the slum-ridden older city hearts nor in the exhaust-fuelled, concrete jungles that replaced them.

By the late 1980s the issue was not just about where to put new houses but the sheer scale of what was claimed to be needed. This was driven by the statistical art of household projections which, just like traffic forecasts, tried to predict how many households there would be in future. As prosperity rose and family structure became more fragmented and diverse, so the trend was towards more, smaller households, many of just one person. CPRE's task became ever more demanding as, in the mid-1990s, the Department of the Environment revised its household projections upwards, suggesting that 4.4 million new households would be formed between 1991 and 2016, and that houses would have to be provided for them all. This triggered many planning applications for new 'settlements' (most no longer even pretending to be more than enormous housing estates) on green-field sites in Hampshire, Oxfordshire and Essex; and proposed releases of green belt around Chester, and in Tyne and Wear, the West Midlands and West and South Yorkshire. Controversies about the quality of what would be built were even greater, because in 1980 the government had instructed local authorities, in its infamous Circular 22/80, that design was none of their business. As Carolyn McGhie and Richard Girling wrote in a publication for CPRE in 1995, *Local Attraction*: 'freed from constraint, developers ran riot . . . a mass of factory-made housing products that smothered local identity, substituted low-density sprawl for clustered village communities and turned everything it touched into a suburb.' It took many years of lobbying and protest before a number of local authorities followed the example of the best, exemplified by Suffolk County Council's *Design Guide*, and began to exercise muscles of taste and offer advice on how to build beautifully, drawing on local dialect and tradition to create a legacy future generations may cherish. As a result the quality of new housing has improved, but we are still a long way from achieving the ideal in many places.

Underlying all the pressures and strains of the 1990s was the newly recognised phenomenon of the reversal of the long process of urbanisation. More people were now leaving the cities than moving there. Between 1971 and 1991 the population of non-metropolitan areas increased by ten per cent, and that of metropolitan areas decreased by between five per cent (South Yorkshire) and twenty per cent (Merseyside). England's major cities lost three hundred people a day over those twenty years. Partly as a result the area of derelict and vacant land in urban areas (in 1993 six hundred square kilometres) was growing, combining the remnants of industrial activity with land abandoned after the demolition of unfit housing. It was not surprising that the poor environment of urban areas was driving people away. At CPRE it was clear that our campaigning focus needed to change.

A rural campaigning group arguing for urban regeneration was, to some, a surprise. But its roots were in our history: having argued for the application of urban planning to the countryside, we now wanted to see proactive urban planning revived.

Advocates for the future of the cities had very similar concerns. Lord Rogers has written:

> by the latter half of the twentieth century urban depopulation, new towns and car-based suburban sprawl had brought their own problems. They created a toxic legacy of hollowed-out cities, scarred with derelict and brownfield sites, abandoned by those middle class families able to make that choice, and with communities deserted by failing local services from schools to shops. These threatening urban voids were not just a terrible waste of land, but also of human potential.

Governments had known since the 1920s that urban sprawl was bad and since the 1940s had aspired to the 'right use of land'. Yet in spite of planning's successes, we risked seeing the worst of both worlds. Cities were spiralling downwards and the countryside was coming under intolerable, suburbanising pressure.

At CPRE our aims were clear: first, that the household projections should inform the debate but not be a target; second, that more new housing should be on brownfield, not green-field sites, forcing a commitment to investment in housing and the environment of urban areas; and third that there should be a determined effort to revitalise the centres of cities and large towns, making them places where people wanted to live. We speculated on a time when people would linger in street cafés in leafy city streets, able to walk to work because they lived locally or 'above the shop' in restored commercial buildings, or could travel easily by improved public transport. Though the idea of street cafés in our chilly climate raised more than one eyebrow these things are no longer dreams.

Though we had to overcome much scepticism, the quality of our research and arguments gained us credibility, and we soon had our first success. John Gummer, who in 1993 had stopped the expansion of out-of-town shopping centres, was now the Secretary of State in charge of household projections and we suspected that privately he liked them as little as we did. In 1996 he introduced the first 'brownfield first' policy, requiring at least fifty per cent of new housing to be built on previously used land.

This decision was transformational. It changed investment patterns and it changed behaviour, forcing attention to be paid to urban regeneration rather than green-field sites. And it stayed. It caught the attention of the new Labour government, elected in May 1997, and within months the new Secretary of State, John Prescott, had increased the target to sixty per cent, and commissioned an Urban Task Force chaired by Lord Rogers of Riverside. CPRE's Tony Burton was asked to join it. And when the Task Force's far-reaching report came out, it argued cogently for an urban renaissance, calling for people and housing to be brought back into the heart of cities; for investment in public goods including green space, public transport, walking and cycling; for an integrated approach for planning the services and facilities people need and to reclaim the brownfield, derelict and abandoned land that compromised the quality of the urban environment and wasted both land and opportunity.

The ideas promoted by the Urban Task Force inspired change.

Public money was poured into regeneration schemes in Sheffield, Manchester, Birmingham and London. Kings Cross and St Pancras stations are beautiful portals to London once again; there is even talk of the Euston Arch being restored. Urban public transport systems – the London tube, and trams and buses elsewhere – have been improved beyond recognition. International sports events like the Commonwealth and Olympic Games have drawn investment and confidence to once-derelict places. The cities that bid for or became Cities of Culture have presided over renewed vibrancy: giant spiders in Manchester, china elephants in London and a burning shrine in Derry have demonstrated the power of cultural regeneration in stimulating pride in and affection for city living. And the Heritage Lottery Fund, the successor body to the NHMF, has dispensed over £640 million to over 700 urban parks since 1996, offering a lifeline to these critical but neglected green spaces, renewing their capacity to refresh people and improve the quality of urban life.

But there is still a long way to go. Beauty is still too low in public bodies' priorities, and while some new architectural commissions are inspiring, the quality of much new urban design, especially housing, remains poor. There is a tension between 'statement' buildings and glitzy shopping centres, which attract inward investment, and the need to provide places where people can live, work and meet their daily needs. Green space and trees, parks and access to nature are too often left out of the equation. The Commission on Architecture and the Built Environment, created to lead the quality of urban regeneration, was abolished in 2010 in the 'bonfire of the quangos', along with the Regional Development Agencies which, though expensive to run, were able to take a strategic approach to development. The 'brownfield first' policy is slipping back to sixty per cent from its height of eighty per cent and once again we have a housing crisis, with renewed calls for protection of the green belt and green fields to be relaxed. Yet as Richard Rogers has pointed out, there is enough brownfield land in East London to build several towns the size of Ebbsfleet, the new commuter dormitory in Kent, and simply by remodelling London's six hundred high streets, space could be found for more than seven years' supply of homes. A 2015 report suggested that a million new homes could be built in London, and would encourage the regeneration of run-down parts of the city. And we are becoming more confident about how to remodel cities for a low carbon future, with work by Future Cities Catapult and ideas about Smart Growth, imported from the USA, offering innovative ideas about how urban areas can be made beautiful, efficient and sustainable.

The same principles apply, of course, to smaller cities and towns, where there is much energy devoted to putting these ideas into practice. The *Transition Towns* movement in particular aims to help communities move towards more sustainable living. Totnes, in the 1520s one of the most prosperous mediaeval towns in England, is now a pioneer Transition Town, describing itself as 'a dynamic, community-led and run charity that exists to strengthen the local economy, reduce the cost of living and build our resilience for a future with less cheap energy and a changing climate'. 'Incredible Edible' Todmorden is an example of a place where vegetable growing in the heart of the community connects people with where their food comes from, and encourages pride and involvement. As the Urban Task Force said, 'in a well governed city, urban living and civic pride go hand in hand'.

But the main lesson we have learned is that, if we are to create and regenerate urban areas that are beautiful and satisfying to live in, thinking about housing is not enough. People also need jobs, shops, doctors' surgeries, schools, parks and green spaces where trees and nature flourish, and good local transport, all near enough

We can build beautifully and sustainably in both town and
country if we choose to (this development is in Cambridge).
Getting both right is critical for our future.

to each other so that city life is not dependent on cars and long
cross-city journeys. The need today is to build beautifully, to
re-shape urban areas within existing city boundaries and to provide
new services and facilities, not only to protect the countryside but
also to provide the best opportunities and quality for urban life. As
the London National Park City movement observes: 'together we
can make London a greener, healthier and fairer place to live.'

And to achieve all that we need good planning. Not just good
land-use planning, which remains one of the best surviving tools of
the post-war objectives for harmonisation, but good *place-based*
planning: planning which makes and sustains good places to live,
not just imposes national housing, health and education policies
on places. And to achieve this, people need to be involved in

plan-making and to shape their own future. There are opportunities here with the commitment, in the new breed of local plans, to neighbourhood planning, and listening to what local communities say. ResPublica's 2015 report *A Community Right to Beauty* goes further, arguing that we should extend the planning process to give people the power to reject ugliness and improve the quality of urban design, and the beauty of their surroundings. And The Prince's Trust has cleverly trounced the often derogatorily used term NIMBY (not in my back yard) with its proposals for BIMBY – beauty in my back yard – developing a toolkit to help local communities identify what is special in their area and what can be enhanced. In other words, its spirit of place.

The prerequisite for all this is good planning, and that requires political support. Yet that too is under pressure. In fact my last fight for beauty at the National Trust, in 2011, was to defend the planning system from an unprecedented assault, in the form of a consultation paper proposing a new draft National Planning Policy Framework (NPPF).

The planning system is easy to criticise, but it has achieved many of the objectives set for it in the 1940s. Uncontrolled sprawl was stopped, urban areas were contained by green belts or strong urban-edge policies, and (especially since the Urban Task Force) new energy was given to urban revitalisation and the provision of well-designed, energy-efficient housing in sustainable locations. We knew the system wasn't perfect, and in the run up to the release of the consultation paper we were aware that there was pressure to relax some of planning's rules, and reduce its complexity. What we were not prepared for was a document that was so transparently pro-development, apparently prepared to cast aside the planning system's long-held and carefully constructed balancing processes designed to harmonise social, economic and environmental goals for the long-term benefit of everyone.

Instead, the draft NPPF emphasised growth, relying on a pitiful and inaccurate definition of sustainable development to argue that the facilitation of development was now planning's objective. A particularly provocative statement suggested that 'decision-takers at every level should assume that the default answer to development proposals is "yes". This placed at risk the achievements of which we felt the country should be most proud: the separation of town from country; the green belt; protection against sprawl; the containment of and commitment to revitalise urban areas; and the protection of the countryside for its own sake.

The National Trust's trustees agreed that we should fight this attack on the planning system. We were clear, however, in doing so that we would be doing more than opposing a poorly drafted government document. We would be honouring the founders of the National Trust and other luminaries whose arguments had initiated then defended good planning and its role in shaping Britain's future: people like G. M. Trevelyan, Patrick Abercrombie and Clough Williams-Ellis. We remembered Trevelyan's impassioned question *Must England's Beauty Perish?* and Octavia Hill's dedicated work to protect green fields and countryside close to her tenants in London. We could not stand by and let their legacy be undermined.

And we didn't. I wrote to every member of the Trust inviting them to support the campaign, and every National Trust property hosted a petition, which members and visitors were invited to sign, under the banner *Planning: up for grabs*. Our members had never been asked to do such a thing before, yet there were almost no complaints. Instead we received phenomenal and generous support for our campaign. I was stopped on the bus, on the train and in the street by people saying 'keep it up!' and 'the National Trust is speaking for us all'. We had struck a nerve and found a voice people wanted to hear.

The National Trust's 2011 planning campaign was one voice among many to which the government listened – but the pressures remain. (Courtesy of Professional Images (UK) Ltd)

Well not everyone, of course. The initial reactions from the government did not become them. Greg Clark, the civilised and intelligent Minister responsible for the consultation, unwisely described those who objected to the NPPF as 'a bunch of nihilists' and soon the Chancellor George Osborne and Local Government Secretary Eric Pickles joined in: 'On controversial issues such as planning reform we will overcome the opposition that stands in the way of prosperity' they said in August 2011. Statements like this, though, only strengthened public support for our campaign. People did not like the government being rude about the National Trust, especially when our campaign made sense to them. It did not go unnoticed that only developers defended the draft NPPF.

We were not, however, against everything in the draft. We accepted that planning guidance needed updating and simplifying, and we supported the delegation of many planning decisions so long as there was a clear, properly balanced strategic framework. So after a few weeks of megaphone dialogue some kind of rapprochement was needed. I wrote to the Prime Minister, appealing personally to him and his party's long record of protecting the countryside. And he wrote back to me. Actually the country saw his reply before I did, because it appeared on the front page of the *Daily Telegraph* (whose own campaign, *Hands off our land*, was hugely effective) on the morning of 21 September 2011. But that did not matter: in his reply, the Prime Minister spoke of his love of the countryside, recognised the legitimacy of seeking balance, and opened the door to constructive dialogue: 'I have always believed that our beautiful British landscape is a national treasure. We should cherish and protect it for everyone's benefit,' he wrote, going on to confirm that 'the purpose of the planning system as a whole . . . is to achieve a balance between environmental, social and economic dimensions.' This was a hint at conciliation, a reassurance that the fundamental purposes of the planning system would not be changed.

So we knuckled down to the detailed work of lobbying to improve the document. We crawled through it and indicated which words were acceptable and which were not, suggesting alternatives. But the government maintained its stance, claiming – astonishingly, given the banking crisis, the mortgage crisis and all the other reasons for the country's recession – that the planning system was a cause of the country's economic problems.

In turn we quoted evidence to the contrary. We pointed out that while the British economy has thrived as well as faltered since the Second World War it had always had a planning system; and that there were over four hundred thousand houses with planning permission that were not being built, not because of the planning system but because of wider economic factors, especially the lack of finance for mortgages. And we showed how, for all its faults, the planning system has a track record of managing the release of land for development in good times and bad in the public interest, balancing the elements of sustainability – social, economic and environmental – as had been envisaged back in the 1940s. In our view the planning system needed strengthening, not weakening.

We stressed that neither the planning system nor the National Trust was anti-development and we agreed that the country needed new houses and development. The question was where and how they should be provided, and how to build in places that would serve our long- as well as short-term needs. And we urged the re-use of previously developed land before the release of green field or green belt land, pointing to evidence provided by CPRE that there was enough underused or idle land within urban areas to build 1.5 million homes.

As time went on it became impossible to read which way the debate was going. The National Trust petition amassed over

230,000 signatures and public feeling remained strongly against the government's proposals. Many other organisations, especially CPRE, were running effective campaigns. Then Greg Clark and his officials went into hibernation, working on the document. We could not predict the outcome.

The revised document was due to come out in March 2012 and for weeks beforehand we were on tenterhooks. Then we began receiving texts, phone calls and snippets as the document was revealed. It was not, of course, perfect. But in section after section wording we had asked for was there, and offending phrases removed. Ministers were briefing the press in terms we supported. It seemed that we – the many bodies who had worked together on this vital campaign – had 'won'. Overwhelmingly that was others' reaction too, and the press coverage the next day provided one of those rare moments of satisfaction for campaigners. We happily credited the government with having listened. It had been a bruising fight and not one we had relished. But it had been so necessary.

Three years on, though, it is clear that although we saw off the worst of the threat, the new guidance has weakened planning's ability to do its job. And while the Conservative Party Manifesto for 2015 promised to 'protect the green belt' and 'ensure this country remains the most beautiful in the world' there is still a propensity to blame the planning system for the slow rate of housing construction and for holding back the economy. And a 2015 review of the NPPF proposed that 'starter' homes should be permitted on green belt sites, once more threatening to breach their protection. So for all our efforts planning once again risks falling prey to 'economism', the state of believing only the economy matters.

What of the future? All that we have seen about the instruments for protecting landscape beauty confirm that planning and good land-use management remain key tools – *the* key tools – for safeguarding that most precious resource, beauty, and enabling us to meet our wider needs. It is not just about countryside protection – critical though that is – but about enabling change and managing the evolution of urban areas in a constructive way. We need housing, jobs, roads and railways, and we need space to breathe and places to love and enjoy. We need beauty in town and country, and we need to believe in the future of our urban areas.

Good planning is how we will achieve these things and reconcile the tensions between them. Good planning is also the means by which we will have the debates and make the decisions that will ensure we leave a legacy that our children may be proud to protect in their turn.

Though the circumstances are very different today, what the 1944 White Paper on land, the 1947 Town and Country Planning Act and the commitment to protect landscape, nature and our cultural history within the post-war reconstruction programme had to say about priorities was right. Human health and well-being, education, jobs and social provision cannot be separated from people's need for fresh air and exercise and for beauty. Planning can help us deliver the right changes as well as stop the wrong ones, so it is not our enemy but our friend, and the sooner we realise this the better will be our chances, in these small and crowded islands, of living happily and sustainably within them.

We face a multitude of challenges and while good planning is not a panacea it will help us make better, fairer decisions that will also satisfy our non-material needs. The decision fully to devolve decision-making, including health provision, to cities like Manchester, under the control of an elected mayor, is a significant opportunity to reappraise priorities and plan in a more integrated, place-based way for people's needs. Similar discussions are taking place across the North, under the banner of the Northern Powerhouse; and in some rural counties, led by Cornwall, the first rural county to achieve the devolution deal. Though growth is the currently stated aim, devolution presents an exciting opportunity to seek harmony. Because if we put beauty into the mix we will get better results. In addition to urban regeneration and infrastructure investment we would get attractive and accessible green space, National Parks as healthy lungs and carbon stores, the protection and revival of the historic fabric of cities, high-quality new development and a better quality of life for all residents.

Beauty is not a luxury we can have only when we are rich; it is a way of shaping the changes we need and want so that they make a positive contribution to everyone's lives, as well as protecting the things and places we most value. To succeed we need to be clear about our objectives: and beauty, sustainability and genuine public engagement must be at their heart.

In less than two centuries Britain has been transformed from a rural to an urban nation. Many countries elsewhere in the world are on the same journey, but travelling faster. With more than eighty per cent of the world's population now living in urban areas, we have to devote more energy and commitment to making them beautiful, satisfying and human places to live in as well as the efficient, prosperous and thriving engines of a new sustainable economy.

10

The case for beauty

'The love of England has in it the love of landscape, as has the love of no other country.' As he wrote this, Hilaire Belloc was thinking of the Sussex Downs where he grew up, but he captured the indefinable but widely shared passion for the landscapes of Britain that this book has revealed. Writing just a few decades later, W. G. Hoskins likened 'the English landscape, especially in a wide view, to a symphony, which it is possible to enjoy as an architectural mass of sound, beautiful or impressive as the case may be, without being able to analyse it in detail or to see the logical development of its structure'. Both were reinforcing what we so love about the British landscape, urban and rural: the way its whole is shaped by multiple elements, some obviously close to nature, others manifestly man-made, and their relationship with each other. This is what makes our landscapes so unpredictable, distinctive, harmonious, varied and – yes – beautiful.

It is for this reason that I have drawn the word 'beauty' widely and not narrowly throughout this book. I have deliberately included not just that which is aesthetically pleasing, but all the natural, cultural and built elements of our country and the forces that shape them. For that is why our landscapes are so different from the miles of spectacular but often homogenous scenery that constitutes large parts of the USA, Australia, China and Africa; and different again, because of the density of our population and remarkably diverse geology, from much of Europe's landscape. As

Hoskins showed us, every inch of our countryside has been shaped, changed and shaped again over the last few thousand years. In today's even more pressurised environment every inch is under pressure again, and the place of beauty ever more important but ever more vulnerable.

But much as we may admire the beauty of Britain, this book has been about what motivates us to defend it. Because as we have seen, time and time again, people have been moved to action by threats to beauty, threats to places they know and love, and threats to the essence, or spirit, of a place.

The shift from admiration to defence was marked by the moment when Wordsworth asked: 'Is then no nook of English ground secure / From rash assault?' as the railway which he saw as noisy and filthy threatened the peace and tranquillity of his beloved Lake District. His was a popular, public voice, and he inspired others to follow his lead. And ever since then voices for beauty have been raised, repeatedly, to defend what we value and to try to safeguard beauty through times of change.

And as we have seen the voices for beauty have not been raised in vain. The fight has, often, succeeded. As builders threatened Stonehenge and quarries Hadrian's Wall, an incremental but increasingly sophisticated defence of the elements of our cultural heritage was put in place, with legislation protecting archaeological and ancient sites and historic buildings. Ruskin's advocacy of beauty led, through Hill, Hunter and Rawnsley's efforts, to the setting up of what has become the world's largest charity for nature, landscape and heritage: the National Trust. In the early twentieth century the horror of uncontrolled sprawl led to planning laws that are envied throughout the world and have, largely, protected our countryside, stopping it from being ruined by unnecessary roads, ribbon development and outdoor advertisements. Passionate amateurs, having watched land drainage and farm improvements destroy precious wildlife sites, achieved wildlife protection laws and launched vibrant statutory and voluntary sector advocates for nature.

After a long campaign, out of the post-war settlement came National Parks, with provisions for public access and spiritual refreshment as well as landscape protection, not just for their own sake but because of the wider human benefits they would bring: 'the enjoyment of our leisure in the open air and the ability to leave our towns and walk on the moors and in the dales without fear of interruption,' said the Minister, Lewis Silkin, introducing the National Parks Bill.

In the 1960s the vision and prescience of public and voluntary bodies, especially the National Trust, led to the safeguarding of our coast; a triumph no other developed country has achieved. Eventually, our National Parks were given the tools and resources which have enabled them to be the innovative champions for beauty that were envisaged but not delivered at the start of their lives. And, more recently, public outrage forced the government to drop plans to sell the public forests and to pull back from a fatal weakening of the planning system.

The fight for beauty has, therefore, achieved a lot. But it has also lost a lot. In spite of heroic efforts we have presided over devastating losses of nature, largely due to intensive farming and the uncontrolled application of pesticides and chemicals in the past. Farming 'improvements' have also damaged the beauty of much of our 'ordinary' but well-loved landscapes, which have been stripped of hedgerows and ponds, wild flowers and ancient pastures. The process of urbanisation has been uncomfortable and imperfect, as is the quality of much of what we have built. Though many elements of our towns and cities inspire us with their beauty, there are still too many parts of them that are not the liveable, sustainable places they need to be.

Yet as we have seen, sympathetic farming and the right kind of forestry can enhance rural wildlife and landscapes as well as producing the food and timber we need; and we can have functioning, sustainable, beautiful cities and towns. It is a question of wanting beauty and working for these ideas to come to fruition. And here we need to look to ourselves.

Because it is not just about beauty lost or beauty saved by this action or that. It is about the extent to which we see beauty as important. And so there is a more insidious story that has been revealed here, too: the decline of beauty as an ideal we strive for. The unashamed championship of beauty in its own terms and for its own sake has become muted. Indeed beauty has so little traction in official discourse that it has become invisible.

The state described as 'economism' – the belief that only the economy really matters – is not the preserve of governments and decision-makers. We are all prey to it. We have become consumers, not citizens, ready to be swayed by marketing messages and with an unrealisable desire for instant gratification. We have become used to mediocrity in the places where we live and the products we use. We have become somewhat embarrassed by the word 'beauty', believing it to be either elitist or so indefinable that it is not useful.

Yet people know what they love and there is a remarkable congruity between people's views on beauty. An IPSOS MORI survey carried out for the Commission on Architecture and the Built Environment in 2010 asked what beauty meant to people from different backgrounds. And while beauty often inspired different responses from different groups, without question it meant something to everyone: to old and young, rich and poor, north and south, and from different ethnic groups. CABE therefore dismissed the idea that a sensitivity to beauty only arises out of a certain level of income or education. As one young person put it: 'when you go to a nice area, it's got colour, it's tidy, it's clean, there's not much in the way of intimidation or crime or litter, mentally it makes you think nice thoughts.' The study concluded: 'the public recognise the time and attention that the study of beauty deserves and they are ready to see public figures and influencers taking beauty seriously.'

ResPublica, in its 2015 report *A Community Right to Beauty*, reached similar conclusions. Though it too heard many personal views about beauty, it also found a remarkable consensus both about what makes a place beautiful (nature, attractive buildings and parks) and what doesn't (crime, vandalism and graffiti – often a clear sign that a place is not valued – and vacant and run-down buildings). People, they concluded, 'like places that feel like places'. Their report, proposing a community right to beauty, was driven by the need to help people protect what they love and make the place where they live more beautiful. In fact it doesn't matter if people disagree about exactly what they find beautiful: the process of debating and discussing it will lift our collective sights and help us strive for better things. As we learned about protecting landscapes and farmland, nature and trees, the coast, our heritage and urban areas, safeguarding beauty is a dynamic, changing and evolving process, not something we fix in stone forever.

But it is in officialdom that we have seen the true abandonment of beauty, not least since we have adopted new words to replace the straightforward concepts which dominated twentieth-century language. Instead of 'beauty', 'nature' and 'access', or 'sprawl', 'ugly' and 'blemish' we hear words like 'ecosystem services', 'natural capital', 'integrated coastal zone management' or 'the environment'. Though these words may, indeed do, have a more precise technical meaning than the old words, few people know what they mean, and even if they do the terms are clumsy and tongue-tying. Concepts such as sustainable development, though adopted for well-intentioned reasons, have been so distorted and colonised by technical experts that they risk becoming meaningless as well as uninspiring.

The adoption of these bureaucratic terms, and the corralling of public dialogue by the focus on the economy, narrowly conceived and desperately short term, means that we, in turn, are tempted to feel we must not use qualitative arguments but must attach a calculated value to nature, or landscapes, or the historic environment. We feel we have to show that there is a business case for protection. We have to show how nature, or beauty, or cultural heritage serves our material needs.

Of course they do, and we should not deny this. And nowhere is this more evident than in the field of health and well-being. Lewis Silkin, the Minister responsible for the National Parks Act in 1949, knew this, remarking on 'the increasing nervous strain of life [that] makes it all the more necessary that we should be able to enjoy the peace and spiritual refreshment which only contact with nature can give'.

These stresses are even more familiar today but we can now more clearly chart the benefits that contact with beauty can bring. There is a growing academic literature which gives us confidence in nature's power of healing and of the value of access to beauty. Roger Ulrich's well-known study showed how, of 160 heart surgery patients at Uppsala University Hospital in Sweden, those given access to pictures of an open, tree-lined stream were less anxious and needed fewer doses of pain-relieving medicine than those who looked at dark forest photographs, abstract art or no pictures at all. In another study the University of Exeter Medical School examined the experience of over one thousand participants and concluded that those who moved to greener urban areas experienced an immediate improvement in mental health that was sustained for at least three years after they moved, while those who relocated to less green urban areas suffered a drop in mental health.

The University of Essex's Green Exercise research shows rising self-esteem, reduced stress and better moods following exercise in green places. Natural England reports that if every household in England were provided with access to good quality green space an estimated £2.1 billion in healthcare costs could be saved.

But beauty is more than a service to us. It fulfils something in us that other things cannot, and it enriches our lives in all kinds of unexpected and vital ways. Because beauty is a perspective, not a transactional experience. As Keats said: 'Beauty is truth, truth beauty, – that is all Ye know on earth, and all ye need to know.' It is a way of looking at the world. Of valuing the things that are priceless: the inspiration of a work of art, a beautiful view, a swallow in flight, breaths of fresh, clean air. In a world where most of us are realistic enough to know that we are unlikely to get much richer, beauty drives the experiences we seek out: the places we go to, the things we surround ourselves with, and the values that make our lives worth living. We live in an era where fewer of us are driven by religious imperatives, but we are not lacking in spirituality, nor the capacity to be moved to strive for better things. Beauty can give shape to that yearning, and as Ruskin intimated, ultimately a search for beauty also helps us to respect the needs of other people and other inhabitants of the Earth, today and in the future.

Those who seek beauty are not, nor ever have been, just from one part of society. Examples abound: the factory worker who sent two shillings and sixpence to the National Trust's appeal for Brandelhow in 1902 saying, 'all my life I have longed to see the Lakes . . . I shall never see them now but I should like to help keep them for others'; the ramblers forcing their way past gamekeepers for the joy and freedom of walking in the hills; the volunteers who join local amenity societies to stop bad development and seek what is good; and amateur naturalists saving wildlife, road campaigners camping in trees and surfers campaigning for safer seas. These stories are not the preoccupations of elitists but represent an enormous movement of people passionate about places, about nature, about landscape and about beauty.

And today, even in a world dominated by the economy, the voices and actions for beauty continue. The established organisations – those whose history and role I have described – continue their good work and new voices are joining in. Local communities who come together to fight fracking; the online campaign group 38 Degrees who, following the success of its campaign for the public forests enables many thousands of people to support local and national campaigns. The Place Alliance, which brings together all those who care about improving the quality of the built environment; and mySociety, which engages people in civic life, especially in urban areas. The Transition Towns and Smart Growth movements are pioneering new ways of involving people in designing towns and cities that will help us live lower carbon, more satisfying lives, true to the spirit of their places. So although beauty has little traction in official discourse, a love of beauty and a passion to protect it is widespread and is energising many people's lives. I suspect also that many politicians and officials know, in their hearts, that these things matter.

So what should those who want to continue the fight for beauty do? As we have seen, protecting beauty is about *whether* we do things, *how* we do things and the *quality* of what we do. So we should talk about beauty, and value what it offers us. And above all we should act as if beauty matters, and draw on it to improve the quality of our lives. We should seek things that make us happy rather than always consuming more. And we should look after the natural beauty – land, nature and natural resources – on which our future depends. In the process we will find that restoring confidence in the word 'beauty' will help us. If people believe we are striving for beauty it will help reduce fears of the unknown, seek solutions that people find appealing, and relieve tensions by seeking a future in which everyone has a stake.

The opportunities for beauty to help us find a better way forward are manifest and clear. Each of the preceding chapters ended with examples. We now have National Parks (and need more of them) whose vision embraces nature, carbon protection and sustainable economic and tourist activity as well as their historic focus on landscape beauty and public access; and we have seen the vital importance of stopping species loss and restoring nature. We need to maintain carbon in soils; harness the potential for a significant increase in woodland cover that would also enhance nature and landscape and renew our links with trees; and designate a deep protected strip, along the entire length of our coast, for the combined purpose of giving people access to beautiful places, protecting nature and helping us adapt to climate change. We know we can achieve more beauty in urban areas, through high quality design of new developments and planning in an integrated way for all human needs, including for green space; and we can develop beautiful as well as functional new infrastructure, from railway lines to wind turbines. Good land use planning, above all, is central to helping us achieve all this.

But to achieve a better future depends on beauty mattering enough to shape both the debate and our decisions. Because we have choices about whether and how we respond to new imperatives, and whether we accept the responsibility of changing our lives to protect the interests of those who will follow us. As John Muir said, our choice must be 'Not blind opposition to progress, but opposition to blind progress'.

And so I come to my final message. It is about the future and its inhabitants. Because if, as Ruskin argued, beauty really is essential to us all, the most important thing we can do is give the next generation access to beauty, to enhance their lives and their wish to pass it on. We remember Octavia Hill, her ragged children and her desire for them to see flowers growing, paddle in streams and feel growing grass under their feet. But they lived in nineteenth-century, grimy, overcrowded London. Surely today's children live in luxury by comparison? Yes, materially. But in terms of access to beauty, no.

In 2005 *Last Child in the Woods* took America by storm, winning its author Richard Louv the Audubon Medal for sounding the alarm about the health and societal costs of children's isolation from the natural world. He argued that children are living increasingly sedentary lives, protected and cut off from experiences in nature through parental fears and misplaced anxieties about health risks and 'stranger danger'. The effects are not just negative but damaging. He coined the phrase 'nature deficit disorder' to explain what he meant.

The equivalent research here in the UK has unearthed some shocking statistics. In the UK, one in four children do not play outside more than once a week; and one in ten children have never visited the countryside. Children spend between six and seven hours a day in front of electronic media and there are growing reports of rickets and other (so we thought) vanished diseases due to children's low exposure to natural light and sunshine. A third of children aged two to fifteen are overweight or obese. A tenth of five to sixteen year olds have been diagnosed with a mental health problem. There are rising incidences of asthma and noticeable declines in heart and lung fitness among children.

Shockingly, the area over which today's parents allow their children to roam unsupervised has shrunk by ninety per cent in a single generation. Two-thirds of parents give their children less physical freedom than free-range chickens, and a child in Britain today is three times more likely to be admitted to hospital for falling out of bed than falling out of a tree. Although the outdoors may appear full of risks the fact is that accidents at home – burns, scalds, poisoning from cleaning products, falling or tripping – are far more common.

We have become frightened for our children. We are not letting them experiment and play, get muddy, climb trees, scrape their knees and learn the limits of their own abilities. Being stuck indoors will not provide the lasting memories, emotional connections or the sense of reward from challenges overcome or imaginations fired through playing outside. And we are depriving children of access to and the inspiration of nature: ninety per cent of children can name a Dalek yet only thirty per cent can recognise a jackdaw.

Children are not, of course, forced to sit in front of the TV and we should not dictate to parents where and how their children should play. But at the National Trust in 2010 we were clear what we *could* do: show that there *are* safe places for children to play, and offer them the chance to share in the joy of experiencing the natural world. One fact that influenced us profoundly was the revelation that unless certain experiences or patterns of behaviour are established by the age of about twelve, they are unlikely to become embedded in later life. These were the origins of our *Natural Childhood* initiative and the campaign *50 Things to Do Before You're 11¾*.

Our *Natural Childhood* report, drawing together all the relevant research, attracted great interest, coming at a time when professional concerns about childhood obesity and rising incidences of mental health problems were coalescing. Its recommendations addressed the range of issues from the formal educational curriculum, in which we argued that nature should play a more central role, to the need for parents simply to let their children play.

And that is what the *50 Things* campaign was about. It was full of ideas for natural play, from climbing trees to flying kites, skimming stones, wading in mud, catching tiddlers and making a leaf trumpet. We were overwhelmed by the warmth of the reaction to it. Among the first to respond were the professionals: in childhood welfare, health, education and psychology, who loved the ideas and have joined with the Trust in partnerships to promote natural childhood.

Even more overwhelming was the reaction of the Trust's members, families and the media. There was an outpouring of emotion, seemingly evidence of a longing for the return to the innocence of lost childhood. Celebrities and columnists spoke nostalgically of their own childhood and of their regret that today's children do not have similar experiences. Families flocked to National Trust properties to pick up the handbook and take part in the activities laid on to help them tick off the list.

We do not know or fully understand the risks of deprivation of exercise, and freedom of the outdoors, but we do know that access to nature and exercise in fresh air can contribute to their solution. The positive effect on physical and mental health, as well as on educational achievement, is increasingly well documented. But it is about our spiritual needs too. So we need to give every child the chance to experience and love the outdoors, develop what has been dubbed our 'Natural' Health Service, including access to green spaces for rest and recreation, and provide beauty close to where people live. That is what will build beauty's champions for the future.

Because, ultimately, the message of this book is a hopeful one. The human spirit needs beauty and can't live without it; and we will all strive for more beauty in our lives if given the chance. The economy on its own, meanwhile, will not save the planet from irreversible damage and will not make us happy. We must learn from the past but our responsibility is to the future, and we should allow beauty to help us find the ideas and actions that will enable us to plan with greater confidence for it.

As David Attenborough once said: 'people will only protect what they care about, and they will only care about what they have experienced.' We should sow the seeds of those experiences so that future generations will know and love the beauty we need to enrich our lives and nurture our souls, now and for ever.

Acknowledgements

They say everyone has a book in them, and this is mine. All my life I've been inspired by and worked to protect beauty, and for a long time I've known that somehow I needed to capture what I've learned and believe about its importance, and advocate for its revival as a human need. This is it. In the process I've drawn heavily on the help and support of my friends, colleagues and family.

The beauty-driven organisations I've worked for – the Campaign for National Parks, Campaign to Protect Rural England and the National Trust – and all their staff, supporters and volunteers have been a profound source of my inspiration and knowledge. There are too many people to thank individually, so I thank them collectively. I am particularly grateful to my numerous presidents, including that well-known champion of beauty, HRH The Prince of Wales, chairs, trustees and close work colleagues, many of whom are dear friends. The National Trust has very kindly let me use some of the stunning pictures from its photo library to illustrate the book, and CPRE has done the same.

During the process of writing, a number of people with whom I've worked over the years have taken the time and trouble to read it, or sections of it, and offer me comments. This – even when the feedback was (rightly) stern – was invaluable, and I couldn't have completed the book without their help. I warmly thank Kate Ashbrook, David Baldock, Tony Burton, Professor David Cannadine, Dr Ben Cowell, Steph Hilborne, Peter Nixon, Professor Adrian Phillips, Tim Sands,

Neil Sinden, Harry Studholme, Laura Vincent, Merlin Waterson and Professor Clive Wilmer. I make special mention of Mike McCarthy, who made two mercy missions to Cambridge to help me when I got stuck. Any errors are, of course, mine.

My colleagues at Emmanuel College, Cambridge have been unfailingly supportive during the process of writing and review, a time during which my respect and admiration for academics, who do it all the time, has multiplied. Along with many helpful steers, three Fellows kindly read it and I am deeply grateful to Dr Sarah Bendall, Dr Phil Howell and Dr Robert Macfarlane for doing so, and offering such helpful comments. My PA, Pauline Martin, has been totally brilliant throughout.

My agent, Caroline Michel and publisher, and editor, Sam Carter and the team at Oneworld, have been incredibly kind, efficient and encouraging.

Finally, I thank my family: Bob, Alice, Rose and Olivia and my mother, Margaret; and the extensive Reynolds and Merrill clans, whose love and support means more than I can say.

Bibliography and further reading

Chapter 1: From admiration to defence

A Tour through the Whole Island of Great Britain, Daniel Defoe, 1724–1727

A Philosophical Inquiry into the Origin of our Ideas of the Sublime and the Beautiful – Edmund Burke, 1757

An Essay on the Principle of Population – Thomas Robert Malthus, 1798

Guide through the District of the Lakes – William Wordsworth, 1810

Modern Painters, Praeterita, The Seven Lamps of Architecture, Unto this Last, The Stones of Venice – John Ruskin

Six Essays on Commons Preservation – Sampson, Low, Son, and Marston, 1867

News from Nowhere – William Morris, 1890

Ruskin: The Great Victorian – Derrick Leon, Routledge and Kegan Paul, 1949

The Darkening Glass: A Portrait of Ruskin's Genius – John D. Rosenberg, Columbia University Press, 1980

The Lake District: A Century of Conservation – Geoffrey Berry and Geoffrey Beard, John Bartholomew and Son, 1980

Founders of the National Trust – Graham Murphy, Christopher Helm, 1987

Octavia Hill: A Life – Gillian Darley, Constable and Company, 1990

The National Trust: The First Hundred Years – Merlin Waterson, BBC Books, 1994

Secure from Rash Assault – James Winter, University of California Press, 1999

Building Jerusalem: The Rise and Fall of the Victorian City – Tristram Hunt, Weidenfeld and Nicholson, 2004

Octavia Hill's Letters to Fellow Workers 1872–1911 – edited by Robert Whelan, Kyrle Books, 2005

The Omnipotent Magician: Lancelot 'Capability' Brown – Jane Brown, Chatto and Windus, 2011

Thirlmere and the Emergence of the Landscape Protection Movement – Ian Brodie, Bookcase, 2012

Uvedale Price: Decoding the Picturesque – Charles Watkins and Ben Cowell, The Boydell Press, 2012

Sir Robert Hunter – Ben Cowell, Pitkin Publishing, 2013

A Brief History of the Civic Society Movement – Lucy E. Hewitt, Civic Voice, 2014

Saving Open Spaces – The Campaign for Public Rights to Enjoy Commons, Green Spaces and Paths – Kate Ashbrook, Pitkin Publishing, 2015

Chapter 2: The calls and claims of natural beauty

The Preservation of Rural England – Patrick Abercrombie, University Press of Liverpool, 1926

England and the Octopus – Clough Williams-Ellis, Geoffrey Bles, 1928

Labour and the Nation – The Labour Party, 1928

Must England's Beauty Perish? – G. M. Trevelyan, Faber & Gwyer, 1929

Our Nation's Heritage – edited by J. B. Priestley, The Temple Press, 1939

Report of the Committee on Land Utilisation in Rural Areas (the Scott Committee) – Cmd 6378, HMSO, 1942

The Control of Land Use – Cmd 6537, HMSO, 1944

'The Calls and Claims of Natural Beauty' – essay in *An Autobiography and Other Essays*, G. M. Trevelyan, Longmans, 1949

As it Happened – Clement Attlee, Odhams Press, 1954

Town and Country Planning in Britain – J. B. Cullingworth, George Allen & Unwin, 1964

Architect Errant – Clough Williams-Ellis, Constable, 1971

The Limits to Growth: a report for the Club of Rome's Project on the Predicament of Mankind – Dennis L. Meadows, et al, Universe Books, 1972

The Evolution of British Town Planning – Gordon Cherry, Leonard Hill, 1974

The Theft of the Countryside – Marion Shoard, Temple Smith, 1980

G. M. Trevelyan: A Life in History – David Cannadine, Harper Collins, 1992

The Expense of Glory: A Life of John Reith – Ian Macintyre, Harper Collins, 1993

Twentieth Century Britain – edited by Paul Johnson, Longman, 1994

Protecting the Beautiful Frame – Melvyn Jones, Hallamshire Press, 2001

Attlee: A Life in Politics – Nicklaus Thomas-Symonds, I. B. Tauris, 2010

GDP: A Brief but Affectionate History – Diane Coyle, Princeton University Press, 2014

Chapter 3: National Parks – a nobler vision for a better world

The Case for National Parks – John Dower, 1938

National Parks – Norman Birkett KC, Cambridge University Rede lecture, 1945

National Parks in England and Wales – John Dower, Cmd 6628, HMSO, 1945

Report of the National Parks Committee – Chairman Sir Arthur Hobhouse, Cmd 7207, HMSO, 1947

Annual Reports of the National Parks Commission, 1950–1967

Leisure in the Countryside – Cmd 2928, HMSO, 1966

Report of the National Park Policies Review Committee (The Sandford Report) – Department of the Environment, 1974

Freedom to Roam – Howard Hill, Moorland Publishing, 1980

National Parks: Conservation or Cosmetics? – Ann and Malcolm MacEwen, George Allen & Unwin, 1982

New Life for the Hills – Malcolm MacEwen and Geoffrey Sinclair, Council for National Parks, 1983

Fifty Years for National Parks – Council for National Parks, 1986

Forbidden Land – Tom Stephenson, Manchester University Press, 1989

A People's Charter? – edited by John Blunden and Nigel Curry, HMSO,1990

Fit for the Future – Report of the National Parks Review Panel, 1991

Chapter 4: How nature and the wider countryside lost out

The Natural History of Selborne – Gilbert White, Benjamin White & Son, 1789

Silent Spring – Rachel Carson, Houghton Mifflin, 1962

Second Nature – edited by Richard Mabey, Jonathan Cape, 1984

Holding your Ground – Angela King and Sue Clifford for Common Ground, Maurice Temple Smith, 1985

This Common Inheritance – HMSO, 1990

A History of Nature Conservation in Britain – David Evans, Routledge, 1992

Wicken Fen: The Making of a Wetland Nature Reserve – edited by Laurie Friday, Harley Books in association with the National Trust, 1997

Ecosystems and Human Well-being – Millennium Ecosystem Assessment for the United Nations, Island Press, 2005

England in Particular: A Celebration of the Commonplace, the Local, the Vernacular and the Distinctive – Sue Clifford and Angela King, Hodder & Staughton, 2006

Making Space for Nature – Professor John Lawton, 2010

The Natural Choice: Securing the Value of Nature – Cm 8082, HMSO, 2011

UK National Ecosystem Assessment – UNEP/WCMC, 2011

Wildlife in Trust: A Hundred Years of Nature Conservation – Tim Sands, Elliot and Thompson, 2012

State of Nature – RSPB et al., 2013

What Nature Does for Britain – Tony Juniper, Profile Books, 2015

Chapter 5: How farming made and destroyed beauty

Rural Rides – William Cobbett, 1830

The Making of the English Landscape – W. G. Hoskins, Hodder and Stoughton, 1955

A New Historical Geography of England before 1600 – edited by H. C. Darby, Cambridge University Press, 1973

A New Historical Geography of England after 1600 – edited by H. C. Darby, Cambridge University Press, 1973

New Agricultural Landscapes – Countryside Commission, 1974

Food from Our Own Resources – HMSO, 1975

Landscape: The Need for a Public Voice – CPRE, 1975

Agriculture: The Triumph and the Shame – Richard Body MP, Temple Smith, 1982

Farming and Food: A Sustainable Future – Policy Commission on the Future of Farming and Food, Cabinet Office, 2002

John Clare – Jonathan Bate, Picador, 2003

Agricultural Landscapes: 35 Years of Change – The Countryside Agency, 2006

Chapter 6: The curious case of trees

Magna Carta, 1215

Charter of the Forest, 1217

Sylva – John Evelyn, 1664

Walking in the Lake District – Rev. H. H. Symonds, W. R. Chambers, 1933

Afforestation in the Lake District – Rev. H. H. Symonds, Dent, 1936

The Lake District and the National Trust – Bruce Thompson, Titus Wilson and Son, 1946

The Case for Control of Afforestation of Open Land in National Parks – Standing Committee on National Parks, 1961

Forest Service – George Ryle, David and Charles, 1969

Trees and Woodlands in the British Landscape – Oliver Rackham, Dent, 1976

Verderers of the New Forest – Anthony Pasmore, Pioneer Publications, 1977

A History of English Forestry – N. D. G. James, Blackwells, 1981

Birds, Bogs and Forestry – Nature Conservancy Council, 1987

John Evelyn – Gillian Darley, Yale, 2006

Independent Panel on Forestry: Final Report – DEFRA, 2012

Chapter 7: The coast – a success story

The English Coast: its Development and Preservation – Wesley Dougill for CPRE, 1936

The Untutored Townsman's Invasion of the Country – C. E. M. Joad, Faber and Faber, 1945

The Sea Coast – J. A. Steers, The New Naturalist, Collins, 1953

The Coasts of England and Wales: Measurements of Use, Protection and Development – Countryside Commission, HMSO, 1968

The Coastal Heritage – Countryside Commission, HMSO, 1970

The Planning of the Coastline – Countryside Commission, HMSO, 1970

The Shell Book of the British Coast – Adrian Robinson and Roy Millward, David and Charles, 1983

Shifting Shores: Living with a Changing Coastline – National Trust, 2005

Coastlines: The Story of Our Shore – Patrick Barkham, Granta, 2015

Chapter 8: Cultural heritage – how caring for the past creates a better future

The Continuing Purpose: A History of the National Trust, its Aims and Work – Robin Fedden, Longmans, 1968

The Destruction of the Country House – Roy Strong, Marcus Binney and John Harris, Thames and Hudson, 1974

The National Trust Manual of Housekeeping – Sheila Stainton and Hermione Sandwith, Allen Lane in association with the National Trust, 1984

Ancestral Voices – James Lees-Milne, Chatto and Windus, 1975

On Living in an Old Country – Patrick Wright, Verso, 1985

The Heritage Industry – Robert Hewison, Methuen, 1987

The Past in Contemporary Society – Peter J. Fowler, Routledge, 1992

The Country Houses of England, 1948–1998 – John Cornforth, Constable, 1998

The Heritage Obsession – Ben Cowell, Tempus, 2008

Men from the Ministry – Simon Thurley, Yale University Press, 2013

The Power of Place – English Heritage, 2000

The Historic Environment: A Force for Our Future – DCMS, 2001

Many Voices, One Vision: The Early Years of the World Heritage Convention – Christina Cameron and Mechtild Rossler, Ashgate Publishing, 2013

Chapter 9: Urbanisation and why good planning matters

Report on the Sanitary Condition of the Labouring Population – Edwin Chadwick, 1842

Wild Wales – George Borrow, John Murray, 1862

Garden Cities of Tomorrow – Ebenezer Howard, S. Sonnenschein and Co., 1902

Greater London Plan – Patrick Abercrombie, 1944

Outrage – Ian Nairn, *The Architectural Review*, 1955

Traffic in Towns – Colin Buchanan, Penguin, 1964

The Country and the City – Raymond Williams, Oxford University Press, 1975

Cities are Good for Us – Harley Sherlock, Paladin, 1991

Urban Footprints – CPRE, 1992

Local Attraction – Carolyn McGhie and Richard Girling for CPRE, 1995

Towards an Urban Renaissance: Report of the Urban Task Force – DETR, 1999

A Community Right to Beauty – ResPublica, 2015

Chapter 10: The case for beauty

Last Child in the Woods – Richard Louv, Algonquin Books, 2005

People and Places: Public Attitudes to Beauty – IPSOS MORI for Commission on Architecture and the Built Environment, 2010

Natural Childhood Report and public engagement campaign *50 Things to Do Before You're 11¾* – National Trust, 2011

Index

References to book titles are in *italics*.

Abercrombie, Sir Patrick 36–8, 41, 44, 46, 280–2
Access to Mountains Act (1939) 70
Adams, Professor Bill 96
Addison, Christopher, Lord 75, 78
agriculture 35, 47, 51, 117, 158–9, 307–8
  and the coast 226
  and disease 149–52
  and history 126–39
  and industrialisation 54
  and landscape 125–6, 142–8
  and National Parks 85–6, 87
  and nature 103–4, 107–9, 111
  and productivity 55, 56, 152–3
  and reforms 139–42, 153–4
  and soil 154–8
  and wartime 100–1
  and woodland 163–5
Agriculture Act (1947) 51, 125, 140–1
Agriculture: The Triumph and the Shame (Body) 143
Ancient Monuments Acts 234–5, 236–7, 238
ancient sites 233–8
Annan, Kofi 114
Antrim, Alexander McDonnell, Lord 208
Archaeological Institute 233
architecture 11, 13, 14, 15, 27–8, 41, 245
Areas of Outstanding Natural Beauty (AONBs) 78–9, 92, 94, 204

art 1–2, 10–11, 13, 15
Attlee, Clement 45, 49–50, 140

Barlow Commission 46
beauty 2–3, 47, 56–8, 59, 62–3, 305–9, 310–13
  and agriculture 126, 158–9
  and the coast 223–5
  and Hill 18–20
  and Morris 15–16
  and National Parks 67
  and National Trust 27, 29
  and planning 302–4
  and Ruskin 10–13
  and technology 53–4
  and trees 161, 169, 174
  and urbanisation 261–2, 264, 275
Betjeman, John 44
Beveridge, William 46
Bewick, Thomas 5–6
birdlife 5–6, 54, 98–100, 101, 180
  and decline 118–19, 179
  and pollution 104
Birkett, Sir Norman 75, 77, 82
Birling Gap 216–18
Black Death 129, 265
Bloom, Bridget 148–9
Blue Flag campaign 215
boat-building 196, 197
Body, Richard 143
Bournville 276

Brecon Beacons 78
British Archaeological Association 233
British Workers' Sports Federation 72
Broads Authority 123, 145
Broads, see Norfolk Broads
Brown, Capability 4, 169
brownfield sites 58, 292–4
Browning, Helen 148–9, 152
Bruce-Lockhart, Sandy 262–3
Bryce, James 69
BSE ('mad cow disease') crisis 149
Burke, Edmund 2–3
Burton, Tony 263, 293

Cadbury family 276
Cairngorms 92
Cameron, David 189, 258, 300–1
Campaign for National Parks (CNP) xiv,
    84–5, 87, 143, 178
Campaign to protect Rural England
    (CPRE) 109–10,175
  and agriculture 142, 144–5
  and the coast 202–3, 204
  and origins 38–41, 44, 75
  and urbanisation 263, 292–4
carbon dioxide 60, 61–2, 155–6, 157,
    185
cars 43, 53, 205, 286–90
Carson, Rachel 104–5
Castle, Barbara 73, 74
cattle farming 129, 130, 135, 150
Chamberlain, Neville 39
Channel Tunnel 261–3
Charter of the Forest 167–8
children 18, 23, 314–16
Chorley, Roger 240
Churchill, Winston 45, 49
cities 9–10, 12–13, 16, 31–2, 245, 293–5
  and industrialisation 264, 270–1
  and National Parks 92–3
  see also London
Civic Trust 245
Clare, John 133–4, 161
Clark, Aitken 122–3, 145

Clark, Greg 300, 302
claylands 136, 137
Clean Air Act (1956) 104
climate change xv, 59–62, 90, 112,
    154–5, 219–21, 223
coal 54, 61, 171, 212, 269–70
coastal landscape 193–203, 208–9, 307
  and conservation 203–8, 209–12,
    224–5
  and erosion 216–21
  and footpaths 225–8
  and pollution 215–16
  and wildlife 212–15
  and wind turbines 221–4
Cobbett, William 132–3, 272
Colston, Adrian 95–6, 100, 113
Committee on Wartime Reconstruction
    45–51
Commission on Architecture and the Built
    Environment (CABE) 295, 308
Common Agricultural Policy (CAP) 58,
    154
Common Fisheries Policy (CFP) 215
Common Ground 110
Commons Preservation Society 21–2,
    69,234
conifers 25, 91, 111, 175–6, 179–80,
    182
conservation xii, 57, 90–1, 96, 106–7,
    146–7
  and buildings 245, 248, 249, 250–3
Control of Land Use, The 48–9, 280
Corn Laws 138
Council of Europe 106
country houses 239–44, 247, 248,
    249–52
countryside 4–6, 30–1, 36–9, 47, 51–2, 53
  and access 68–70, 72–3, 74–5
  and leisure 150–1, 257
Countryside and Rights of Way Act
    (2000) 74–5
Countryside Character Programme 111
Countryside Commission 81, 82, 89–90,
    106, 112

and agriculture 141–2, 145–6, 147–8
and the coast 207
and forests 186
Countryside in 1970 conferences 106
CPRE, *see* Council for the Preservation of Rural England
Cripps, John 204–5
crop farming 130, 131, 138
Crossman, Richard 245
Crowe, Dame Sylvia 177
Crown Estate 135, 222
Cuckmere Haven 218–19
Curry, Don 152, 153

dairy farming 139
Dartmoor 78, 80, 82, 88
Dawber, Sir Guy 36–7, 39
Defoe, Daniel 3, 132
Department for Culture, Media and Sport (DCMS) 255–7
Department for Food and Rural Affairs (DEFRA) 153, 187
devolution 303–4
Dickens, Charles 271–2, 273–4
Dinas Oleu 14, 27–8, 200, *201*, 207
Domesday Book 127, 163–4, 198
Doughty, Sir Martin 113
Dougill, Wesley 202–3
Dower, John 76–7, 78, 79, 176
Dower, Pauline 78
Durham Coast 211–12

Earth Summit 1992 60, 112
economism 63–4, 302, 308
economy, the xv, 31, 35, 53–4
ecosystems 114–16
Edwards, Ron 89, 90
egg collecting 99, 100
electricity 283–4
Eliot, George 137–8, 273
Ellis, Tom 69
England and the Octopus (Williams-Ellis) 41–2

English Heritage 253, 256
English Nature 112
Enterprise Neptune 207–11
Environment Acts (1990/95) 90, 112
environmental movement 56–8
Environmentally Sensitive Areas (ESAs) 146
Epping Forest 18, 22, 69
European Landscape Convention 92
European Union (EU) 58, 105, 154
Evelyn, John 22, 170–1
Exmoor 66–7, 78, 84, 85–6, 204

farming, *see* agriculture
Fedden, Robin 247, 249
fens 95–6, 100, 119, 130–1, 136, 157
Finn, Hugh 261, 262, 263
First World War 30, 33–4, 138, 173, 237
fish 54, 104, 128, 196, 197, 214–15
flooding 131, 157–8, 220–1
Flow Country 111–12, 179–80, *181*, *182*, *183*
food supplies 8–9, 117, 125–6, 138–9, 140, 154
  and quality 149, 150, 151, 152–3
  and surpluses 147
foot and mouth disease 149–52, 257
footpaths 25, 70, 73, 90, 225–8
Forest of Dean 160, 170
Forestry Commission 111, 160–1, 173–4, 175–7, 178–9, 182–4
  and sales 187, 188–90
Forestry Panel 190–2
forests 103, 165–8, 169–70, 177–8, 179–80, 182
fossil fuels 55, 59, 61
fracking 88–9
Friends of the Earth 56
Friends of the Lake District 41, 175

Garden Cities 278–80
gardens 3–4, 16, 248–9
Geddes, Sir Patrick 36–7
General Enclosure Acts 133–5

geological sites 103, 197
Gibbs, Christopher 208
Gilpin, William 5
Glasgow 92, 93
Gower Peninsula 204
grant schemes 243–4
green belts 44, 58, 280, 302
greenhouse gases 60, 61
Greenpeace 56
Griffin, Sir Herbert 36–7, 39
Grove-White, Robin 109
Guild of St George 13–14
Gummer, John (Lord Deben) 58, 149, 293–4

Hall, Chris 86
Halvergate Marshes 123, 145–6
Hampstead Heath 22, 69
Hardy, Thomas 34, 138, 172
health 9, 46, 64, 185, 272–3, 275
    and children 314
    and nature 310–11
heritage 229–30, 232–9, 244–6, 253–60, 306
Heritage Coasts 206–7, 212
Heritage Link 256
Heritage Lottery Fund 253–4, 294–5
hill farming 143–4
Hill, Octavia xii, 15, 17–21, 22–3, 64, 239, 275
    and National Trust 25, 26, 28, 200
historic buildings 54, 232–3, 234, 235–44, 246–54
Historic Buildings and Ancient Monuments Act (1953) 243–4
Historic England 253
history 255–6, 257–60
History of British Birds (Bewick) 5–6
Hobhouse, Sir Arthur 77–8, 102
Hoskins, W. G. xiv, 123–5, 141, 161
housing 7, 8, 19–20, 32, 33, 58–9
    and back-to-backs 230, 231, 232, 252–3
    and London 281–2

and New Towns 285–6
and philanthropy 275–6, 278
and planning 290–1, 296, 292–5
and post-war 34, 35, 36
and sprawl 41–3, 44, 40, 45
and wood 185–6
Housman, A. E. 1, 33
Howard, Ebenezer 278–80
Hunter, Robert 15, 20–1, 22–3, 25, 26
hunting 98, 165, 166
Hussey, Christopher 239, 244
Huxley, Julian 102, 103

industrialisation xii, 1–2, 8–10, 30, 254–5
    and the coast 205–6
    and urbanisation 265–6, 267–71
Intergovernmental Panel on Climate Change (IPCC) 60–1
Internal Drainage Board 123, 145
International Union for Conservation of Nature (IUCN) 114, 246
iron industry 269

John, King of England 166–7
Joint Nature Conservation Committee 112
Jones, Rt Rev. James 190
Jurassic Coast 92

Kent 261–3
Kirby, Esmé 82
Kyoto Protocol (1997) 60
Kyrle Society for the Diffusion of Beauty 16–17, 245

Lake District 5, 12, 28, 78, 91, 92
    and administration 79, 83
    and the coast 204
    and Rawnsley 23–6
    and trees 172–3, 174–6
    and Wordsworth 6–8, 68
land
    and access 68–70, 72–3, 74–5

and development 32–3, 35–6, 45, 48–9

and planning xii, 58, 297–8, 300–4, 306–6

and reclamation 200

Land Utilisation in Rural Areas 47

landscape 1, 2, 96–7, 101–2, 123–5, 305–6

and agriculture 125–9, 130–1, 132–3, 142–8

landscape gardens 4, 169

Lansbury, George 238

Larkin, Philip 287

Last Child in the Woods (Louv) 314

Lawson, Nigel 111, 182

Lawton, John 115–16

Lees-Milne, James 240–1, 242–3

leisure 53, 68–9, 150–1, 177

Letchworth 279–80

Letwin, Oliver 62

Lever Brothers 276

Limits to Growth, The 54–6

Lincoln, Abraham 67

Lloyd George, David 31, 173

Loch Lomond and the Trossachs 92

London 16, 19–21, 22, 92–3, 266–7, 271–3

and green belts 280

and post-war 280–2

and trees 187

Longland, Jack 82, 84

Louv, Richard 314

Lundy 213, 214

Macdonald, Ramsay 75

MacEwen, Malcolm 86

Macmillan, Harold 52–3

Magna Carta 166–7

Making of the English Landscape, The (Hoskins) 123–5

Malthus, Rev Robert 8–9

Manchester Corporation 24–5, 175

Marine and Coastal Access Act (2009) 224, 225

marine environment 212–15

Mass Trespass 72–3

Matheson, Donald 240

Melchett, Lord 108

military occupation 194, 203

Millennium Ecosystem Assessment 114–15

Ministry of Agriculture, Fisheries and Food (MAFF) 142, 144, 145–6, 148, 149, 153

Montreal Protocol (1987) 60

Morris, William (artist) xii, 15–16, 25

Morris, William (car designer) 287

motorways 288, 289

mountains 69–70

Muir, John xv, 68

National Character Areas 111

National Ecosystem Assessment 115–16, 154, 185

National Farmers' Union (NFU) 87, 140, 144

National Forest 186

National Grid 80, 283–4

National Health Service 46, 51

National Heritage Memorial Fund (NHMF) 248, 252

National Land Fund 243

National Nature Reserves 103

National Parks xiv, 54, 90–1, 92–4, 120, 284

and administration 79–84, 86–90, 91–2

and agriculture 143–4

and cities 92–3, 296

and the coast 203–5

and creation 75–8, 307

and Exmoor 66–7, 85–6

and forests 177–8

and USA 67–8

National Parks and Access to Countryside Act (1949) 51–2, 74, 78

National Planning Policy Framework (NPPF) 297–8, 300–2

National Trust xii, xiv, 43, 153, 256–8
  and children 315–16
  and the coast 193–4, 200, 204,
    207–12, 216–21, 223, 225
  and forests 187–9
  and foundation 15, 17, 23, 26–9,
    306
  and historic buildings 230, 232, 238,
    239–44, 246–53
  and nature 95–6, 100, 105–6
  and peat 155–7
  and planning 298, 299, 300–2
Natural Capital Committee 116, 117
Natural England 113
Natural Environment White Paper 2011
  116
Natural History of Selborne (White) 5,
  97–8
Natural Resources Wales 184
nature 5–6, 51, 95–8, 100–4, 307,
  310–11
  and agriculture 107–9
  and children 314–16
  and the coast 212–14
  and conservation 110–11, 112–21
  and pollution 104–6
  see also birdlife; plantlife; wildlife
Nature Conservancy 102–4, 213–14
Nature Conservancy Council (NCC)
  106–7, 108–9, 111–12, 180, 182
Nature Improvement Areas 116, 117
Neville, Charles 201, 202
New Forest 5, 78, 89–90, 92, 170, 177
New Lanark 276
New Towns 48, 281, 282, 283, 285–6
non-native species 119–20
Norfolk Broads 91, 92, 122–3, 145–6
North Downs 79
North York Moors 78, 80, 92, 204
Northern Ireland 208
Northumberland 78, 204

Office of Works 235
oil 54, 104, 212–13, 215

open-field farming 128, 129, 130, 133–5
Owen, Robert 276

Packer, Richard 148
Parker, Barry 279
parks 3–4, 16, 81, 271, 294; *see also*
  National Parks
Patten, Chris, Lord 58
Peacehaven 44, 200–2
Peak District 40, 70, 71, 72–3, 74, 78
  and administration 79, 80
  and peat 91, 155–6
peat 91, 97, 122, 131, 155–7, 180
Peek, Henry 21
Peers, Charles Reed 235, 237
Pembrokeshire Coast 78, 80, 204, 208
Pennine Way 73, 74, 97
pesticides 104, 105
Planning Acts (1909/19/32) 31–2, 33,
  44
plantlife 54, 120, 179
poetry 2, 6, 30, 33–4, 133–4, 287
pollution 9, 54, 55, 104–5, 215, 289–90
population growth 8–9, 55, 264, 265, 267
Porchester, Henry Herbert, Lord 86–7
Port Sunlight 276, 277
Potter, Beatrix 26, 150
poverty 9, 23, 35, 139
Prescott, John, Lord 58, 293
Preservation of Rural England, The
  (Abercrombie) 37
Price, Uvedale 5
Priestley, J. B. 35–6
Public Forest Estate 187–90

quarrying 7, 24, 25, 88

Rackham, Oliver 161–2, 164, 169
railways 12, 24, 139, 230, 261–3, 273–4
ramblers 70, 73, 151
Rawnsley, Conrad 211
Rawnsley, Hardwicke 15, 23–4, 25–6
regionalism 46, 127–31, 136–7
Reilly, Sir Charles 36–7

Reith, John, Lord 47–9, 76–7, 282
religion 2, 265, 275, 311
renewable energy 221–4
Repton, Humphry 5, 169
ResPublica 297, 309
Restriction of Ribbon Development Act (1935) 44
ribbon development 36, 37, 41, 44, 280
Rivers (Prevention of Pollution) Act (1951) 104
roads 25, 87–8, 205, 287, 288–90
Rogers, Richard, Lord 263, 292–3, 295
Rothman, Benny 72–3
Rothschild, Charles 100, 101
Rowntree, Joseph 278
Royal Agricultural Society of England (RASE) 136
Royal Forests 165–8, 176–7
Royal Society for the Protection of Birds (RSPB) 100, 101, 105, 118, 179, 180, 182
rural planning 36–9, 47
Ruskin, John xii–xiii, 1–2, 10–15, 17–18, 23, 25, 64
  and legacy 31, 50
  and National Trust 26–7

Sandford, Lord 82–4
sandlands 136
Sandys, Duncan 244–5, 280
sanitation 32, 33, 272–3
Sayer, Sylvia 82
Sayes Court 22–3, 170
science 101–3
Scotland 39, 69, 92, 111, 112, 179–80, 182
Scott Committee 47, 103–4, 125, 203
Sea Birds Preservation Act (1869) 99–100
seaside resorts 199–200, 205, 271, 274
Second World War 45–6, 140
set-aside schemes 147, 148
sewage 215–16
Shaw Lefevre, George 234–5
sheep farming 128–9, 130, 135, 144, 150

Sheffield Association for the Protection of Local Scenery 41
shipbuilding 170, 196, 197
Shoard, Marion 56, 143
Shropshire Lad, A (Housman) 1, 33
Silent Spring (Carson) 104–5
Silkin, Lewis 30, 51–2, 73, 74, 77
Sites of Special Scientific Interest (SSSIs) 88–9, 102, 103, 106–7, 109
slum clearances 33, 35, 275
Snowdonia xiii–xiv, 78, 79, 80, 82, 83, 204
Society for the Promotion of Nature Reserves (SPNR) 100–2, 105
Society for the Protection of Ancient Buildings (SPAB) 15, 28
Society of Antiquaries of London 233, 234
soil conditions 154–8
Somerset, Guy 66
Somervell, Robert Miller 24–5
South Downs 78, 79, 91, 92
sprawl 30–1, 35–6, 41–2, 275, 280
Standing Committee on National Parks (SCNP) 81, 82, 178
Steers, J. Alfred 203, 208
Stephenson, Tom 73, 74, 78, 225
Stockholm Conference on the Human Environment (1972) 54, 60
Stukeley, William 233
sustainability 63, 91, 185, 309–10
  and agriculture 147, 152–3, 155
  and fish 214–15
Symonds, Rev H. H. 176

Talbot, Fanny 14, 27, 200
tax breaks 111, 142, 180, 182
technology 53–4, 61–2, 131–2, 135
textile industry 269
Theft of the Countryside, The (Shoard) 56, 143
Thirlmere 24–5
timber 138–9, 168, 170–2, 173–4, 185–6

Tomorrow! A Peaceful Path to Reform
(Howard) 278
Torrey Canyon, SS 104, 212–13, 215
tourism 5, 24, 150–1, 232–3, 257
    and the coast 193–4, 199–200, 205
    and historic buildings 246–50
    and National Parks 81, 82, 90
    and woodlands 177, 184–5
Town and Country Planning Acts
    (1932/44/47) 51, 75, 76, 244,
    282–3
Transition Towns 295
trees 25, 91, 111, 160–5, 168–9, 170
    and benefits 184–5, 190–1
    and controversies 54, 172–3, 174–6,
    179–80, 182
    and forestry 169–70
Trevelyan, Charles 69
Trevelyan, G. M. 42–3, 76
Turner, J. M. W. 1, 10

ugliness 41, 43, 63
United Nations Educational, Scientific
    and Cultural Organisation
    (UNESCO) 246
United Nations Environment
    Programme (UNEP) 60, 114
United States of America 67–8, 104–5
Unwin, Sir Raymond 36–7, 279, 280
uplands 136, 137, 174
urban regeneration 263–4, 292–7
urbanisation 9–10, 12–13, 30–1, 33,
    35–6, 135–6, 261–2, 307–8
    and decline 291–3
    and history 264–9, 270–5, 284–6
    and planning 297–8, 300–4
Uthwatt Committee 46

Vermuyden, Cornelius 130, 131

Waldegrave, William, Lord 109, 148
Wales 39, 69, 112, 184

    and coastal path 225, 226–7
war poets 30, 33–4
Weaver, Sir Lawrence 36–7
Webb, Mary 34
Wembury Point 193–4
wetlands 98, 119
White, Gilbert 5, 97–8
Whittow, Dr John 208–9
Wicken Fen 95–6, 100, 157
Wild Birds Acts 99–100, 101
wildlife 51, 91, 96–7, 98–100, 115–16,
    307
    and the coast 194, 212–14
    and decline 118
    and pollution 104–5
    and woodlands 185
Wildlife and Countryside Act (1981)
    86–7, 107–9, 213
Wildlife and Countryside Link 113
Wildlife Link 108
Wildlife Trusts, The 119, 214, 225
Williams-Ellis, Clough 36, 41–2, 280
Williamson, Henry 34
Wilson, Woodrow 67–8
Wimbledon Common 21, 22, 69
wind turbines 63, 221–4
Woodland Trust 185, 187
woodlands 54, 90, 161, 162–5, 168–9,
    171
    and benefits 184–7, 190–2
    and decline 170–2, 173, 179
    and new creations 186–7
wool industry 265–6
Wordsworth, William 6, 7–8, 12, 24, 68,
    306
    and trees 172–3, 175
World Heritage Sites 92–3, 246
Worldwide Fund for Nature (WWF) 56

Yorkshire Dales 78, 80, 91, 92
Young, Arthur 132, 133, 268